HEAVY FREIGHT LOCOMOTIVES OF BRITAIN

Other books by the same author:
Brunel's Great Western
Locomotive Engineers of the GWR
Classic Locomotives
Raising Steam
Power of the Great Liners
Locomotive Engineers of the LMS

Patrick Stephens Limited, a member of the Haynes Publishing Group, has published authoritative, quality books for enthusiasts for a quarter of a century. During that time the company has established a reputation as one of the world's leading publishers of books on aviation, maritime, military, model-making, motor cycling, motoring, motor racing, railway and railway modelling subjects. Readers or authors with suggestions for books they would like to see published are invited to write to: The Editorial Director, Patrick Stephens Limited, Sparkford, Nr Yeovil, Somerset, BA22 7JJ.

HEAVY FREIGHT LOCOMOTIVES OF BRITAIN

Denis Griffiths

Patrick Stephens Limited

This book is dedicated
to my sisters
Mrs Euphemia Mercer and Mrs Colette Khalifa
for being there when they were needed
and
to the memory of
Arthur Griffiths,
Our Dad

First published 1993

British Library Cataloguing in Publication Data
A catalogue record for this book is available from the British Library

ISBN 1-85260-399-2

Library of Congress catalogue card No. 93-77249

Patrick Stephens Limited is a member of the
Haynes Publishing Group plc, Sparkford, Nr Yeovil, Somerset, BA22 7JJ.

Typeset in Great Britain by Wyvern Typesetting Ltd, Bristol.
Printed and bound in Great Britain by
Butler & Tanner Ltd, Frome and London

Contents

Acknowledgements

For any book dealing with the history of railways the records held at the National Railway Museum provide valuable information, and the author would like to thank Mr C.P. Atkins and other members of the library staff for the assistance and courtesy offered. Liverpool City Library and the library of the Institution of Mechanical Engineers have also been extremely useful and thanks must be expressed to the staffs of both establishments.

Many individuals have provided information and guidance during my researches and in the writing of this book including Gill Harrison, batting for the Lancashire & Yorkshire Railway, and Stan Utting, on the side of Crewe and British Railways. The electrical enlightenment imparted by Joe Watson and Frank Smith has been most useful, whilst Keith Naylor has shown enthusiasm for anything steam. Geoff Johnson, Jim Stopforth and Martin Harrison have provided information and have been kind enough to encourage the author in his efforts. Will Adams, formerly of PSL, must also be thanked for getting the project off the ground in the first place and being enthusiastic about its progress.

David Russell, Railfreight Engineer at BR, has been extremely helpful with respect to the diesel locomotives and has shown a keen interest in the book as a whole. His introductions to others who have offered assistance have been most valuable. Russell Sharp of General Motors has provided photographs and much useful information concerning the Class 59 locomotives, whilst Ivor Mason and Steve Hannam of Foster Yeoman have been similarly useful with information regarding operation of the class. Neville Maze and others at Brush Electrical Machines guided the author with respect to the Class 60s and imparted much useful information not available elsewhere. To the above thanks are also due for enabling the author to tour the various sites and depots.

It is usual for an author to thank his family for encouragement and patience whilst working on a book and in that respect I am no different. As any author knows, research and writing are invariably solitary pursuits from which families are generally excluded and it is right that family members be thanked for their silent part in any work of this type. For my wife Patricia, daughter Sarah and son Patrick I offer my sincere thanks, but will not promise never to do it again.

Introduction

With but a few exceptions the railways of Great Britain were constructed primarily for the carriage of freight, with passengers being a secondary, albeit lucrative, consideration. Mergers, takeovers and amalgamations brought about larger conglomerates culminating in the single nationalized British Railways, but the carriage of goods not passengers swelled the coffers. Throughout their existence all four of the post-Grouping railway companies derived most of their revenue from freight; at least 60 per cent came from the carriage of minerals, general freight and parcels, compared with at most 40 per cent from the carriage of people. Where heavy mineral traffic was involved, such as on East Coast lines, revenue from freight approached 70 per cent. Even in the early post nationalization years freight still provided the larger share of railway income but the loss of much traffic to road haulage resulted in a dramatic decline. By the late 1980s income from freight barely reached 20 per cent if the government operating subsidy is considered as income from passenger operations. Reasons for such a decline are many, but ineffective management and marketing played an important part. However, the 1990s could well see an improvement as newer and more cost effective diesel locomotives become available for the specialized purpose of hauling heavy freight trains.

Freight trains, despite their revenue earning capability, played second fiddle to passenger services as far as a railway's operating department was concerned. They were shunted into sidings to allow passenger trains to pass, frequently operated at night to avoid delaying passenger services and were often allocated run-down passenger locomotives for haulage purposes. There were many good reasons for such action not least being the fact that passengers could, and would, complain over delays. As a perishable commodity the passenger could not be kept hanging around indefinitely, especially without creature comforts such as food, water and toilet facilities. A train load of coal or general merchandise did not complain nor did it deteriorate during prolonged transit; obviously railways did take special care of goods such as fruit, fish and livestock.

Despite the apparent emphasis on passenger trains railway managers were not unaware of the advantages to be derived from the carriage of goods, particularly in long and heavy trains. Towards the latter part of the 19th century some locomotive engineers were becoming aware of the needs for specialized heavy freight locomotives for such trains and that gave birth to the eight-coupled, and subsequently the ten-coupled, locomotive on the railways of Britain. Double heading could be employed for heavy trains but single locomotive haulage was more cost effective and so the dedicated freight locomotive found favour on most lines. Although much of the technology developed for passenger classes could be applied to heavy freight locomotives there were restrictions with respect to loading gauge, axle weight and wheel base. The clever locomotive engineer could find ways around these restrictions and still meet the needs of his masters.

Heavy freight steam locomotives were still steam

locomotives but as a group they seem to have been ignored in railway writings. Passenger locomotives were certainly more accessible both to the enthusiast and the journalist: very few freight runs were ever timed or analysed in the railway press but then very few freight trains were afforded the luxury of an unhindered run, passenger trains having priority. Freight locomotives were not as glamorous as express passenger engines which, at least prior to nationalization, were maintained in a very clean condition. Often, however, the only sight an enthusiast had of a heavy freight locomotive was on shed, from the window of his passenger carriage, or a distant view from a station platform as the freight took the avoiding line. During the era of steam preservation and in the dedicated diesel locomotives the heavy freight engine has come into its own and is at last being recognised as a valuable unit in the continuing history of British railway traction.

During two world wars the people of Britain relied upon the railways for the movement of goods and of servicemen. Throughout those conflicts freight and military trains had priority and only the construction of freight and mixed traffic locomotives would be sanctioned. Movement of troops and supplies across mainland Europe could only be effectively carried out by rail but the quality of any railway was not guaranteed after years of conflict. Locomotives had to be supplied to the Continent from Britain and America, as existing engines would certainly have been destroyed by retreating armies. The story of those conscript locomotives is as interesting as they were important, particularly those moved to Europe in 1944 and later. Low axle loading, ease of maintenance, cheapness of construction using available materials and simplicity of operation were the hallmarks of these machines. They were more-or-less 'throw away' locomotives, the 'Liberty ship' of the rails, but they did the job required of them and, like the 'Liberty ships', continued in active service long after their expected lifetime; both ships and locomotives found extended life in the service of Greek owners.

This book illustrates the development of the heavy freight locomotives employed on the railways of Britain, from the first eight-coupled engines to British Rail's Class 60 diesels. It is not an operating book describing services but is oriented towards the technical for it was, and is, technicalities which set the heavy freight engine apart from its passenger or mixed traffic brother. Simply increasing power potential does not produce a heavy freight locomotive, power must be transferred to the rail in order to start and then haul the heavy load.

1
The Heavy Freight Locomotive

As a basic machine the steam locomotive designed for heavy freight work is essentially the same as a steam locomotive designed for any other form of work; it consists of boiler, power cylinders, wheels, etc. A steam locomotive, or a diesel electric locomotive for that matter, is much the same in concept no matter what its design purpose. Having stated the fairly obvious it is important to realize that the ability to do a certain job requires particular attributes which must be built into the design and the characteristics required for a fast express train are not the same as those needed for heavy freight haulage. Fundamentals such as boiler, cylinders, wheels, etc. are essential to both designs but there is more to effective locomotive design than simply assembling a collection of parts. That machine might function, but it will not be much use unless care has been taken in choosing the right parts. For a number of reasons it is not possible to design a locomotive which is equally at home hauling passengers at express speed and a heavy mineral train on a start-stop service. Mixed traffic locomotives have been produced which could satisfy the middle ground but haulage of heavy freight trains was and is very much a specialized task which demands a special locomotive, the heavy freight locomotive.

For the purposes of this book the heavy freight steam locomotive has been considered as one having eight or ten coupled wheels, together with the Garratt articulated form. Diesel electric locomotives of this power are those designated Type 5 in the British Rail classification system. Only main line locomotives will be considered, thus excluding a small number having the indicated wheel arrangement which were specifically designed for shunting work. Of the four Grouped railway companies only the Southern did not construct any main line eight or ten coupled locomotives although the Z class 0-8-0 was designed for shunting work in the large marshalling yards of that railway. Because of restrictions, which also applied to main line locomotives, eight or ten coupled shunting engines could only be used in the larger marshalling yards or at specific locations, thus their application was limited. Numbers constructed in such classes were small and on the other railways designs were frequently based upon main line locomotives.

From time-to-time heavy freight designs were proposed by the Southern, particularly for haulage of coal trains in Kent, but the length of train which could be handled was always limited by the size of refuge siding available. Six-coupled locomotives were satisfactory for trains which could be accommodated in existing refuge sidings and the Southern was not willing to spend money lengthening the sidings. Eight and ten coupled main line locomotives did operate on Southern metals, especially during wartime, but these were on loan from the other railway companies.

The above illustrates that heavy freight locomotive design did not exist in isolation from the railway, locomotives were not produced to satisfy some engineer's desire for fame, but they were constructed to meet a need. Needs existed within the operating limits of a railway and one of those limits was the length of train which could be reasonably managed. Large and very powerful steam locomotives have been constructed for service world wide but if the largest train they can haul will block a line, or require splitting before it can enter a marshalling yard, then haulage problems are simply replaced by operational problems. The good designer would give the power required, with a little in reserve to account for deterioration. Other factors in design included route restriction due to weight, track curvature and loading gauge. These restrictions could be satisfied by design but in many cases at the expense of incurring other restrictions. Reducing weight to limit axle loading could be achieved by fitting a smaller boiler but that would limit hauling power up prolonged gradients; increasing the number of axles would spread the weight and so reduce axle loading, but a longer wheelbase would limit route availability due to track curvature. Locomotive designers were able to overcome these problems and produce designs which satisfied their railway's needs, in doing so they constructed some of the finest locomotives to operate on the railways of Britain.

Several factors influencing locomotive design apply to all railways but the way in which individual designs overcame restrictions differed with the design team. The remainder of this chapter is devoted to considering common aspects, thus avoiding the need for repetition in the chapters concerning the designs of individual companies.

By virtue of its definition a heavy freight locomotive must be capable of hauling heavy loads and hence needs to be able to develop considerable power. Actual power developed in the cylinders is termed indicated power, a device known as an indicator being used to produce a diagram which relates cylinder pressure to cylinder volume. The governing equation for indicated power is;

$$\text{Power} = \frac{P \times A \times S \times N}{\text{constant}}$$ units of power being watts (or horsepower)

P = average cylinder pressure in N/m^2 (or lbs/in^2)
A = area of piston in m^2 (or in^2)
S = length of piston stroke in m (or feet)
N = number of power strokes per second; units s^{-1}

Constant is 1 for power in watts (or 550 for power in horse power)

A steam engine cylinder is double acting and so the power per cylinder is almost double that obtained from the above equation. Almost double because the area of the under side of the piston must be reduced by the area of the piston rod. Total power per locomotive must be multiplied by the number of cylinders on that locomotive. In practice steam

A typical 0-8-0 Heavy Freight design. Former LNWR G1 class rebuilt with a G2 boiler. No 49094 at Bletchley in 1962. (D.K. Jones Collection)

pressure for each cylinder is slightly different and so the indicator must be used on each cylinder in order to obtain the average steam pressure. During operation a driver may adjust the regulator and cut-off, thus influencing the average steam pressure, but in general terms the power potential of a locomotive depends upon steam pressure, diameter of piston, length of piston stroke and operating speed.

Many factors govern each of these and the designer must organise their combined effect to produce the desired result. Over the years boiler steam pressure increased as that allowed for greater expansive working and thus improved overall economy. Length of stroke and piston diameter also changed over the years as the designers aimed for higher power development. Cylinder power can, however, only be produced by steam and as power output increased so did steam consumption. Adoption of superheating raised the specific energy per unit of steam and so reduced steam, and coal consumption per unit of power developed but in general terms the higher the power requirement the larger the demand for steam and the bigger must be the boiler. The above applies to all steam locomotives but the heavy freight locomotive must also be capable of sustained high levels of power for hauling heavy loads at relatively slow speeds up prolonged gradients.

Ability to actually haul a load requires power but a high powered locomotive is not necessarily capable of starting a heavy load or hauling one at slow speed. Power developed in the cylinders must be translated to hauling ability at the drawbar and it is in this respect that the heavy freight locomotive differs from its express passenger counterpart. Both might have cylinders of the same size and boilers operating at the same pressure but it is the size of their driving wheels that will differ. Wheel size acts like gearing on a bicycle or car, large diameter wheels being similar to a high gear ratio with small diameter wheels being similar to a low gear ratio. When bicycle pedals are turned at a particular rate a high gear allows for fast progress along the flat but a low gear enables steady progress to be made up an incline without undue strain being imposed on the legs. If a car is towing a trailer or caravan a lower gear must be selected than would be the case under similar conditions if that load was not applied. Unlike these other forms of transport the steam locomotive is not provided with gearing and so tractive ability must be organized through driving wheel size. As wheel diameter cannot change it follows that an express passenger locomotive cannot usefully be employed for heavy freight haulage and vice versa. By virtue of its wheel size the freight locomotive is defined.

The ability to start and haul a load is designated by the vague concept of tractive effort. The Phillipson formula used to determine theoretical tractive effort is;

$$\text{Tractive effort} = \frac{0.85\, d^2\, s\, n\, p}{2w}$$

Units of tractive effort are Newtons (or lbs)

d = cylinder diameter in metres (or inches)
s = piston stroke in metres (or inches)
n = number of cylinders
p = boiler pressure in N/m^2 (or lbs/in^2)
w = wheel diameter in m (or in)

Actual tractive effort or tractive force is a maximum when starting but it falls as the train picks up speed and the driver reduces cut-off or shuts in the regulator.

The drawbar power or power available at the rail may be calculated for a particular speed if the tractive force at that speed is known:

$$\text{Power available at the rail} = \frac{\text{tractive force} \times \text{speed}}{\text{constant}}$$

Power will be in watts (or horsepower)
Tractive force (or effort) in Newtons (or lbs)
Speed in kilometres per hour (or miles per hour)
Constant is 3.6 (or 375)

A similar relationship may be used for drawbar power, in this case the drawbar pull is used instead of tractive force.

In order to make full use of available tractive effort a locomotive must keep its driving wheels fully in contact with the rails and that is only possible if there is sufficient adhesion. High force between wheels and rails allow for this as does a high coefficient of friction. Steel wheels upon steel rails give a low coefficient of friction and hence a low adhesive force, particularly in wet conditions. The use of sand increases friction between wheel and rail thus enabling heavy loads to be started, but sand cannot be used perpetually. High levels of adhesion can be obtained by providing a high contact force between wheels and rails thus the entire weight of the locomotive should be on the driving wheels. That is not always possible and

The first 2-8-0 Heavy Freight design in the UK, Churchward's GWR 2800 class No 2821 on Dainton Bank in June 1958. (D.K. Jones Collection)

sometimes leading pony trucks are used to provide support for the front end and guide the locomotive into bends. When a locomotive starts to haul a load there is a tendency for it to 'sit down' on its rearmost wheels thus increasing the adhesion between those wheels and the rails. If those wheels are driving wheels no adhesion is lost but if a pony truck or bogie is fitted behind the rear driving wheels then adhesion is lost. Such additional wheels are frequently fitted to provide support at the rear under a wide firebox but the smaller diameter driving wheels of a heavy freight locomotive can generally be carried as far back as is necessary, thus avoiding the need for a trailing bogie or pony truck.

A factor of adhesion, or adhesive coefficient, relates weight on the driving wheels to tractive effort:

$$\text{Factor of Adhesion} = \frac{\text{Adhesion weight}}{\text{Tractive effort}}$$

The factor of adhesion is a coefficient and has no dimensions. Adhesion weight is in Newtons (ie mass in kg $\times$ 9.81), (or lbs). Tractive effort is in Newtons (or lbs).

In order to minimise the risk of slipping the factor of adhesion should be greater than 4.0 for two-cylinder engines and above 3.5 for three-cylinder engines. It follows from the above that the higher the adhesion weight the lower will be the risk of slipping for any particular tractive effort, however, there is a limit to the weight which can be put on any axle. For the locomotive to have wide route availability the axle loading needs to be kept reasonable and that can have a restricting effect on tractive effort. It is not, therefore, a case of trying to obtain maximum values for everything; there are limiting factors.

Axle loading for heavy, and hence powerful, locomotives is kept reasonable by spreading the weight over a number of wheels and if these are all driving wheels then the total adhesive weight is the actual weight of the locomotive; any pony trucks or bogies reduce adhesive weight. Means of minimising the actual weight of a locomotive will be discussed for individual classes in subsequent chapters but the axle loading for any given total weight falls as the number of axles increases. Although this book only considers eight- and ten-coupled wheel arrangements the principle applies to any number of coupled axles.

With four, and more particularly five, coupled axles there are certain restrictions which must be observed with any good design. With larger driving

Heavy Freight Tank design, No 7206 of the Collett 7200 class 2-8-2T. (D.K. Jones Collection)

wheels axle spacing must be increased in order to give adequate clearance between wheels for brake blocks and hangers. Positioning smaller diameter wheels close together may not overcome problems as there are restrictions on loadings per metre run of rail as well as on individual axle loadings. The actual size of wheel is chosen for particular purposes not least of which is intended maximum operating speed while factors such as hammer blow need to be considered.

Weights are applied to wheels in order to balance out reciprocating masses of piston assemblies but those weights can actually introduce problems of hammer blow on the rail due to the vertical

The most extensively built British Heavy Freight design, Stanier's 8F class 2-8-0, No 48762 in BR days. (BR LM Region)

component of their centrifugal force. The value of centrifugal force increases with wheel diameter and with the square of the rotating speed. For a particular speed along the track smaller wheels produce higher values of centrifugal force. However, freight locomotives operate at relatively low speeds and in most situations the problem was never considered to be of major significance. Should the locomotive be expected to work fast freight trains a portion of the reciprocating mass would be balanced with the balance weight being spread amongst all of the coupled axles. The larger the number of coupled axles the smaller the balance weight applied to each wheel, thus the lower would be the hammer blow effect. A number of LMS Stanier 8F class locomotives had 50 per cent of their reciprocating masses balanced in order that they could run on fast freights and these were identified with a star painted below the cabside number.

Eight and ten-coupled locomotives had relatively long wheel bases and that could restrict the curvature of track they could safely negotiate. In order to allow movement over tightly curved track some flexibility had to be arranged and a number of possibilities were available to the designer. One was to allow a degree of sideways movement on one or more of the axles but that presented problems with respect to coupling rods, thus limiting its application. Reducing wheel flange thickness or eliminating them altogether allowed that flexibility without the penalty of mechanical restriction and many designers adopted this ploy, although there was no rule which governed which of the middle axles would be so treated on an eight-coupled locomotive. The ten-coupled BR Class 9F engines had flangeless centre wheels whilst those either side had flanges of reduced thickness.

Whilst these arrangements satisfied requirements for curvature, problems could exist with such locomotives when passing over indifferent track. Imperfections in the laying of rails could make the ride extremely uncomfortable with four or five axles even when these were correctly sprung. During the 20th century most British lines over which heavy freight trains operated were of reasonable standard but during the 19th century that was not always the

The final British steam Heavy Freight design, Standard 9F class 2-10-0, No 92144 on a typical mixed goods. (D.K. Jones Collection)

case and Webb provided compensated levers for his early 0-8-0 locomotives. Adequate springing avoided the need for such arrangements with later engines but care was always necessary in design and setting in order to avoid loss of adhesion as one wheel encountered a 'trough' in an indifferently laid track.

The above deals with certain general aspects of heavy freight steam locomotive design and these points should be borne in mind when considering individual designs outlined in later chapters. Each of the locomotives was designed for a purpose and to suit particular conditions thus it is not realistic to compare designs of one company with those of another. In most cases heavy freight locomotive designs lasted much longer than those for other types of service and that in itself should be justification enough for any design. Weight saving, ease of construction, minimum maintenance, etc. were all requirements of heavy freight designs for use by the War Department, but the locomotives produced proved to be extremely effective for peacetime operations. There was, in fact, no single ideal heavy freight steam locomotive but each design was special in its own way and they should be considered as separate entities.

Limitations are also imposed upon the design of diesel locomotives for heavy freight haulage and, as with the steamer, these can be overcome in a number of different ways. The difference with respect to the diesel is that there are few designs which can be compared. Although it is true to say that a diesel electric locomotive consists basically of an internal combustion engine driving an electric generator which powers electric motors used to turn the wheels, the approach is too simplistic. A similar set of remarks can be made about the steam locomotive but the steamer has more parts exposed and most people can see that there is more to it than a boiler, cylinders and wheels. The same is true of the diesel but most is hidden from view.

The power developed by a diesel engine could be measured in the same way as for a steam engine but there is no necessity for that as the useful power can be monitored through the output of the electric generator, or alternator if alternating current is being produced. This is the power which is supplied to the traction motors and these turn the driving wheels

Class 56, first of the BR Heavy Freight diesel designs

The second generation BR diesel Heavy Freight locomotives, Class 58. No 58024 on a merry-go-round coal train, for which it was designed.

through gearing. The traction motors cannot provide sufficient torque at the axle to produce the necessary tractive effort and hence gearing is required. A motor which could provide the desired torque directly to the axle would be extremely large and present considerable problems. Single reduction gearing with a ratio of about four to one is usually sufficient for heavy freight locomotives which do not have high maximum speeds but are required to provide a high starting torque. Tractive effort is the force exerted by the wheels on the rails and this is related to the power supply to the motors and the speed of the motors; diesel locomotives having an electric motor on each driving axle.

Because there are no reciprocating parts to the drive mechanism on a diesel electric locomotive there are no problems of balance or hammer blow but effective springing is still essential. Wheels, axle, gearing and motor represent unsprung masses directly in contact with the rails and the higher the

Overseas Heavy Freight for Britain. GM-EMD Class 59, a compact version of the American classic diesel to fit the British loading gauge. Foster Yeoman's No 59001 Yeoman Endeavour.

The British answer to the American challenge. Brush built Class 60, No 60055 Thomas Barnardo, *in the builder's yard at Loughborough.*

value of these masses the greater the potential for track and tyre damage. There is also an increased risk of vibration transmission due to indifferent track and that can influence the quality of ride. Effective springing must also be used to even out loading on individual axles, this being achieved through a combination of primary springing between axle and bogie, and secondary springing between bogie and structure. As with the steam locomotive incorrectly set springing can produce instability and may even result in derailment.

Weight limitations exist but unlike the steam locomotive it is usually possible to adjust springing so that each axle takes approximately the same loading. Each bogie can turn in relation to the locomotive body structure but by allowing the centre axle on the bogies to float sideways it is possible for the locomotive to operate on tightly curved track. Similar problems existed with steam locomotive operation and, as mentioned above, solutions were found but the diesel electric locomotive does have a number of advantages over its steam counterpart and one of these is in its ability to vary power to suit loading.

Steam locomotives require close cooperation between driver and fireman but the diesel only has a driver, although he is aided by sophisticated control systems. For a merry-go-round train the load is steadily increased at the colliery and gradually reduced at the power station, but a requirement of the service is that speed must be maintained within narrow limits. Control systems can, generally, maintain speed under such conditions but it is not easy to imagine even the most skilful steam locomotive driver keeping his train moving at a steady slow speed with the load changing as each wagon is discharged.

This chapter has aimed to provide a general introduction to the actual heavy freight locomotives to be discussed. There are of course many more aspects of locomotive design and for further details on general steam locomotive construction the reader is referred to one of the more specialized texts such as the author's *Raising Steam*, also published by Patrick Stephens. Heavy freight locomotives served and still serve a very useful purpose, their longevity being a testament to that usefulness. Considerable effort went into the designing of such machines and that attention was rewarded by their earning power. Express passenger locomotives had the glamour but heavy freight engines possessed the guts. The succeeding chapters tell the story of these unsung classes and hopefully give credit where it is due.

During the pre-Grouping period a number of heavy freight designs were formulated at about the same time and to follow a strict chronological format might result in confusion, particularly as a number of designs were modifications of earlier classes. For this reason the succeeding three chapters consider designs on a pre-Grouping company basis, each dealing with companies under a post-Grouping heading, ie GWR, LMS and LNER.

2

Heavy Freight Locomotives on GWR Lines

Originating as a means of fast transport to and from London for the citizens and merchants of Bristol and Bath the Great Western Railway soon expanded its sphere of influence to other parts of the kingdom. As far as the western areas were concerned these offered considerable scope for the South Wales pits produced vast quantities of high quality coal. Not only was this useful to the railway for operating its trains but the homes and industries of London had an insatiable appetite for the black gold. During the early years of the railway boom many small companies were formed to exploit the mines and provide ready access to the ports on the Bristol Channel. The GWR had influence in South Wales but did not attempt to dominate by taking control of all lines in the area. Coal traffic from pit to port was handled very well by the smaller railway concerns but any shipments by rail had to go via the GWR. Coal was a major freight commodity but it was by no means the only cargo carried by the Great Western. However, whilst the broad gauge still existed there were many problems concerning the carriage of freight.

As in other areas special freight locomotives were developed and the small railway companies also indulged in the exercise. Their needs differed somewhat from that of the main line concern as route mileage was low and locomotive design could reflect the requirements of short distance running. Over the years many types of engine were supplied to the South Wales railways by assorted manufacturers and amongst these were a number of primitive eight-coupled tank locomotives. These were neither main line engines nor significant in heavy freight locomotive development but in 1889 the Barry Railway took delivery of the first 0-8-0 main line tender engines to work in this country.

Barry Railway

The Barry Railway was incorporated in 1884 as a result of the growth in the coal trade which caused congestion in Cardiff Docks and on the Taff Vale Railway. The first dock at Barry opened in 1889 and the railway provided access to this via connections with Taff Vale lines and other railways in the area. Subsequent expansion enabled trains to run from many parts of South Wales directly to the docks at Barry. However, with the opening of the docks there was an urgent need for heavy freight engines to haul coal trains. Sharp, Stewart & Co. had been contracted to construct a number of 0-8-0 engines for the Swedish & Norwegian Railway and this it did to a standard design of its own with a few modifications to suit the requirements of the purchaser. Unfortunately for that Scandinavian concern, and for Sharps, financial problems prevented payments being made and the final two engines of the order were not delivered. These were purchased by the Barry Railway becoming Nos 35 and 36. Two others, Nos 92 and 93, of identical design were also purchased in 1897 when they were repatriated following prolonged litigation.

As originally constructed the engines had 20in (50.8cm) by 26in (66cm) cylinders outside the frames. Inside Stephenson link motion, fitted with a screw reverser, operated the slide valves. The boiler

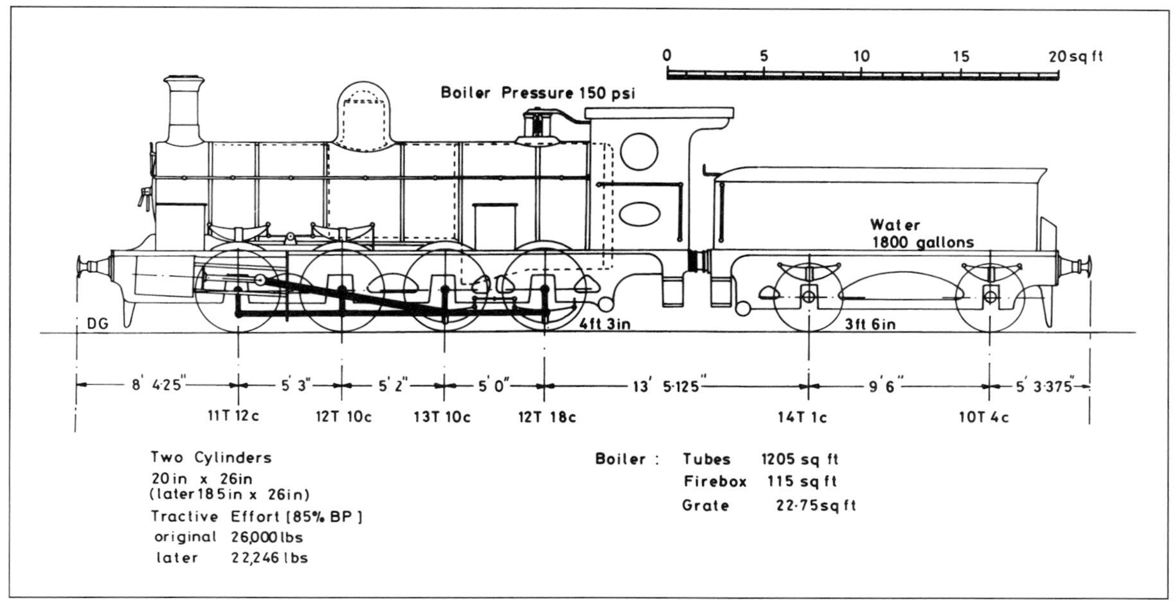

Barry Railway 0-8-0 design.

provided steam at 150psi and the 4ft 3in (1.3m) diameter driving wheels had a wheelbase of 15ft 5in (4.7m), the third pair being flangeless. Boilers were fitted with three Ramsbottom safety valves over the firebox casing and a Salter spring balance safety valve on the dome. These were, obviously, a requirement of the Scandinavian company but they were retained until new boilers, almost identical to the original in terms of heating surface, were fitted during rebuilding in 1901–2.

Minor variations did exist between the locomotives and particularly between the two batches but they were essentially the same engine design and fulfilled the same duties. These consisted of hauling heavy coal trains between storage sidings around Barry and the docks although work on main line duties was undertaken as required. In 1909 it was decided that Nos 92 and 93 should be used only for main line duties. Rebuilding to equip them for that duty included the fitting of new boilers whilst cylinders were lined up to a diameter of 18½in (47cm) thus reducing tractive effort. Cylinders of the other pair of engines were subsequently lined up to 19in (48cm). At the same time as these partial rebuildings locomotives received thicker tyres increasing the wheel diameter to 4ft 4in (1.3m), the third pair of driving wheels being provided with thin flanges.

Just prior to Grouping plans were made to fit these engines and the 0-8-2 tanks with new boilers, the work being completed after the GWR had taken over ownership. Being non-standard they presented certain problems for Swindon especially as no standard items of equipment, particularly boilers, could be used during subsequent overhaul. They did, however continue to perform valuable service around the docks at Barry until being scrapped between 1927 and 1930.[1]

In addition to constructing the 0-8-0 tender engines Sharp, Stewart & Co. also constructed a tank version for hauling heavy coal trains on the Vale of Glamorgan Railway. This line was nominally independent but its operations effectively came under Barry Railway control and as the six locomotives on order were ready before the line was completed they were put to work on Barry metals. These 0-8-2 tank engines were designed for heavy coal train working but were employed by the Barry Railway on shunting duties and so do not really come within the scope of this book. However, a brief description is worthwhile as it allows the nature of South Wales heavy freight locomotives to be covered more completely. The Barry engines were delivered in 1896 but three very similar locomotives were constructed for the Port Talbot Railway in 1901 for similar shunting and short trip working.

Cylinders, motion, driving wheel diameter and

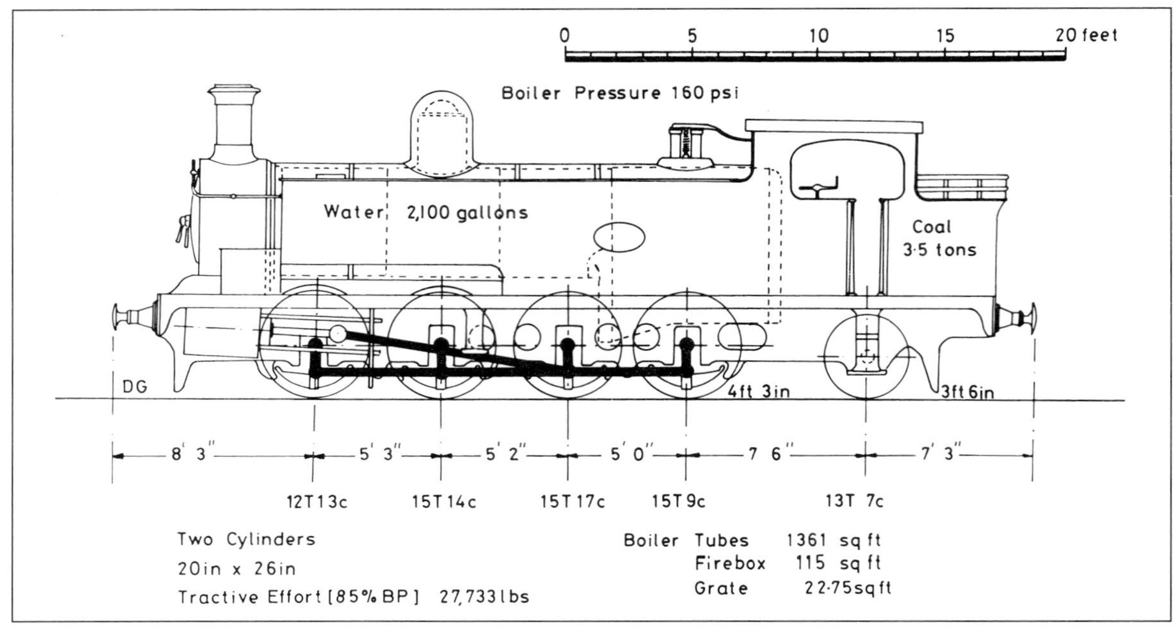

Barry Railway 0-8-2 tank design.

spacing were identical to the 0-8-0s and of the major components only the boiler differed. This is to be expected as the seven years between the classes had resulted in a number of boiler design improvements, even the 0-8-0s being reboilered in 1901. Due to the effects of water and coal, axle loading for the tanks was greater than for the tender engines but still within track restrictions. The higher adhesive weight did, however, allow for improved hauling ability and they could handle 100 loaded wagons easily.

Barry Railway 0-8-2T as modified and working in GWR days. No 1380 at Barry in June 1930. (D.K. Jones Collection)

Originally flangeless tyres had been provided on the third pair of wheels, as for the 0-8-0s, but this caused the other tyre flanges to wear badly and the same solution of providing tyres with thin flanges was adopted. During later years of operation a number of locomotives received modifications including lining up of cylinders to 18½in (47cm) diameter, fitting of coal rails to the bunker and replacement of exhaust steam injectors by live steam injectors. The latter was probably as a consequence of shunting duties which did not allow for prolonged operation of the exhaust steam type. Some locomotives were provided with new boilers of the type eventually fitted to the 0-8-0s, but others simply had the boiler modified to the new tube arrangement. All boilers then operated at 160psi.

As shunting engines they performed their duties well but by the mid-1920s their non-standard nature made repairs expensive and they were withdrawn for scrapping.[2]

Great Western Railway

When George Jackson Churchward became CME the Great Western had an extensive fleet of locomotives for passenger and freight duties but it was only just getting over the traumas of broad gauge conversion and there was considerable scope for improvement. Churchward grasped the nettle bravely and set about giving the railway a modern stable of locomotives which could meet current and anticipated traffic demands. The scheme showed considerable foresight but the fact that he developed the different classes around a stock of standard parts indicates deep engineering understanding and a degree of courage. Others, including his immediate predecessor William Dean, had applied standardization of parts to locomotive construction but only on a limited scale. Not since Daniel Gooch set about giving the GWR its first real fleet of engines had there been such a well defined plan for wholesale reconstruction of the stock. It is wrong to believe that Churchward simply sat down and drafted a scheme for a range of locomotives using a limited number of set parts. That it eventually turned out to appear that way belies the considerable amount of thought, design, planning and experimentation which went into the process but then the consumer, or observer, only sees the final product; skill makes the engineering effort look easy.

The initial concept for a series of main line engines making use of standard parts appeared in 1901 and concerned six types, one of which was a 2-8-0 for freight duties. The boiler was the same as the 4-6-0 in the series as were the length of connecting rod and pony truck wheels; all engines were to make use of standard sized cylinders 18in (45.7cm) diameter by 30in (76.2cm) stroke and 8½in (21.6cm) diameter piston valves. One of the 4-6-0s was never constructed but the remaining locomotives in the plan were, including No 97 the prototype 2-8-0, which appeared in June 1903. This was the first locomotive with that wheel arrangement to

Churchward's 2800 class 2-8-0.

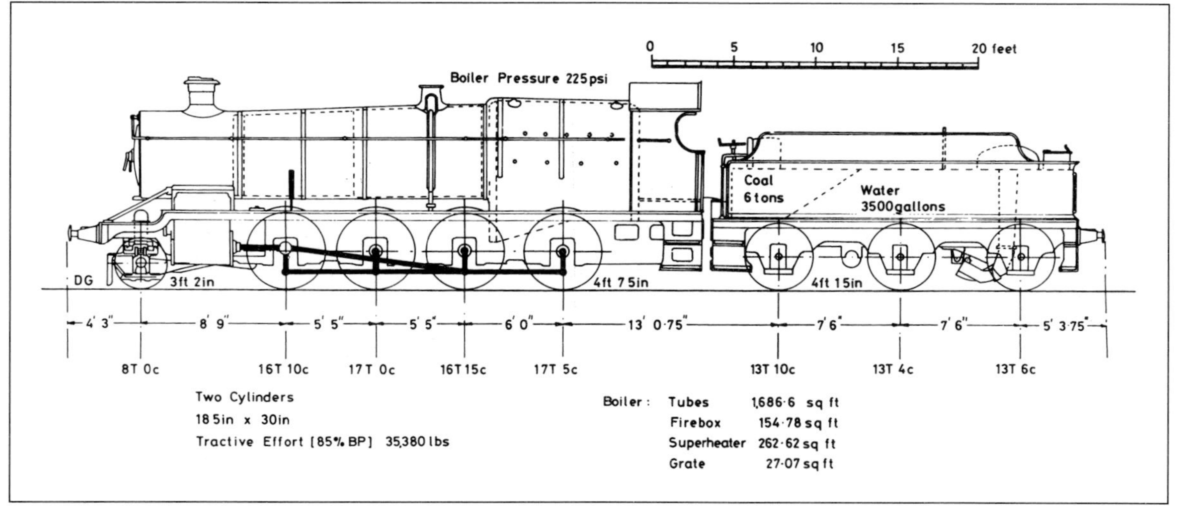

operate in Britain. After testing proved the anticipated operational performance and construction had confirmed the suitability of standardization it was but a small step to a more detailed scheme for nine standard locomotives.[3]

The boiler fitted in No 97 was subsequently developed as the standard No 1 boiler which was fitted in many GWR locomotives over the following years. At the time superheating had not been applied and boiler pressure was 200psi; construction consisted of two ring sections, that next to the smokebox being parallel and that attached to the Belpaire firebox being coned above its horizontal centre line. A feature of Churchward's design philosophy was the use of a minimum number of identical parts and that applied to castings, even when those castings were to be fitted to opposite sides of the locomotive. By making castings which incorporated a cylinder, valve chest, steam passages and half of the smokebox saddle as a single unit the number of castings could be reduced. If castings for left and right hand sides were identical that would reduce the number of standard parts even further, although there was a price to be paid for such an advantage and Churchward was prepared to pay it. To enable left and right hand cylinder block castings to be identical and bolt together the cylinders had to be horizontal and the centre needed to be raised 2½in (6.35cm) above the axle centre line in order to clear the loading gauge. That arrangement stayed for all GWR construction even though it presented certain problems and despite the fact that other railways overcame similar difficulties by inclining the cylinders. Inclining cylinders would have required the two cylinder block casings to be machined differently thus losing an advantage of standardization.

Inside Stephenson link motion operated the valves which had large lap and were of the long travel type. Motion was transmitted to the valves, positioned above the cylinders outside the frames, by means of rocking levers but long valve extension rods had to be used to link valve spindles with the levers.

One aspect of the 2-8-0 design which separated it from the other engines in the initial scheme was the size of its driving wheels, no other engine having them of 4ft 7½in (1.41m) diameter. In order to allow for some flexibility over the 16ft 10in (5.13m) wheelbase the tyres on the second and third pair of driving wheels had thinner flanges and the leading axle was allowed some side play. To accommodate this a swivel joint was provided at the coupling rod connection between leading and second driving wheels. Drive from the cylinders was onto the third axle. To improve the quality of riding compensating or equalizing levers were used to connect spring hangers on first and second and third and fourth coupled wheels. The pony truck with its 3ft 2in (0.97m) diameter wheels employed a swing link arrangement for control.

Experience with the running of No 97 and the other prototypes allowed a more definite scheme for standard locomotives to be formulated, but again the number of parts was limited. To some extent that restricted each of the designs which then had to compromise on parts available but the advantages it introduced in terms of scale of production, availability of spares, familiarity for maintenance, etc. far outweighed the slight disadvantages there might have been. The fact that these standard designs generally lasted a long time and performed efficiently and effectively indicates that the compromise worked.

An order for 20 new 2-8-0s was placed early in 1905 and delivery commenced later that year with these production engines varying only slightly from the prototype. The smokebox saddle was extended upwards in order to put the boiler centreline 8ft 2in (2.49m) above the rail and the cab was modified to suit this higher positioning of the boiler. Increased boiler pressure of 225psi enabled a higher tractive effort to be developed as cylinders and driving wheel diameter remained the same as the prototype. In order to provide for an easier steam flow Churchward decided that the 10in (25.4cm) diameter piston valves fitted to some early 4-6-0s offered considerable advantage and this size was provided for the production 2-8-0s. A further ten engines appeared in 1907 and these had 18.375in (46.7cm) diameter cylinders but in other respects they were identical to the first production batch. During 1909 superheating was introduced to the class, No. 2808 being the first so fitted, and at the same time cylinder diameter was once more increased, this time to 18½in (47cm) which became standard for these engines. It was soon discovered that the frame overhang at the front was too weak to withstand buffing forces and from 1908 onwards support struts were fitted. These connected the front end of the frames with the smokebox and provided the necessary additional strength.

Over succeeding years slight changes took place but the design remained fundamentally that as devised by Churchward. Weight distribution was improved by the addition of weights to the frames,

'28xx' No 2887 at Taunton in October 1946. (D.K. Jones Collection)

superheater areas changed as different patterns of superheater were tried, and outside steam pipes were fitted when a new pattern of cylinder block was introduced. This latter modification came about from 1934 onwards in order to make high pressure steam lines more accessible for rejointing should that be necessary. The actual cylinder block casting also became simpler and less costly to produce. With the development of better and more flexible springs the use of compensating levers was abandoned and modification of the engines to remove such levers commenced in 1931.

Churchward ceased construction of this 2800 class of 2-8-0s in 1919 and no further members of the class were constructed until 1938. By this time trade was increasing, thus producing a need for larger numbers of heavy freight engines, but war clouds were also gathering and the demand for such locomotives enabled construction to continue until 1942. Apart from the modifications already mentioned and some minor improvements such as side cab windows the '38xx' engines were fundamentally

With a typical 1950's mixed goods train No 2822 at Patchway in July 1957. (D.K. Jones Collection)

the same as the design derived by Churchward nearly 40 years earlier[4] but were classified 2884, from the first example to appear with such modifications.

The 83 locomotives of the class constructed between 1903 and 1919 proved to be highly successful on the traffic for which they were designed. This was mainly coal traffic originating in the South Wales area but other heavy freight duties were also undertaken, and in later years the 2-8-0s acted as relief engines on passenger trains. For operating coal trains many were based at sheds in the Newport division with others being located at Old Oak Common and Bristol. Following Grouping heavy freight traffic did not expand very quickly due to the depression and the 2800 class could manage the work available, including services north to Birmingham.

Expansion in trade during the 1930s and the scrapping of older engines resulted in a necessity for more powerful freight locomotives but Collett was satisfied with performance of the '28xx' locomotives and so further batches were ordered. Although nominally the same as the Churchward design, apart from the modifications mentioned above, the new engines were constructed to a higher standard than had been possible with their predecessors. During overhaul the pre-Grouping batches were also treated to the improvements which included optical alignment of cylinders and axles. Collett had not indulged in the production of many new designs as the former CME had left the GWR well provided for and he devoted much of his energy towards the improvement of assembly and workshop techniques. Correctly he presumed that a locomotive which was constructed to a high degree of precision would perform more effectively and require less time in the repair shop. All locomotives were to benefit from the introduction of optical alignment and similar techniques, the '28xx' as much as any. One advantage claimed for optical alignment of axles and finer clearances at bearings was that the interval between shopping could be increased, thus giving the locomotive increased availability; the corollary of this was that increased availability required fewer locomotives to be constructed.

Although figures can be misinterpreted and may even be used to mislead it is possible to appreciate how good the '28xx' engines were by considering figures presented by R.C. Bond in 1953.[5] Between periodical repairs members of the class achieved an average running distance of 86,981 miles (139,169km); by this time many of the engines were over 40 years old although, admittedly, a number had not yet achieved ten years in service. LMS Class 8 2-8-0s could only manage 50,361 miles (80,578km) between periodical repairs, the LNER O1 class 2-8-0s 55,616 miles (88,986km) and the War Department 2-8-0s in service on the LNER 62,624 miles (100,198km). Even allowing for some data gathering discrepancies the GWR heavy freight engine was way out in front as far as its availability was concerned. Similar figures for passenger locomotives indicate that GWR types were good but their advantage is not so pronounced as that for the heavy freight engine. From the figures provided by Bond it is noticeable that mileages for heavy freight engines were, apart from the GWR 2800 class, consistently lower than for other types, indicating the arduous nature of their duties and tendency towards neglect not afforded passenger classes. For GWR engines the '28xx' mileage was very close to the 'Castle', 'Hall' and 'County' classes and marginally better than the 'Kings'.

The fine mechanical condition of these heavy freight engines was also backed by performance as proved by the interchange trials of 1948. During these comparative trials on tracks formerly owned by the GWR, LMS, LNER and Southern Railway the best locomotive stock was operated on similar services in order to assess, if possible, the best types then available. Whilst observers witnessed and timed passenger runs the freight trains performed away from public gaze but their operations were closely watched by staff of the recently formed British Railways. Examples of the GWR 2884, LMS 8F, LNER O1 classes were put through their paces alongside representative locomotives from the War Department (by then Ministry of Supply), 2-8-0 and 2-10-0s. The GWR engine was by far the oldest design under test although more recently constructed examples were used. The O1 design, as will be seen from later chapters, was a Thompson rebuild of an earlier GCR design originally introduced in 1911. The LMS design was barely twelve years old, whilst both War Department engine designs were produced that decade.

Obviously much depended upon the state of individual locomotives but considerable efforts were made to ensure that the trials were as fair as possible because it was knowledge which was the aim, not proof of the superiority of one or other of the railways. With testing carried out on the open road using normal service trains there were problems

Collett version of the '28xx', 2884 class No 3801 with minor modification from the original design. (D.K. Jones Collection)

such as signal checks and weather which afflicted one or more of the engines but not others, at least to the same degree. Allowance was made for these effects and for route conditions as trials were undertaken on all regions. Special additional tests were carried out for the GWR engines using Welsh coal for which their fireboxes were specifically designed, normal trials being made wth South Kirkby Hards and Blidworth Hards. Both of these coals had a lower calorific value than the Welsh coking coal but in the additional tests carried out on the Western Region allowance was made for this fact in the calculations. Only the GWR engines were tested with Welsh coal as they were specifically designed for its combustion but it would have been interesting to see how other locomotives performed using this 'foreign' fuel.

The four test routes were chosen to provide different characteristics and so enable a realistic trial to be achieved. On the Western Region 119 miles (190km) were covered between Acton and Severn Tunnel Junction whilst on the Eastern Region the route between Ferme Park and Peterborough was 74 miles (118km). The London Midland provided the longest run, 127 miles (203km) between Toton and Brent, and the final route was a combined Southern and Western affair between Eastleigh and Bristol via Salisbury. Because of the nature of the route the actual mileage in the latter case varied between 75½ and 77 miles (121km to 123km). All routes had sections of gradient. Loads applied were approximately the same for each test but they varied over different sections of the run in a number of cases. Actual values were given in the official report and other publications,[6] these also giving accounts of conditions and the actual tests. The interested reader is referred to these texts for full accounts of the trials.

Analysis of any test results are always open to misinterpretation and as figures can be manipulated in a number of ways they may be used to prove almost anything. A mass of data was gathered allowing, amongst other things, fuel and water consumption to be determined for each route. Route figures can deceive due to particular problems encountered but the overall figures, probably, give a good indication as to locomotive performance although any such figures must be treated with caution.

Aggregate consumption figures obtained for the heavy freight engines were as follows:

	Coal Consumption		Water Consumption		Evaporation
	lb/hp hr	(kg/kW hr)	lb/hp hr	(kg/kW hr)	lb/lb or kg/kg
LMS 8F	3.52	1.19	27.26	9.24	7.73
LNER O1	3.37	1.14	25.73	8.72	7.68
WD 2-8-0	3.77	1.27	28.75	9.73	7.65
WD 2-10-0	3.52	1.19	28.05	9.49	8.03
GWR '28xx'	3.42	1.16	26.8	9.08	7.93
(Welsh coal)	2.64	0.895	25.5	8.64	9.67

As far as coal consumption is concerned, although they performed very well, it would be wrong to infer that the '28xx' was markedly superior to the rest. In fact no firm conclusion was drawn from the trials apart from the fact that variations in performance existed between the locomotives tested and that there was no single design, heavy freight, express passenger or mixed traffic, which could be considered far better than the rest in its type.

These exchange trials did, however, prove that the 2800/2884 class still had plenty left and, despite its age, the design was still a very good one. When assessing suitability it is assumed that the desired power will be available and that the locomotive will be effective in hauling the load but factors other than coal and water consumption must also be considered. As was shown above, the GWR 2-8-0 had an excellent record of availability judging by the mileage between overhauls but costing had to be considered and it was an accepted fact that GWR engines were more expensive to construct than similar classes on other railways. Unfortunately no figures were produced from the data which must have been available to show relative total costs and that would probably have put the '28xx' lower down the list. A further fact mitigated against the class being chosen as a British Railways standard and that, as E.S. Cox put it, must be blamed on Brunel. The generous loading gauge he had provided allowed successive CMEs to construct locomotives of ample external dimension. This would simply not do for the remainder of the railway system.[8]

This factor, amongst others, probably mitigated against their use by the War Department even though they were recognised as good locomotives. Axle loading was high compared with many other eight-coupled engines, the need to supply Welsh coal would have presented logistical difficulties, and the high standard of mechanical construction could not be maintained in crude wartime workshops. The 2800 class was a breed apart but it suited the GWR and that is what really mattered. Many of the class lasted into the 1960s being forced out by the Standard 9Fs and the onset of dieselization. At withdrawal some of these engines were over 50 years old and could still haul heavy freights; they had well paid their construction cost.

In Great Western terms '28xx' locomotives were given the power classification 'E' and route availability 'Blue'. During British Railways service the power classification was '8F'. Performance would more than justify the power classification but it was a pity that axle loading and width so restricted their use in the wider theatre of British operations. Apart from service during the 1948 exchange trials one engine did venture further afield, again to show its paces to another railway. In January 1921 No 2804 went north to perform on the Glenfarg Bank, part of the North British Railway's track. The first trial with a load of 590 tons (600 tonnes) was successful, time taken being the scheduled 33 minutes, some 20 seconds less than taken by the railway's 0-6-0 on an earlier run with a 400 ton (407 tonne) load. However, the second with a load of 686 tons (698 tonnes) was not a success as the train came to a stand after a series of bad slips. There was no shortage of steam, failure being attributable to the weather, the snowstorm raging at the time resulting in loss of adhesion. Unfortunately there was no opportunity for a further test in better conditions. The trial was arranged in order for the Scottish railway to assess the suitability of an eight-coupled locomotive to work on its lines, the Operating Superintendent being of the opinion that considerable savings could be made by having longer trains hauled by more powerful locomotives than the railway's 0-6-0.

Neither the trials with the GWR eight-coupled engine nor those using the NER 0-8-0, to be described in Chapter 4, produced any change in North British locomotive design. One thing that the first set of trials did confirm, however, was the limited application of GWR engines on other routes. In order to reach North British metals No 2804 had to take a rather circuitous route as the LNWR would not allow passage over its northern main lines. Due to width and weight the Midland Railway would not take it and so a route had to be devised via Banbury onto the Great Central as far as Mexborough. North Eastern and Midland Joint metals allowed passage as far as Milford Junction where the North Eastern line was joined allowing the final run through to Berwick. The engine left Swindon at 11am on Saturday January 8th and reached Edinburgh, Haymarket, at 6.15pm on Monday 10th.[9]

Following World War II hostilities the financial state of Britain was not good and a need existed to earn foreign exchange. Good quality coal commanded high prices abroad and a scheme was instituted to convert some British locomotives to oil firing, thus freeing coal for export. As the GWR made use of high quality Welsh coal it is natural that early interest should centre on that line and the '28xx' engines were prime candidates for conversion. Initially it was proposed that 63 members of the class would be so treated but ultimately only 20 received oil burning equipment, principally because it was soon realized that oil had to be purchased from overseas and that cost much of the valuable foreign exchange the export of coal earned.

No 2872 was the first to be converted in October 1945 with the other 19 following over the next two

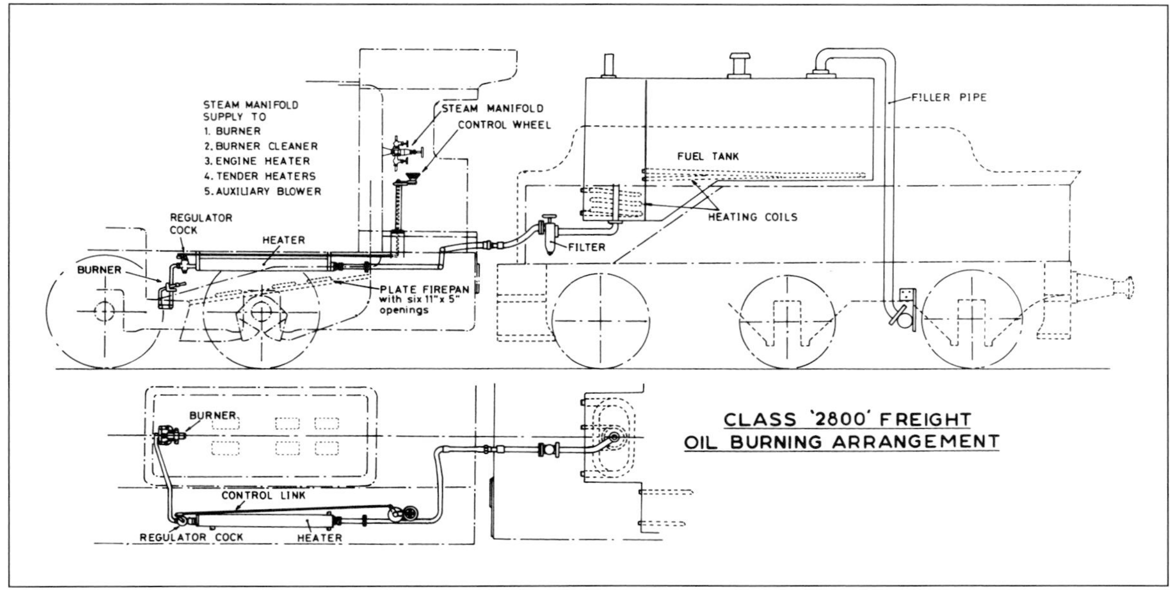

Oil burning arrangements for 2800 class.

years; all reverted back to coal firing by January 1950. Conversion required the tender to be modified in order to accommodate 1,800 gallons (8,228 litres) of fuel oil, the oil tank being lagged and provided with steam heating equipment. Modifications to the firebox included fitting of firebrick and installation of a plate in the ashpan to allow for control of combustion air. The firehole was arranged so that it

No 4809, formerly No 2845, operating on oil-firing at Hilmer Halt, 25th September 1948.
(J. Russell-Smith Collection/NRM, York)

formed a seal when shut but provided a small observation hole so that combustion conditions in the firebox could be observed. Gravity fed the oil from the heated tank through a further heater to the burner unit positioned at the front end of the firebox floor. Steam was used to atomize the oil and spray it into the firebox. A minimum oil flow was always maintained in order to sustain combustion but the fireman could regulate the size of the flame by means of an oil flow cock fitted at the outlet from the heater, the control handwheel for this being conveniently positioned in the cab. As the oil burning engines were to be employed in the South Wales area only two fuelling depots were considered necessary, one at Severn Tunnel Junction and the other at Llanelly. Under normal circumstances locomotive fuel tanks had capacity for 250 miles (400km).[10]

Although individuals have their own preferences it would be conceded by most that the '28xx' engines were exceptional by any standards. They certainly lived up to the expectations of their original designer and served both the GWR and British Railways consistently over many years. Few would, or could, argue against their hauling capacity or their efficiency and the '28xx' must be considered as one of the great British heavy freight locomotive classes.

The 1905 standardization scheme also called for a 2-8-2T which was to have been a tank version of the 2800 class using the standard No. 1 boiler. For various reasons, probably including the belief that the wheelbase was too long for the areas in which it would serve, it was never constructed. However, a 2-8-0T version did see the light of day and it proved to be very effective on the short mineral traffic which existed in South Wales. Standard parts were used in keeping with the plan and many of these were identical to the '28xx' engines, including driving and pony truck wheels, cylinder block castings, piston valves, and the Stephenson valve gear. In keeping with the usual practice a prototype was constructed during 1910 and quickly proved its worth. Construction of the production engines commenced in 1912 and batches appeared each year until 1917. Many more were constructed during the final Churchward and the early Collett years, the last batch coming from Swindon during 1940, these differing but little from the pilot engine of 1910.

Introduction of the 2-8-0T actually completed the nine standard classes of the original standardization scheme. A No. 4 boiler replaced the No. 1 boiler of the 2-8-0 thus allowing space for the coal bunker, whilst the driving wheelbase was extended in order to provide support for the bunker. Cylinders drove the second axle thus the connecting rods were shorter than those fitted to the 2-8-0, within the standardization scheme there being only two sizes of such rods.[11] Because these 2-8-0T engines, designated the 4200 class (the later engines being 5205 class), were designed for operation in South Wales with its tightly curved track it became necessary to provide for some flexibility in the rather long coupled wheelbase of 20ft (6.1m). Second and third coupled wheels had tyres with thin flanges, there was some side play in the trailing coupled wheels and trailing coupling rod bushes were provided with spherical seatings at their fork ends; bushes were split and provided with distance pieces to allow for easy removal. Such arrangements allowed the '42xx' locomotives to negotiate curves down to 2 chain radius, ie 66ft (20.1m).[12] LNWR 0-8-4 tanks operated similar duties in the South Wales area but they were unable to negotiate such tight curves giving the GWR engines a positive advantage.

Prototype engine No 4201 had bunker capacity for 3 tons (3.05 tonnes) of coal but that was considered insufficient and production versions carried about ½ ton (0.51 tonnes) more: a general uprating of bunker capacity to 4 tons (4.07 tonnes) commenced in 1919. As with the 2800 class minor modifications took place over the years including lengthening of frames at the rear to increase bunker capacity, introduction of outside steam pipes and new cylinder blocks, and an increase in cylinder diameter to 19in (48.3cm). The latter had the effect of increasing tractive effort. Superheaters underwent changes over the years and minor variations in the standard No. 4 boiler did take place but its overall size remained much the same as it had at introduction. Support for the frame at the front end had to be provided by means of struts attached to the smokebox.

Specifically designed for coal traffic in South Wales the class spent most of its working life in that area although a few examples did find work elsewhere. Main duties entailed haulage of coal trains from pit to port, coking plants for the steelworks or distribution sites. Runs were relatively short and the locomotives were ideal with some 72½ tons (73.8 tonnes) of adhesive weight being on the coupled driving wheels. Classed by the GWR as 'E', 'Red', in BR days they were designated as 7F or 8F depending upon cylinder diameter. GWR 'E' group-

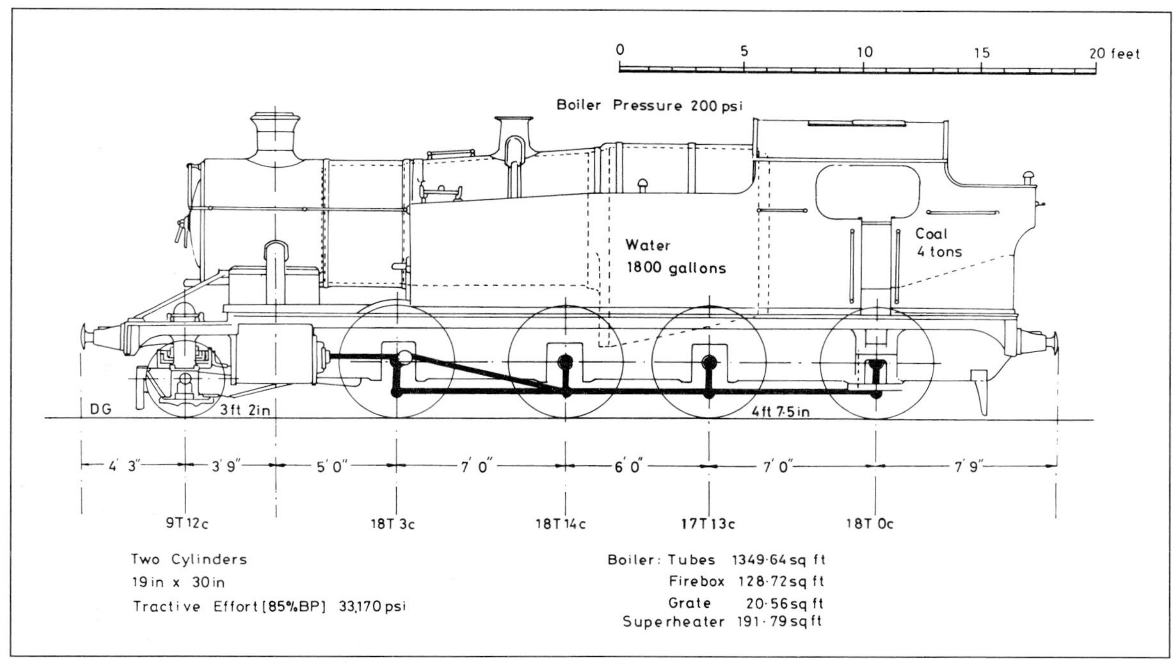

Churchward standard design 2-8-0T for Heavy Freight duties.

ing applied to locomotives up to 38,000 lbs tractive effort whilst route colour 'Red' signified engines having axle loading in excess of 17.6 tons (17.9 tonnes); 'Blue' route classification of the '28xx' engines signified axle loading up to 17.6 tons (17.9 tonnes).

5205 class Heavy Freight 2-8-0T No 5225 at Cardiff General in May 1962. (D.K. Jones Collection)

4200 class 2-8-0T No 4264 at Pontypool Road during July 1939. (D.K. Jones Collection)

Construction of the '42xx' tanks continued throughout the early 1930s, but a reduction in coal export traffic caused many of them to lie idle as they were of limited use elsewhere due to their small coal capacity. Improvement in general trade provided traffic on intermediate cross country routes primarily operated by mixed traffic 2-6-0s, some of which were then nearing the end of their useful lives. Collett took the decision to modify some of the 2-8-0T engines in order to provide increased coal and water capacity thus enabling them to undertake duties then performed by the ageing 'Aberdare' 2-6-0s. The first 20 rebuilt engines appeared in 1934 as 2-8-2 tanks and were designated the 7200 class. Modification was quite simple in that the frames of the 2-8-0T engines were extended by 4ft 1in (1.24m) to the rear using bolted on extension pieces. This located a trailing radial axle and allowed the bunker and side tanks to be extended. This conversion increased coal capacity to 6 tons (6.11 tonnes), the same as a tender engine, and increased water capacity to 2,500 gallons (11,429 litres).

Trailing wheels were of 3ft 8in (1.12m) diameter, a non-standard size in the Churchward scheme but by this time Collett was moving away from rigorous adherence to the old policies. As mentioned, the 1905 Churchward scheme had actually proposed a 2-8-2T engine using the standard No. 1 boiler but this was not constructed and in the '72xx', with its No. 4 boiler, the project reached fulfilment. So useful did the initial 20 engines prove to be that the Operating Department requested more of the same and Collett complied with two further batches, also converted from '42xx' engines taken out of service. The third batch made use of earlier, and hence older, Churchward engines necessitating more substantial reconstruction including the fitting of new cylinder blocks with 19in (48.3cm) diameter cylinders. Fuel and water capacities were revised with this batch being 5 tons (5.09 tonnes) and 2,700 gallons (12,343 litres) respectively.[13]

In terms of power the '72xx' engines were identical to the '42xx' series and so came under the same GWR classification of 'E' 'Red': BR class 8F. Adhesive weight on the coupled wheels was 72.75 tons (74.1 tonnes). The additional coal and water capacity did exactly what Collett had required and increased the operating range of the engines although they were still mainly stationed in South Wales. That allowed them to operate heavy coal trains to London and the South West which they did throughout the 1930s. During later years large numbers of former War Department 2-8-0s became available and the 2-8-2 tanks were put to work on the iron ore trains in South Wales. Expansion of the steel making industry in the region resulted in

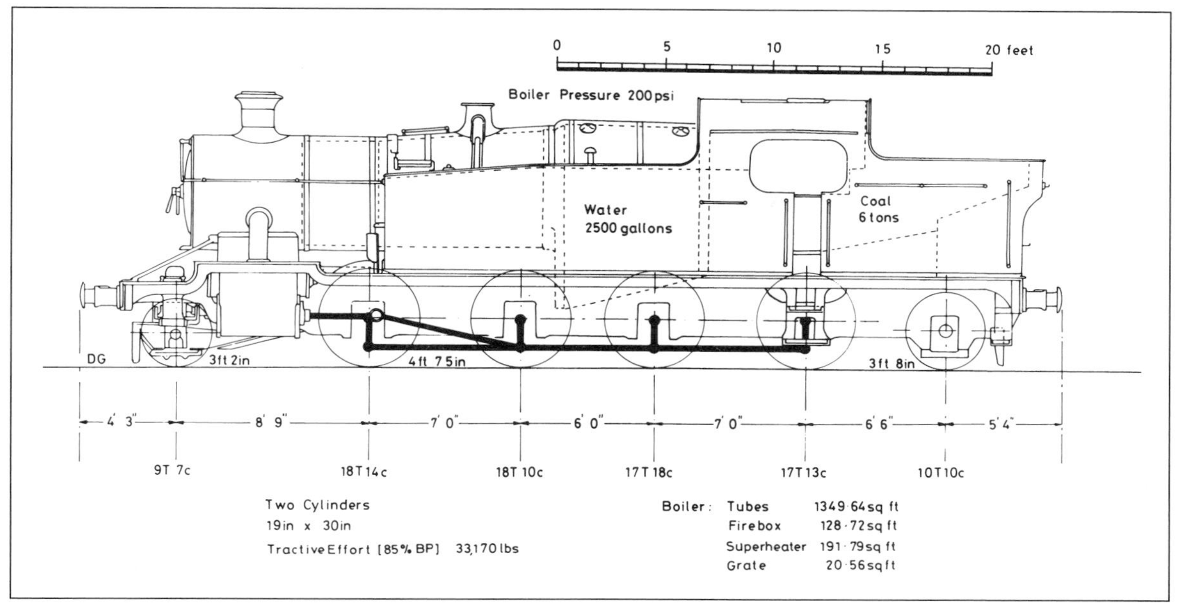

2-8-2T Heavy Freight design, Class 7200.

massive imports of iron ore and the 7200 class engines proved themselves to be ideal for hauling the heavy trains from dockside to blast furnaces. It was in effect a reverse of the role for which the '42xx' engines had been designed; haulage of coal from colliery to dock.

An interesting adjunct to the GWR heavy freight tank engine story is the 1938 proposal to construct a 2-10-2T engine for the iron ore traffic to Ebbw Vale. It would have made use of the standard No. 1 boiler and other standard features such as cylinder blocks and wheels as used for the 7200 class. With a total weight of 109.6 tons (111.6 tonnes) it would have been the heaviest tank engine, apart from the

7200 class 2-8-2T, No 7250 at Radyr in May 1964. (D.K. Jones Collection)

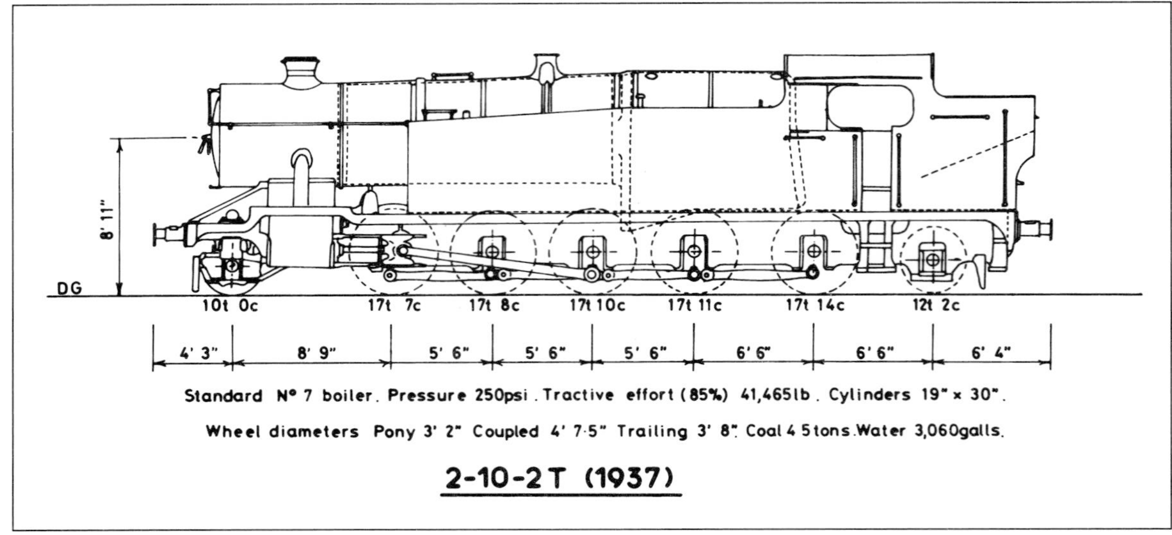

Proposed 1938 Collett design for a 2-10-2T locomotive.

Garratts, to operate in Britain and with a tractive effort of 41,465lbs also the most powerful. Wheels on the driving axle were flangeless whilst adjacent wheels had flanges of reduced thickness. Post war availability of other heavy freight engines removed the necessity for such construction.[14]

Churchward's standardization scheme also proposed another 2-8-0 but with larger diameter driving wheels and larger boiler than the '28xx'. For a variety of reasons the locomotive was not constructed immediately but it did appear shorty before Churchward retired as CME. Construction was eventually requested by the Traffic Department in order to deal with fast vacuum fitted freight trains which were demanded by certain sections of industry. The large wheels and arrangements for dealing with vacuum fitted stock enabled the class to work passenger trains as required, so in effect the design

Large, wheeled 2-8-0 for mixed traffic. The 4700 design.

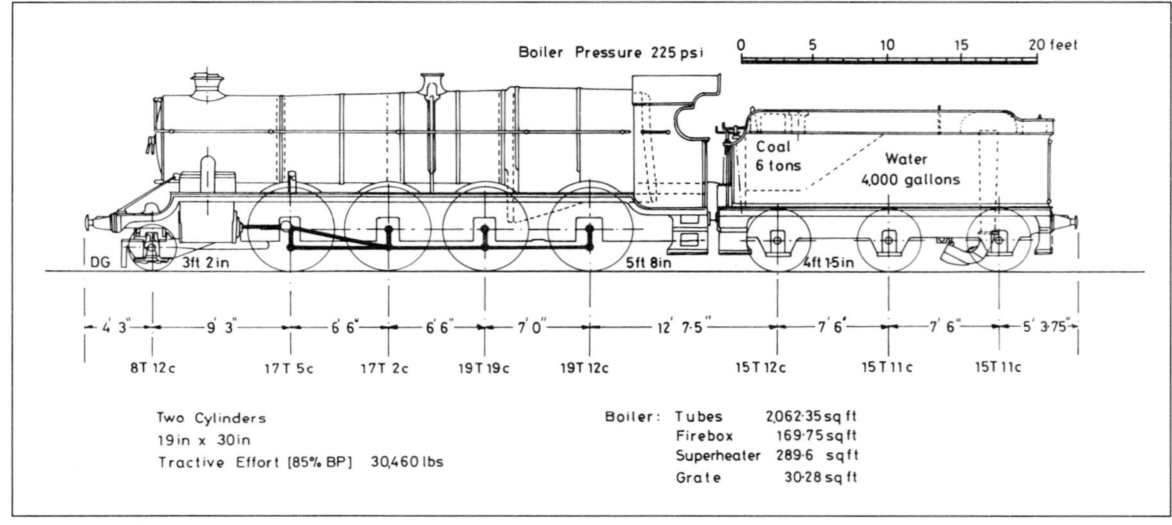

4700 class No 4704 at Shrewsbury in 1960. (D.K. Jones Collection)

was for mixed traffic rather than heavy freight, however, the wheel designation and the fact that heavy freights were operated is reason enough for inclusion in this book.

As formal plans were made for construction it soon became apparent that the intended No. 1 boiler was not large enough but no suitable boiler was available in the standard range, the No. 6 boiler from the solitary 4-6-2 being too large. In order not to delay construction of the prototype Churchward decided to fit the No. 1 boiler but provided it with an extended smokebox so that the length was correct. No 4700, the first member of the 4700 class appeared in 1919 and was put to work on the services for which it had been designed. A new standard boiler, the No. 7, was designed for the class

The imposing sight of the 4700 class locomotive – the first member of the class, No 4700. (D.K. Jones Collection)

and when the first of these became available in 1921 it was fitted to No 4700. Outside steam pipes were introduced at this stage and became standard. Eight other members of the class were constructed during the following two years and all found immediate employment on heavy fast freight services between London and the Midlands and between London and the West Country.

In terms of construction they followed the usual Churchward practice and apart from the boiler incorporated standard parts already available. In order to allow negotiation of curves, tyres on the middle two sets of driving wheels were provided with thinner flanges, a practice introduced with the 2800 class. Coupling rod bushes were also given spherical seatings to allow for flexibility when negotiating curves. It is a generally accepted fact that they were very useful engines permitting the working of heavier trains than could be undertaken by the 2-6-0 mixed traffic locomotives. High axle loading, 19.6 tons (19.95 tonnes), and a long coupled wheelbase, 20ft (6.08m), restricted these engines to certain routes and that limited usefulness attesting against further construction. Collett considered that his 'Hall' class 4-6-0 engines were more suitable for such duties as they had greater route availability. In British Railways service they were classified 7F, having been designated 'D' 'Red' during GWR days.

Great Western heavy freight and 2-8-0 mixed traffic engines lasted well and their performance was more than adequate even at the end of their days. Whilst the generous dimensions allowed by the GWR loading gauge prevented more widespread use throughout Britain they proved themselves to be well suited to operations right up to the end of steam. Use of standard parts and the high quality of construction and maintenance practised at Swindon allowed what were essentially elderly designs to last. They may have had their faults, and they certainly had limitations, but longevity in the work for which they were originally designed indicates a degree of usefulness which few would deny. It is true that many ageing locomotives were set to freight duties as their performance failed but the GWR eight-coupled classes stayed with their duties, requiring very few modifications throughout their long lives. That is a tribute to the initial design and the quality of maintenance.

3

Pre-Grouping Heavy Freight Locomotives on LMS Lines

Of the companies which formed the London Midland & Scottish Railway four had constructed eight-coupled locomotives for main line freight haulage, namely the Caledonian, Lancashire & Yorkshire, London & North Western and the Somerset & Dorset Joint railways. Each of these companies dealt with extensive mineral traffic, particularly in the form of coal, and gradients were severe on many parts of their route mileage. The LNWR was the only one with lines into London and it carried considerable quantities of general freight in heavy trains along its trunk routes. The industrial revolution had given birth to railways and developing industry demanded better facilities for movement of its goods and raw materials. Coal was the life blood of industry for it powered the factories but it was also an essential to trade as the movement of passengers and goods on land and sea required fuel and that meant coal.

Just to operate its trains the railways required an abundant supply of coal and that had to be collected from pits and distributed throughout the system. The British naval and merchant fleets were the largest in the world and prior to World War I all steam ships were coal fired: liners such as *Lusitania* and *Mauretania* consumed 1,000 tons of coal per day during an Atlantic crossing and that coal had to be moved to the ports as quickly and economically as possible. Large wagons and long trains were ideal but powerful locomotives had to be provided, hence development of heavy freight locomotives. Coal was not the only freight commodity carried by the railways but consideration of the tonnage illustrates its value to the railways and the country in general.

During 1913, the last full year of peace before World War I and probably the last full year of stable trade for a considerable period, the mines of Britain produced over 287 million tons of coal. Of this 26.9 per cent was shipped abroad as coal or coke, whilst 7.3 per cent was used to provide bunkers for ships trading overseas. Although some of this would have been moved around the coast in colliers the coal still needed to be transported from pit to port, usually by railway. During that same year the railways consumed over 13.5 million tons of coal which, obviously, had to be transported by rail. The remainder served Britain's blast furnaces, industry and domestic fires, and in general it all had to be moved by rail. It is no surprise, therefore, that those railways with considerable coal traffic developed heavy freight locomotives. In 1913 the LNWR carried almost 23.5 million tons of coal, the Caledonian 13 million tons and the LYR 9.4 million tons.[1] A notable exception in developing heavy freight locomotives was the Midland Railway which, although moving almost 28 million tons of coal that year, stayed firmly with its small engine policy.

Caledonian Railway

Close links with the LNWR provided continuity for passenger and freight trains north of Carlisle to Glasgow and beyond, thus the Caledonian needed at least to keep pace with certain aspects of locomotive development undertaken by its English ally. It also

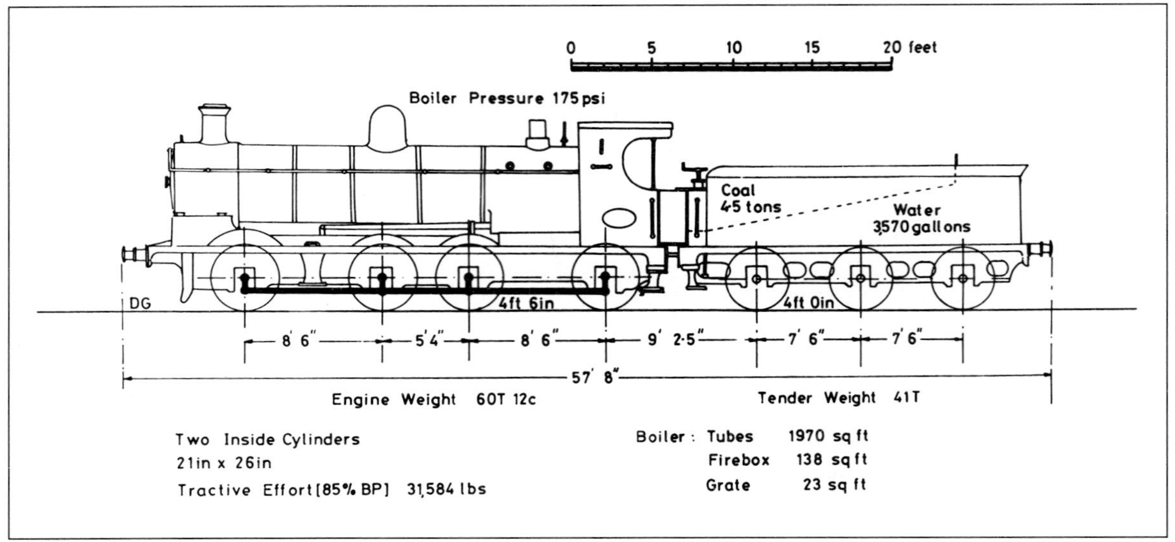

Caledonian Railway 600 class 0-8-0.

needed to consider its own traffic and take steps to meet those requirements. The Lanarkshire coal fields had been a rich source of mineral traffic but acquisition of the Solway Junction Railway in 1895 provided a route for bringing iron ore to the steel works of Lanarkshire which bypassed Carlisle. As was the case in most other areas 0-6-0 locomotives were employed for freight haulage until in 1901 two 0-8-0 locomotives were constructed at the railway's St Rollox Works. These locomotives were designed by the railway's Chief Mechanical Engineer, John F. McIntosh, for the specific purpose of hauling heavy mineral trains composed of 30-ton bogie open wagons which McIntosh had also introduced at the same time. The initial two locomotives were supplemented by six more two years later thus giving the 600 class a strength of eight.

Powerful locomotives with a tractive effort of 31,584lbs had been developed in order to haul trains comprising 35 of the 30-ton wagons giving a total train load of some 1,500 tons (1,527 tonnes).[2] Unfortunately the Traffic Department experienced difficulty in finding suitable sidings for trains of that length and usually a limit of 15 large wagons was imposed; not for the last time did operating restrictions interfere with haulage capability. Due to the weight, and anticipated length of train, Westinghouse air braking equipment was applied to the wagons, and hence to the locomotives, which in turn were fitted with air pumps at running plate level on the right hand side just in front of the cab.

Two inside cylinders 21in (53cm) diameter by 26in (66cm) stroke were supplied with steam from a large boiler working at 175psi. That boiler was a lengthened version of the one employed for the 'Dunalastair III' series locomotives, being some 15ft 4in (4.67m) long. Four Ramsbottom safety valves were grouped in a cylindrical casing. Slide valves, placed above the cylinders, were actuated by eccentrics acting through rocking levers.[3] With a total weight, engine plus tender, of just over 100 tons (102 tonnes) McIntosh's 0-8-0s were powerful and attractive above the frames but the unusual wheel spacing created a rather odd appearance. Cylinders drove the second axle which was positioned only 5ft 4in (1.62m) from the third axle, leaving barely enough room between the 4ft 6in (1.37m) wheels for the brake gear. A distance of 8ft 6in (2.6m) separated the outer wheels from the adjacent inner wheels thus producing a long wheelbase which offered support over the locomotive length with very little overhang at the front end. McIntosh must have been well aware that such a long wheelbase would cause problems on tightly curved track for he allowed a degree of flexibility at the centre axle coupling rod joints.[4] This flexibility would only be effective if side play at these axle boxes had also been provided. Even this does not explain the unusual axle spacing but it is possible that McIntosh considered close spacing of the

McIntosh 600 class No 605 with oddly spaced wheels. (Nevitt Collection/NRM, York)

middle pair of wheels to be the best arrangement for negotiation of tight curves without excessive flange wear. Position of the coupled axle was dictated by the location of the cylinders and length of connecting rod to be employed, whilst close spacing of the second and third axles would produce an effect approaching that of an 0-6-0 locomotive. During the 1903–4 period McIntosh constructed six eight-coupled tank engines for shunting and banking duties but these do not fall within the scope of this book which is concerned with main line locomotives. Apart from the fitting of Westinghouse brakes and the use of eight-coupled wheels they owe little to their main line brothers.

Overall the 600 class 0-8-0s performed well, in fact too well for the operating system then available, but they must have been inefficient when operated below designed load, the loads generally offered being within the capacity of an 0-6-0. Usually stationed at Motherwell to cover the mineral traffic they did see service on other goods trains and four of the class were used for hauling the heavy 'Buffalo Bill' circus trains from Stranraer to Carlisle during 1904. McIntosh certainly understood the needs of his railway in providing air braked, high capacity, bogie mineral wagons and the locomotives to haul them economically. Unfortunately the railway itself did not appear to appreciate its own needs or, perhaps, railway departments just did not communicate effectively with each other.

Lancashire & Yorkshire Railway

Straddling rich coalfields in two counties and with ports on both sides of the country put the LYR in an enviable position as far as goods traffic was concerned. That traffic was not purely of a mineral nature as extensive shipments of fish took place whilst imports of timber from Scandinavia also required moving. The main traffic was, however, coal and towards the turn of the century it had reached such proportions that the 0-6-0 goods engines were no longer able to cope. LYR cross-country routes offered heavy gradients and powerful locomotives were necessary for even moderate loadings. The Aspinall 0-6-0s could deal with through loads of up to 475 tons on the moderately graded route between Sowerby Bridge and Goole but could only handle 120 ton loads on the steeply graded line between Middleton Junction and Bacup.[5]

In order to provide additional hauling power to meet the rapidly increasing coal shipments Aspinall set in motion plans for construction of an eight-coupled coal engine which entered service during 1900, shortly after H.A. Hoy became CME. In order to provide the necessary power two inside cylinders 20in (51cm) diameter by 26in (66cm) stroke were supplied with steam from a large boiler working at a pressure of 180psi. The boiler was similar to that fitted to the Aspinall 4-4-2 express passenger locomotives being of the same diameter and having

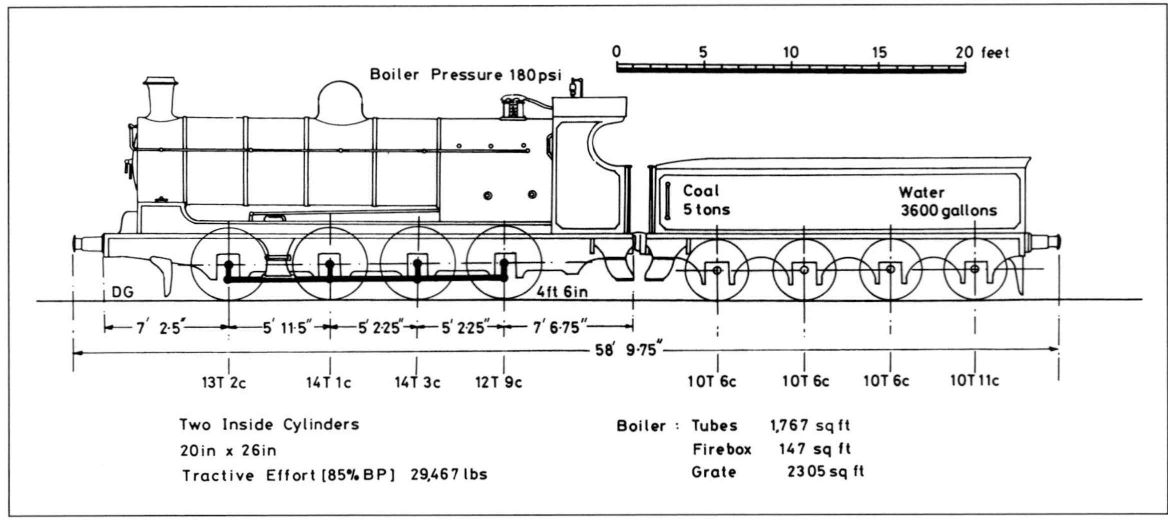

Aspinall 0-8-0 Heavy Freight design for the Lancashire & Yorkshire Railway.

the same length of tube, 15ft 0in. Unlike the 4-4-2s, however, there was no recessed smokebox and so the 0-8-0 boiler was shorter externally. The large Belpaire firebox had a shallower depth than that fitted to the 4-4-2 thus reducing firebox heating surface by some 14 sq ft.

Joy valve gear operated Richardson balanced valves placed on top of the cylinders with exhaust taking place through the back of the valves. Drive from the cylinders was through the second axle to the 4ft 6in (1.37m) diameter coupled wheels. With a tractive effort of 29,467lbs the engines were a definite improvement on the 0-6-0s, being able to haul greater loads and sustain higher speeds. For the same sections of route mentioned above equivalent loads for the 0-8-0s were 790 tons and 206 tons respectively. These are just typical figures quoted by George Hughes to illustrate the ability of the new goods engines and higher through loads could be taken with assistance available in certain sections. On normally graded routes 60 loaded wagons, equivalent to 1,000 tons, were hauled with ease.

The initial 40 locomotives had standard six-wheel tenders which held 5 tons (5.6 tonnes) of coal and 2,290 gallons (10,469 litres) of water. On long hauls water became something of a problem and subsequent examples were fitted with Hoy designed eight-wheeled tenders. These held 5 tons (5.1 tonnes) of coal but contained 3,600 gallons (16,457 litres) of water. Because of the long wheelbase, 15ft 9in (4.8m), the inner pairs of wheels had thinner flanges in order to reduce friction on curves.

On 11 March 1901 engine No 676 was running tender first with a heavy coal train to Goole when its boiler exploded near Knottingley. The driver and fireman were killed, the locomotive and 24 wagons becoming derailed. The entire left hand side of the firebox and part of the crown sheet had given way, resulting in a blast of steam which forced the boiler out of the frames onto the lineside from where it toppled into a field. At the subsequent enquiry Hoy claimed that shortage of water had resulted in the firebox crown overheating but the enquiry decided that defective stays were to blame. The copper based alloy used for the stays had been devised by Hoy and it turned out to have low elasticity and a tendency to cracking. The fault, therefore, lay with the LYR and its engineers. If stays were a problem then a design which avoided the use of stays must present the best solution. This view was certainly held by J.A.F. Aspinall, formerly CME and by then General Manager of the LYR, who during discussion of a paper by F.W. Webb on locomotive firebox stays stated, '. . . it was mentioned how frequently stays had to be renewed and he (Aspinall) thought that pointed to the desirability of getting rid of the stay altogether, if possible. Engineers ought to look forward to a time when they could get rid of the rectangular firebox and adopt something 'circular'.[6]

Marine practice with Scotch boilers and land practice with Lancashire boilers had long employed

Aspinall 0-8-0 No 12715 in LMS days. (Author's Collection)

circular corrugated fireboxes and such a form did not require staying as only flat surfaces required support. Circular fireboxes were not new to locomotive practice, F.W. Webb having designed one a number of years earlier, but it had not proven to be successful.[7] Many years before that John Ramsbottom had used a corrugated circular firebox in a shunting engine design.[8] Hoy, most likely at Aspinall's instigation, set about producing a design for a boiler incorporating a corrugated firebox.

Locomotive No 392 was fitted with the new boiler during February 1902 and after a series of tests Hoy declared himself satisfied and decided that 20 more 0-8-0s with that form of boiler could be constructed during 1903. Tube leakage soon occurred and several remedies were tried including changes in tubeplate thickness and material. After 5 years in service cracks developed in the tubeplates near the flange whilst fireboxes developed a tendency to become oval. Jacking back to circular form corrected that defect but it soon reappeared. Problems were experienced with priming and several means were adopted to overcome this, including increasing the size of dome, placing baffles across the base of the dome and inserting perforated plates in the dome, but none of them overcame the problem. Poor circulation was also evident and overall the boiler compared very unfavourably with the Belpaire type.[9] From an operational point of view it was priming and poor circulation which caused most problems. The latter resulted in the need to light a fire early on Saturday if the locomotive was required for service on the Monday morning. Steaming problems and leaks did not endear them to footplate crew or shed staff and they earned themselves the nickname of 'Sea Pigs'.[10] Needless to say the boilers were replaced as soon as economically possible with most locomotives receiving Hughes large Belpaire boilers by 1914.

These 0-8-0s in what can be considered as a small boiler form were constructed steadily until January 1908 by which time George Hughes had taken over as CME. Without doubt, apart from problems with the corrugated firebox boilers, these coal engines were successful at hauling heavy mineral and other freight trains throughout the system but Hughes wanted more than just success, he wanted economy. During presentation of his paper 'Compounding and Superheating in Horwich Locomotives' to the Institution of Mechanical Engineers in 1910 he made a statement to the effect that economy in locomotive working did not necessarily imply a reduced coal bill as the whole aspect of locomotive operation had to be considered.

Hughes had studied compounding in marine and stationary plant and concluded that its advantages were so well proven as to ensure adoption. Locomotive application was a different matter and he considered that the comparatively good results from simple locomotives and the meagreness of published data on the working of compounds made locomotive engineers cautious of adopting the principle. Hughes was a cautious man but he would make up his own mind from the results of his own work. Careful consideration of the facts directed him to the conclusion that very little benefit would result from compounding an express passenger locomotive as the pistons moved too quickly for condensation to occur within the cylinder anyway. It was his view that the advantages of compounding lay in reducing the temperature range between the steam at inlet and exhaust. For large temperature ranges condensation takes place with a consequent loss in efficiency. This, he considered, was the case with slow moving goods engines where piston speeds would fall below 600 feet per minute (183 metres per minute), a figure he believed to be significant. Observations of goods locomotives at speeds of 20mph (32km per hour) and 30mph (48km per hour) gave piston speeds of 480 to 716 feet per minute (146 and 218 metres per minute) for the 0-6-0 and 540 to 809 feet per minute (165 and 247 metres per minute) for the 0-8-0.

Piston speeds and other aspects such as cut-off and cylinder compression convinced Hughes that the goods engine was a more promising vehicle with which to test compounding. Exhaust ports are closed before the piston reaches the end of its stroke during the exhaust period and that produces compression of steam remaining in the cylinder. Such compression exerts a cushioning effect for fast moving pistons but it also exerts a back pressure on the piston thereby reducing the total work output. The amount of compression is determined by valve lap and lead, which in turn is influenced by the cut-off. Earlier cut-off as used for express engines produces earlier closing of the exhaust with consequent increase in compression.

From the above figures it might appear that the 0-6-0 offered greater scope as piston speed would tend to be below the 'magic' 600 feet per minute for a longer period, however, Hughes decided that the 0-8-0 would be more suitable because of its higher power and greater length. During 1906 locomotive No 1452 was converted into a four-cylinder compound, all four cylinders driving the second axle. Cylinder dimensions were chosen in order to make the hauling capacity of the compound the same as the simple, this gave two 15½in (39cm) diameter HP cylinders outside the frames and two 22in (56cm) diameter LP cylinders between the frames. All pistons had 26in (66cm) strokes and Joy valve gear was provided for each set of pistons. HP inside admission piston valves were used whilst the LP valves were of conventional Richardson type. Hughes wished to avoid the risk of high compression pressures in the HP cylinders when running at high speed with earlier cut-off and so he took the precaution of providing greater clearance between piston and cylinder cover at the end of the stroke than was normal with a simple engine. Even then it was found that excessive compression pressure did

Hughes Compound 0-8-0 design, LYR.

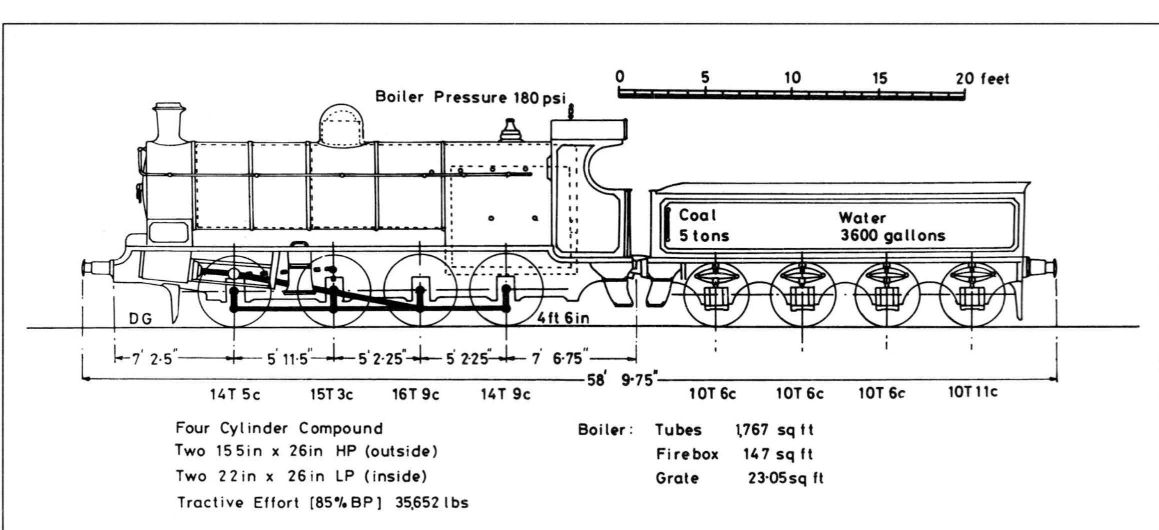

result in the HP cylinders when cut-off was less than 40 per cent.

Cranks for pairs of pistons, one LP and one HP, on the same side of the locomotive, left or right hand side, were placed at 180° to each other in order to provide a degree of balance. Equivalent left and right side cranks were at 90° to each other thus providing an even driving torque. Two sets of Joy gear were fitted just inside the frames, one each side of the locomotive, and each set of gear operated the valves on its side of the locomotive by means of a two-arm rocking shaft. Both valves moved in the same direction at the same time.[11]

Extensive testing of the compound took place during 1906 and 1907, with loads and conditions similar to those used for testing the simple during 1904 and 1905. From the dates of the tests it is obvious that Hughes was dedicated to obtaining extensive data on his locomotives and had plans for improvements as early as 1904. Test trains operated on routes from Aintree to Accrington and Goole to Smithy Bridge. Full details of the results and analysis were published by Hughes in his paper 'Compounding and Superheating'. It is not necessary to give full details of those results here as interested readers can consult the paper but the conclusions are worthy of repetition. Hughes analysed the data and produced comparisons between the compound and simple, giving water and coal consumptions on the basis of loads and output power. In all cases the compound proved to be the most economical, the degree of economy depending upon a number of factors including route and load. Fuel savings per horse power (kW) developed amounted to 16 per cent on the Aintree section whilst on the Goole section it was 8.3 per cent. As the compound developed less power than the simple total fuel savings amounted to 36 per cent and 23.7 per cent respectively. During certain tests the compound hauled the same load as a simple with the same coal consumption but in 13 per cent less time.

Approval was given for construction of a further 20 compounds as a result of the trials, but only ten were actually built, the other ten locomotives of the order being constructed as simples. Why Hughes did not construct all as compounds is unknown but it is possible that he still wished to perfect the design before committing himself to extensive construction. Heavy freight power was urgently needed and the ten simples would add to the total stock, rebuilding in compound form being possible at a later date. In order to perfect the design testing still continued and showed up some interesting points in respect of compound operation.

Hughes had designed the cylinders in order to obtain approximately the same power from both HP and LP but indicator card analysis showed that less power was developed in the HP cylinders than anticipated. Valve gear was linked thus it was not possible for the driver to vary LP and HP cut-off independently. The difference between powers increased with speed and lateness of cut-off; an unexpected falling off in anticipated power also occurred in the LP cylinder with cut-offs greater than 65 per cent. Hughes concluded that the problem was due to cylinder compression and considered solutions. Negative valve lap would avoid compression but was only suitable at high speed, being positively detrimental at slow goods train speeds. Spring-loaded relief valves on cylinders could be used to relieve compression but they only released a small amount of compressed steam, maintaining at least full boiler pressure and so were unsuitable if the engine was operating with the regulator throttled. The only solution as far as Hughes was concerned lay in relieving pressure directly to the steam receiver between HP and LP cylinders and that could be achieved by means of special spring loaded valves in main the HP piston valve.

In respect of the power fall off in the LP cylinders Hughes believed that the port area ratio of 1 to 12.6 was too small and that a larger ratio should have been provided, although the use of standard valves had dictated that ratio. Regarding the unequal distribution of work he considered that equalization could be achieved by allowing separate adjustment of cut-off for HP and LP cylinders as was the usual practice on the Continent.[12] He understood the need for careful handling by the driver and the fact that he made no moves to apply such mechanisms indicates a belief that British locomotive drivers were, generally, not as skilful as their Continental brothers. Certainly the nature of training and education of drivers on the Continent was superior to that in Britain, there they really were 'engineers'.

An aspect of the compound design which illustrates the Hughes attitude to driver intervention was his auxiliary valve for use when starting or running at high values of cut-off on gradients. Power and torque requirements during such periods were high and could not be provided by compound working, so it was necessary to operate as a simple with steam being supplied to the LP cylinders only. The device consisted of two slide valves mounted back-to-back and situated in an auxiliary chamber within the LP steam chest. That chamber was supplied with steam directly from the boiler and movement of the auxiliary valve directed steam to the LP chest from where it could pass to the LP cylinder via its valve; steam could also pass through the receiver pipes to the HP cylinder acting on the exhaust side of the HP piston thus equalizing pressure and putting the HP side in equilibrium. Although full boiler pressure was applied to the auxiliary chamber pressure on the LP piston was somewhat lower as the relatively small area of the auxiliary valve produced a throttling effect. The valve was operated by means of a linkage connected to the reversing shaft and so it was not under the direct control of the driver. Operation as a simple was automatic whenever cut-off exceeded 73 per cent.

The production batch of compounds differed but slightly from the prototype, the most significant alteration being that the outside HP cylinders connected with the third axle whilst the inside HP provided drive for the second. The running plate was also higher than the simples and there was no long splasher. Many other features were the same, including the use of compensating levers for the spring gear of the front three axleboxes, which according to Eric Mason was a very good feature of the 0-8-0 design. The boiler was identical for simples and compounds but Mason believed that the compounds suffered due to inadequate steam supply. Apart from that he considered them to have been very successful.[13]

Testing did not cease when the production compounds entered service as Hughes insisted on the collection of full operating data in order to provide evidence to assist with future decisions. This information was comprehensively given in the paper ‘Compounding and Superheating’ but at the time of its publication, March 1910, Hughes still believed that data from three more years of operation was required before true figures for coal consumption and maintenance could be determined. He was prepared to state, however, that operations up to that time pointed towards maintenance costs for compounds being lower than for simples. Unlike most other engineers he was also prepared to put values on costs and charges thus his simple analysis provides a valuable indication as to locomotive operating costs. Compounds cost £260 more than simples to construct but they indicated a 9 per cent improvement in economy of coal and water. Taking 10 per cent as annual charges for depreciation, interest and repairs the additional annual cost for a compound would be £26; his presumption was that compound repairs cost no more than for simples. As the LYR had direct access to coal from local pits during the period, costing 8s 4d (42p) per ton and based on average annual consumptions he was able to determine a cost saving for coal. Similar analysis allowed the cost of saving on water to be obtained and, allowing for an increase in lubricating oil at a cost of 10s (50p), it was possible for him to arrive at a total saving of £28 4s 10d (£28.24p). The difference between this and the higher annual charge for compound construction was marginal, although it would have been higher if coal cost more.[14] The LYR obtained its coal at a lower cost than most other railways and Hughes was well aware that the savings made did not justify the additional complication involved. He believed that traffic had to be handled more expeditiously and that the first cost of a compound needed to be reduced if compounding was to be perpetuated.

It would appear that construction costs could not be reduced as the LYR built no more compounds. Hughes did not cease his experimentation and ideas towards further improvement with compounding utilising higher boiler pressures and superheating certainly crossed his mind. During 1913 when simple 0-8-0s with larger superheated boilers were under construction approval was given for construction of ten compounds with that type of boiler. Unfortunately the order was cancelled but it would have been most interesting to compare the results from such engines with the earlier type compounds.[15]

Construction of 0-8-0s continued until 1920, a total of 295 being built in all forms. Later groups were provided with larger boilers and many of these were fitted with superheaters. Hughes carried out experiments into the economy of superheating and benefits were also explained in the paper on the subject but at the time of its delivery no eight-coupled locomotive had been so fitted. Cost and savings analysis were also applied to superheating and the same conclusion drawn, namely for the idea to be effective first cost had to be reduced.

Initially trials had been carried out using Schmidt superheaters on which a royalty had to be paid. Hughes was not particularly happy with that form of superheater and by the time the principle was applied to the 0-8-0 coal engines in 1914 he had devised his own. In fact Hughes developed two different types of superheater, the plug type and the top and bottom type. The latter came in two versions, the early form with 20 elements and the later form with 28 elements, the latter becoming established as the standard LYR superheater. Plug type superheaters caused many maintenance problems as elements became jammed in position. The top and bottom form was developed to overcome this problem and to maintain the smokebox relatively free of steam pipes. That it was a successful design is evident from its continued use by the railway. Several heavy freight engines were provided with Robinson superheaters, again to test the system but this type proved no more effective than the Hughes type.

Construction of saturated boiler 0-8-0s continued alongside those with superheaters and many remained in that form until they were scrapped. This does not indicate any lack of benefit from superheating but merely that some operations on the LYR did not justify its application. Routes on this railway varied considerably as did services. Short haulage with frequent stopping was not suited to superheating and a place for saturated boilered heavy freight engines could still be found on such services. Externally there was no obvious difference between superheated and non-superheated engines but over the years certain changes had been made in design. Twenty large boilered, saturated locomotives built in 1910–11 had been provided with a very heavy Joy valve gear, strap type bottom end bearing keeps and a large, heavy crosshead. The reasoning behind this is unknown and it was not perpetuated in other batches.

As with all designs there were a number of problems including a tendency for driving axleboxes to fail, particularly on the superheated engines. This resulted from knocking between axleboxes and hornplates due to excessive clearance caused by incorrect setting. If clearances were too tight however, there was a tendency for axleboxes to seize in their horn blocks. In general they were good locomotives, Eric Mason considering them to be simply designed and easy to work. During his long experience of them he was not aware of any serious or persistent complaints being made regarding performance or maintenance.

The 0-8-0s worked throughout the system, easily handling any load which could be accommodated in loops or refuge sidings. The LYR appears to have organized its interdepartmental communications better than other railways as its heavy freight locomo-

Aspinall 0-8-0 as rebuilt by Hughes with larger boiler. No 52782 at Abergavenny during 1949, still in LMS livery. (D.K. Jones Collection)

tives were not over powered for the work involved. Loads applied suited the gradients and assistance could be made available if necessary. In keeping with the Hughes philosophy of experimentation a number were provided with feed water heating apparatus employing Weir's feed pumps. Although that practice was short lived further trials of Dabeg feed water heating equipment was carried out during LMS days. Neither form improved efficiency sufficiently to warrant continued use.

Following Grouping the former LYR 0-8-0s continued to operate cross country routes but they were outnumbered in the enlarged fleet by former LNWR 0-8-0s. Introduction of the Garratts and Fowler's 0-8-0 7Fs made them non-standard and dispensable. Withdrawals commenced in the mid-1920s but a number did survive until Nationalisation.

Despite the fact that the 0-8-0s could meet LYR heavy freight traffic needs there was always room for improvement and neither Aspinall nor Hughes relaxed in their pursuit of efficiency. Double heading with 0-6-0s was still employed but that could be eliminated on certain heavy coal trains by the use of very powerful locomotives and just prior to the outbreak of the First World War Horwich produced an outline drawing of a four-cylinder 2-10-0. It was never built nor did it get past the outline stage but the fact that such a scheme was under consideration illustrates the advanced nature of Horwich locomotive thinking. This four-cylinder machine would have had a tractive effort of 53,328lbs making it easily the most powerful locomotive in Britain at that time.[16] How the 4ft 10in (1.47m) diameter driving wheels on a wheelbase of 22ft 10in (6.96m) would have negotiated LYR curves is open to question, however, kept to certain main lines the locomotive could have been a most effective solution to a problem faced by most railways. Other factors including length of loops and refuge sidings would have required attention but co-operation between departments on 'Aspinall's' railway was as good as anywhere.

London & North Western Railway

An extensive trunk route system and major freight haulage dictated that the LNWR would require a large stud of dedicated goods engines. Ramsbottom's six-coupled DXs had been introduced in 1858 and Webb subsequently constructed updated versions of this class in the form of his 17in and 18in goods engines. These could deal with traffic then offered but by the end of the 1880s it was becoming apparent that a more powerful locomotive design was required in order to meet expanding trade. Running more trains hauled by 0-6-0s was not ideal as these would occupy lines which were already dominated by passenger traffic, and operating freight at night could not meet service needs. The only solution was to run longer trains hauled by more powerful locomotives; Webb had quickly realized that double heading was not an economic proposition and economy of working was always to the fore in Webb's thinking. Several factors had to be taken into account regarding any new freight locomotive not least being the fact that it should be capable of working throughout the extensive LNWR system on track with high gradients and sharp curves. Much LNWR track at the time was laid in indifferent ballast which resulted in frequent fishplate failures and must have caused problems with locomotive springing. Replacement with stone ballast during the 1890s reduced the incidence of such failures but conversion was a long process and locomotives needed to cope with sections of poor track for many years.[17]

Faced with this situation Webb set about designing an eight-coupled freight engine and in October 1892 No 2524 entered service, the first 0-8-0 specifically built for heavy freight duties in Britain. In view of Webb's enthusiasm for compounding it has often been thought that construction of this locomotive as a simple was out of character but the fact is that there were no freight compounds at that time and anyway, the compounds formed but a small part of the LNWR locomotive stock. Many features of existing freight engines applied to No 2524 and Webb drew on already proven practice. Valves and motion were based upon the 18in goods; two 19½in (49.5cm) diameter by 24in (61cm) stroke cylinders being placed between the frames. The boiler, operating at a pressure of 160psi, was of the type fitted to the express compound *Greater Britain* and contained a combustion chamber in the middle section with an associated ash chute.

The eight-coupled wheels were of 4ft 5½in (1.36m) diameter with new tyres and employed cast iron centres, a practice common to the six-coupled coal engines. For the first time on a goods engine metal brake blocks were provided and all wheels were braked. On the locomotive sanding gear was arranged only in front of the leading wheels but additional sanding was fitted at the leading wheels of the tender, obviously for use when operating tender first. The second axle was used for driving and, in addition to the two axleboxes on the frames there was a central bearing carried in a casting extending from the motion plate to the frame stretcher in front of the firebox. Valves were positioned above the cylinders and actuated by means of Joy gear. Coupling rods provided an interesting feature as they were made up of three interchangeable lengths, one end having an eye and the other having a fork into which the eye of the mating rod would fit. The weight of the engine alone was 46.84 tons (47.7 tonnes).[18]

Without doubt Webb considered this machine as a 'one off' to be used for testing purposes and it is likely that many trials were conducted on various sections of the system, both to test locomotive performance and suitability for a particular section. One such trial has been documented by C.J.B. Cooke[19] and it illustrates Webb's interest in obtaining operating data from his locomotives. No 2524 ran a special coal train between Rugby and Willesden, a distance of 77 miles (123km), on 16th July 1893 with a load of 777 tons behind the tender. The total train length was 1,263ft (385m). Within the train formation was Webb's dynamometer car, or tractometer car as it was sometimes called. This section of line with its maximum gradient of 1 in 326 was not particularly severe but it was typical and allowed data to be gathered on heavy freight operation. Cooke provided tractometer diagrams of the trip and these illustrate the drawbar pull throughout the run. On the steepest section the drawbar pull was 5 tons (5.09 tonnes) and the locomotive developed 557 horsepower (416kW) whilst moving at 13 miles per hour (20.8km per hr).

This, and other tests, must have convinced Webb as to the usefulness of an eight-coupled freight locomotive and may even have convinced him that a compound could perform even better. There is no evidence to indicate that, like Hughes in later years, he believed the slow speed goods engine to be more suitable for compounding than the express locomotive. He had faith in compounding and it is likely that the trials with No 2524 confirmed his opinions. Whatever the thinking plans were already afoot for construction of a compound eight-coupled freight engine as the first of the A class three-cylinder compound 0-8-0s entered service in September 1893. Although of similar arrangement to No 2524 the compound was radically different. The two 15in (38cm) by 24in (61cm) HP cylinders were positioned outside the frames driving the second axle whilst the single 30in (76cm) by 24in (61cm) LP cylinder was between the frames, also driving the second axle. Stephenson gear, positioned inside the

Webb A class 0-8-0 three-cylinder compound Heavy Freight design, LNWR.

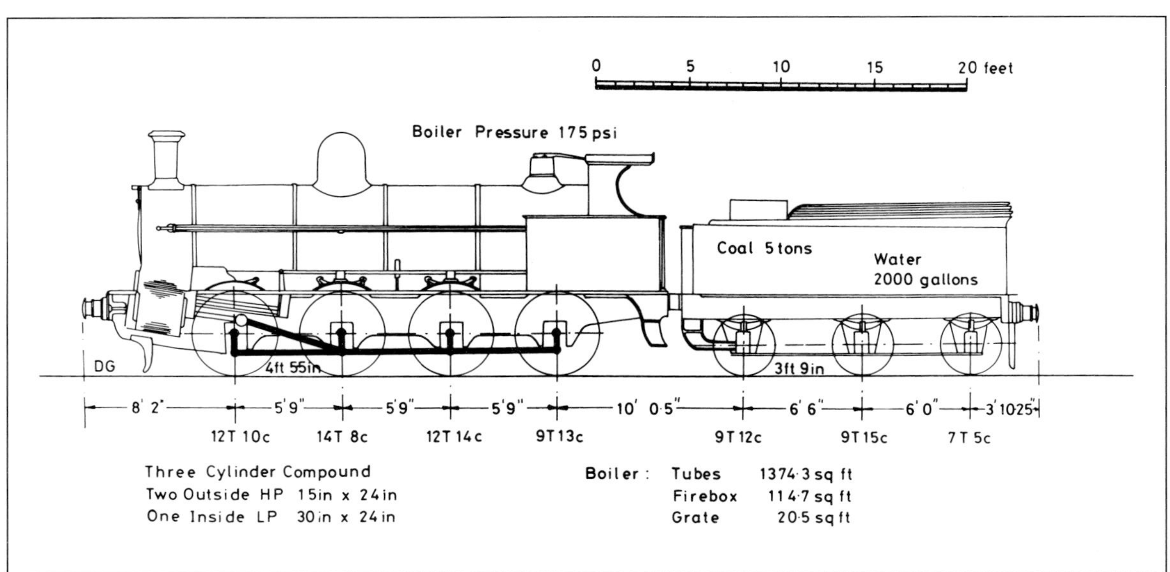

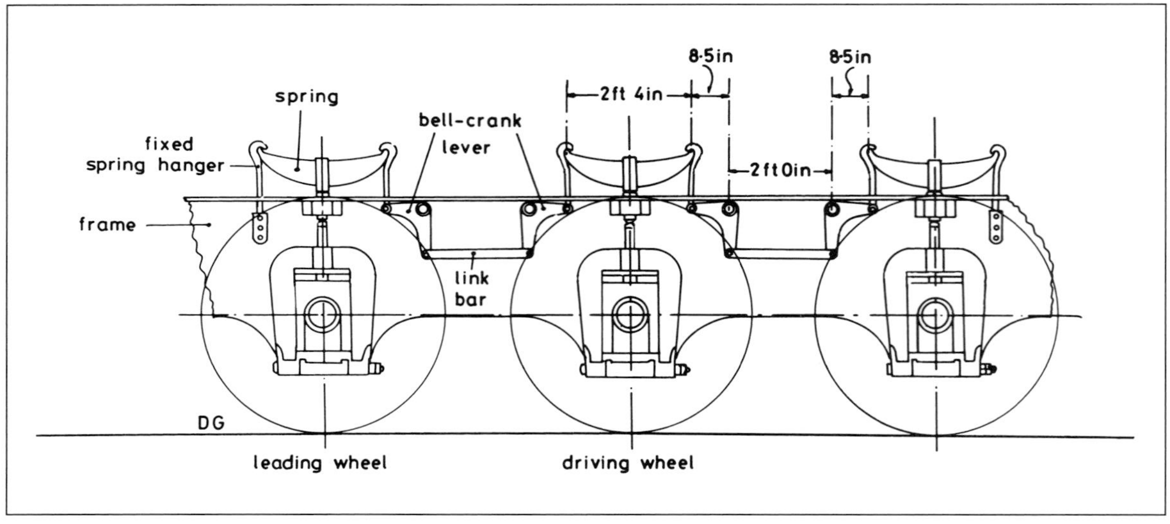

The arrangement of equalizing levers as fitted to Webb's A class 0-8-0s.

frames, operated the HP valves placed alongside the cylinders, whilst the LP valve, above the cylinder, was driven by a slip eccentric. These arrangements had applied to a number of three-cylinder compound passenger engines. HP cranks were placed at 90° to each other with the LP crank at 135° to these.

The long boiler was similar in external arrangement to that of the simple but differed internally as no combustion chamber was provided. Its pressure was also higher at 175psi making subsequent comparative running trials an unequal affair. Other features of the simple, and other freight engines, found their way onto the compound, including sanding gear, cab, and driving wheels. In order to deal with the indifferent LNWR track equalizing levers were provided for the springing on the first three axles thus allowing for automatic adjustment of weight between the wheels. Webb has publicly stated that he designed these engines to operate heavier trains with increased numbers of wagons over steeply graded lines thus allowing the number of trains run to be reduced and enable a large number of banking and assisting engines to be dispensed with.[20] Compounding, he always believed, produced economy of working but larger locomotives did the same as it enabled longer trains to be run and assisting engines to be eliminated.

The merits, or otherwise, of compounding as applied to locomotives is always the subject of debate, but Webb firmly believed in the principle and would frequently carry out trials to test his convictions. Results would be made public and from an engineering point of view they generally backed the Webb line but that is to be expected as compounding was the order of the day at Webb's Crewe.

On 1 April 1894, the date might now be looked upon as appropriate, Webb arranged comparative trials between simple and compound versions of his 0-8-0. The test runs between Crewe and Stafford were carried out with identical loads and, as far as possible, under identical firing conditions. Because of the short distance and the relatively level track the results cannot be taken too seriously but they did indicate a positive advantage for compounding. Coal consumption for the compound was 46.48lbs per mile (13.2kg per km) whilst that for the simple was 60.66lbs per mile (17.23kg per km).[21] To what extent those trials were useful is unknown but it is highly unlikely that Webb required any further convincing as to the merits of compounding for heavy freight use. However, comparative trials were a useful way of gathering evidence to sway reluctant directors, although Webb never appeared to worry himself too much about what directors thought. Between 1894 and 1900 some 110 three-cylinder compound 0-8-0s were built and they appear to have been successful in hauling traffic throughout the system.

The original intention had been to make use of these locomotives for heavy freight haulage on the main line north to Carlisle but Webb evidently considered them suitable for use elsewhere and on other traffic. On 29 December 1896 No 2525 was tried between Crewe and Carlisle with a passenger train consisting of 25 six-wheeled coaches and the Webb dynamometer car. The total weight of the train including locomotive was 354.5 tons (361 tonnes) and it observed a passenger schedule with seven stops. Throughout the run readings of drawbar pull, speed and engine indicated power were obtained, whilst water and coal consumption was measured. The true reason for the trial was never disclosed but the locomotive consumed a creditable 55.1lbs of coal per mile (15.65kg per km) during the actual trip and developed a maximum 781 horse power (583kW). Timings were not up to passenger locomotive standard but a mean speed excluding stops of 32.53mph (52km per hour) was achieved.

A second test, using the same locomotive, was undertaken two days later on the scheduled 10.15am goods train between Edgeley Junction, Stockport and Heaton Lodge, on the Leeds branch. This time the load consisted of 45 loaded wagons, a brake van and the dynamometer car giving a 991ft (302m) long train of 445 tons (453 tonnes), both including locomotive and tender. No fuel or water consumption measurements were made, it only being Webb's intention to determine the suitability of that type of locomotive on the heavy gradients in the Pennines.[22] It obviously proved to be suitable as the class was subsequently used extensively over that route and in the South Wales district as well as on Carlisle trains.

Webb has frequently been accused of never listening to any criticism of his locomotives thus he was not aware of their defects. The fact that many modifications were made to various classes refutes that claim. A number of modifications were made to the three-cylinder 0-8-0s during their construction period and these must have been as a result of problems detected during running. Originally all wheels were fitted with flanged tyres and the long coupled wheelbase must have caused difficulties on tightly curved track. Such problems will certainly have been reported back to Webb who would then have taken the necessary steps to minimize the problem. His solution was to fit flangeless tyres to the third pair of wheels and that arrangement remained for all future LNWR eight-coupled engines and many other heavy freight designs. Starting problems must also have been experienced as the LP stage bypass valve was also incorporated in the design and existing engines so modified. This

Flangeless driving wheels on the third coupled axle, as seen on the preserved LNWR 0-8-0 locomotive, No 485.

valve, already fitted to the three-cylinder passenger locomotives, allowed exhaust steam from the HP cylinders to pass directly to the blast pipe thereby making starting easier. Nobody but Webb would have had the authority to modify any current design in so detailed a manner and so he must have been well aware of how his locomotives performed; test results would also have shown that.

Throughout the history of LNWR eight-coupled engines only one coupled wheelbase was used, the 17ft 3in (5.25m) evenly divided arrangement as devised by Webb with his original design. Driving wheel diameter also remained the same at 4ft 5in (1.35m) with new tyres: tractive effort was always calculated using, and designations given with, partly worn tyres of 4ft 3in (1.29m) diameter. At this point it is worth mentioning that the classification using capital letters A to G was only introduced in 1911 but is used here for continuity purposes.

Four cylinder compounding was applied to passenger locomotives in 1897 and by 1901 a heavy freight form was under construction. The three-cylinder variety had performed well but the advantages of four cylinder compounding were obvious and it was reasonable to apply the principle to an 0-8-0. Apart from cylinder arrangement, and necessary gear to support the arrangement, the four-cylinder B class 0-8-0 differed from the three-cylinder version in its boiler, this operating at a pressure of 200psi and being 5in (12.7cm) larger in diameter. Webb still adhered to wooden framed tenders. Outside HP cylinders were of 16in (40.6cm) diameter, inside LP cylinders 20½in (52cm) diameter, the stroke in each case being 24in (61cm), all cylinders connecting with the second axle. Piston valves replaced slide valves for HP cylinders but flat valves were retained for LP cylinders. Two sets of inside Joy gear actuated the valves, one set for each HP and LP pair, that form of gear being used as it occupied less space than Stephenson gear and with two LP bottom ends to accommodate the crankshaft was cluttered enough. A central bearing was once again possible on the driven crankshaft. LP valves were directly operated by the Joy gear but HP valves were moved via rocking levers driven by front end extensions of the LP valve spindles. These rocking levers were placed in front of the cylinders and housed in a curved casing below the smokebox. The shape of this casing resulted in the nickname 'piano-fronts' or 'pianos'. Adjacent pairs of HP and LP pistons were at 180° to each other with the cylinders on the opposite side of the engine being at 90° to these. No bypass valve or other special starting assistance was provided.

Between introduction and 1904 some 107 engines of this type were constructed for duties similar to

LNWR B class four-cylinder compound 0-8-0 No 2024 of 1903 vintage at Buxton. (Courtesy NRM, York)

LNWR B class four-cylinder compound No 18 fitted with leading pair of wheels by Whale to form E class 2-8-0. (Nevitt Collection/NRM, York)

those of the three-cylinder 0-8-0s. There are no records of comparative trials between three and four-cylinder 0-8-0s but the latter lasted much longer in compound form, a number into the early 1920s, one even taking part in the Stockton & Darlington Railway celebrations during 1925. For Eric Mason it evoked memories of earlier main line goods trains but he was most impressed by the fact that there was no sign of steam leakage at the front end.[23] Apparently the four-cylinder 0-8-0s were very prone to this fault and the front of an engine would frequently be shrouded in steam making the view from the cab rather indistinct. Certainly a four-cylinder locomotive would have twice as many piston rod and valve spindle glands than a two-cylinder engine but the compounds also had glands at the front end of the LP valve spindles as these operated the rocking lever. Careful maintenance should have avoided undue leakage and the fact that such excessive leakage did occur is indicative of poor attention, not necessarily bad design.

Operation of compounds always required more care than simples and skilful driving was essential for good performance. British drivers, unlike their Continental brothers, were simply drivers and not footplate engineers and the fact that French compounds performed better than those in Britain is more indicative of better footplate attention than it is of better design. There was nothing essentially wrong with the British way of training footplate crew but compounds and sophisticated equipment required more skilful handling than could generally be expected from locomotive drivers in Britain. Webb, and later Hughes, probably understood that and made the controls as simple as possible. E.C. Poultney made the comment that he had met drivers at Camden shed who would be quite content to have a Webb 'Greater Britain' compound and could do anything with it from running a coal train upwards, but other men would not be able to operate those engines at all.[24] Undoubtedly there were faults with compounds but then the same applies to all locomotives. It must be concluded that it was not always the fault of the locomotive.

When Webb retired compounds fell from favour although classes under construction were completed and the B class continued operating throughout the system. In its special edition celebrating the LNWR's Diamond Jubilee *The Railway Magazine* reported that they had done and were continuing to do good work. During the Whale anti-compound era that was surely praise indeed. Whale quickly set about changing matters at Crewe and passenger locomotives were not the only compounds to receive attention. An early modification was to the four-cylinder version but that did not concern the steam side but consisted of the fitting of a leading pony truck. The new CME disliked the concentrated load on the leading coupled wheels due to the overhang at the front end. There were also reports of excessive

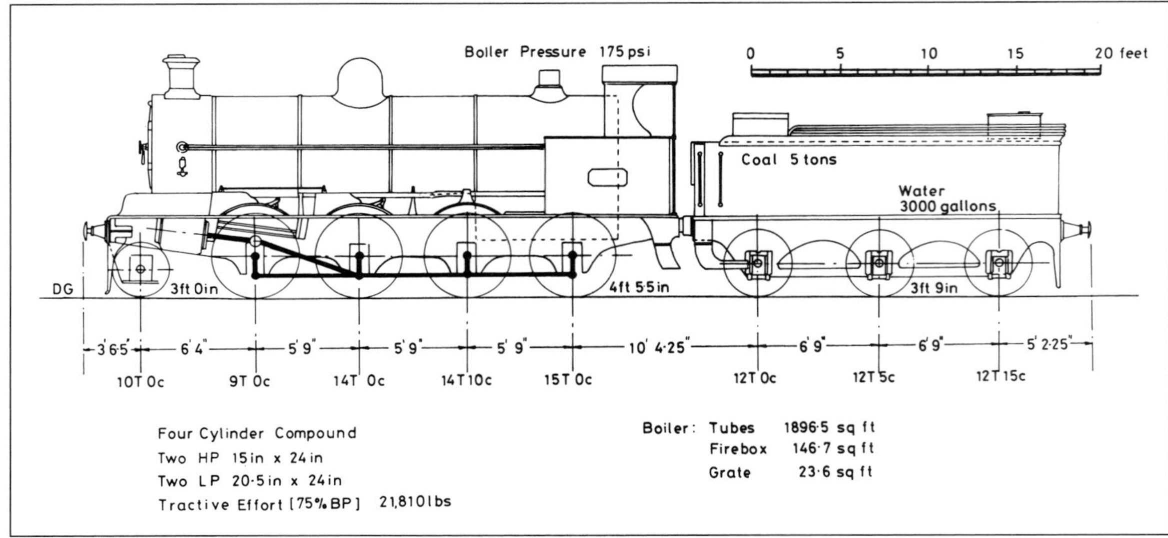

LNWR F class design, basically an E class with larger boiler.

tyre wear on the leading wheels which could well have been attributed to that weight but no such modifications were applied to subsequent D and G class 0-8-0s, and they had higher axle loadings.

These 2-8-0s were designated the E class but were essentially B class engines in all but wheel arrangement. Ten engines were treated to this modification during the four-year period to 1908, the small number involved and leisurely pace indicating that the modification was not that essential. A further ten were similarly treated but they also received the larger boilers thereby producing the F class: subsequently two of the E class engines were given the larger boiler, thus the F class comprised twelve engines and the E class eight.

It was the three-cylinder A class which came in for drastic treatment as no sooner had Whale become CME than he set in motion a scheme to convert them to simples. During November 1904 No 2541 had its compound cylinders replaced by two inside 19½in (49.5cm) by 24in (61cm) cylinders and apart from the provision of new valve gear the locomotive remained much as Webb designed. In all 15 locomotives were given this treatment producing the C class but in 1906 Whale decided that a larger boiler was required to supply the 19½in (49.5cm) cylinders. The boiler which had been designed for the F class was ideal and a further 62 A class locomotives had their compound cylinders replaced by simple cylinders but the larger boiler was fitted. This produced the D class but Whale had still not finished messing about. These later conversions resulted in a surfeit of still useful smaller A class boilers which Whale had discovered were not suitable for the larger cylinders. In order to retain the smaller boiler he fitted 18½in (47cm) diameter simple cylinders to the remaining 34 A class engines thereby producing the C1 class. Three effectively different classes from one former class was certainly some conversion work, especially as cylinder and/or boiler power was different and so they could not all be designated for the same loads or duties as the A class had. Whale's policy appears to have been the antithesis of standardization.

With the A class conversions achieved Whale returned to the four-cylinder compounds and commenced rebuilding them along similar lines. Modifications to structure were again to be minimal and the essence of the machine was retained but compounding had to go. In the light of experience with the three-cylinder conversions it was decided not to fit new cylinders but simply to remove the outer HP cylinders and retain the inner LP units, but rate them for HP. As these 'new' HP cylinders were 1in (2.54cm) larger in diameter than those of the D class it was necessary to reduce boiler pressure to 160psi so that tractive effort remained approximately the same. A restriction on tractive effort was necessary due to the adhesive weight and any significant increase in tractive effort would have

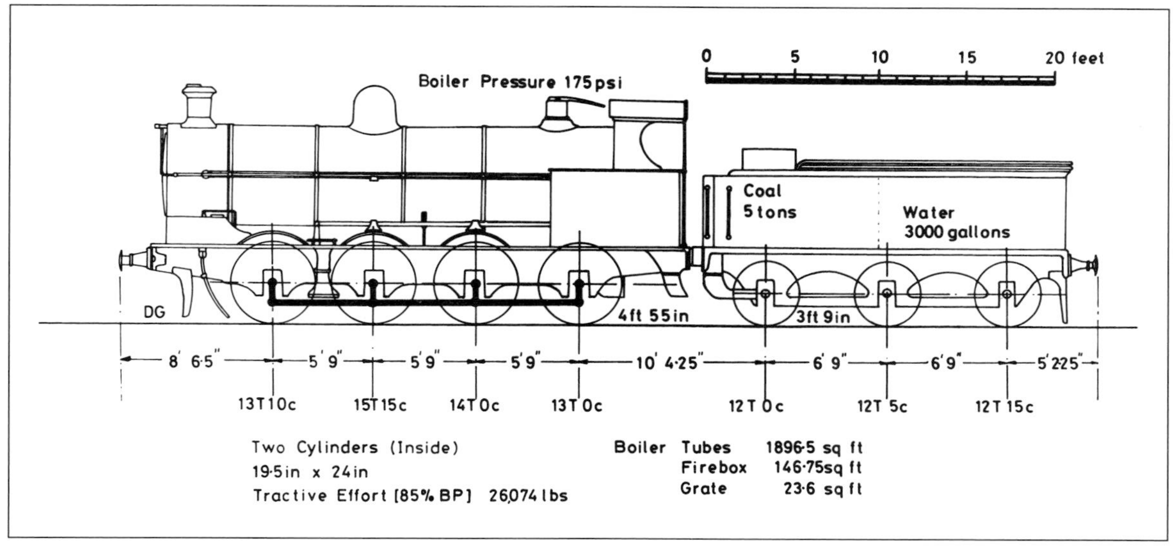

D class LNWR 0-8-0 simple, converted from A class compound, but with larger boiler.

resulted in slipping.

Conversion of this type presented fewer practical problems and must have been achieved at minimum cost as well as resulting in a smaller number of working parts. However, operating costs could only have risen as the thermal efficiency would have fallen due to reduced boiler pressure. Such aspects do not appear to have been any concern of Whale, improved loading and operating speeds being the new criteria for performance. In this form the G class, as they became known, were, according to C.J.B. Cooke, able to haul five more loaded wagons with an increase in coal consumption of only 1.2 pence per mile.[25] Few could argue against that being an improvement worth having.

So useful were G class engines that in 1910 the first of 60 newly constructed engines was delivered from Crewe Works. In basic terms the new and

LNWR G class design based upon the original Webb 0-8-0 concept.

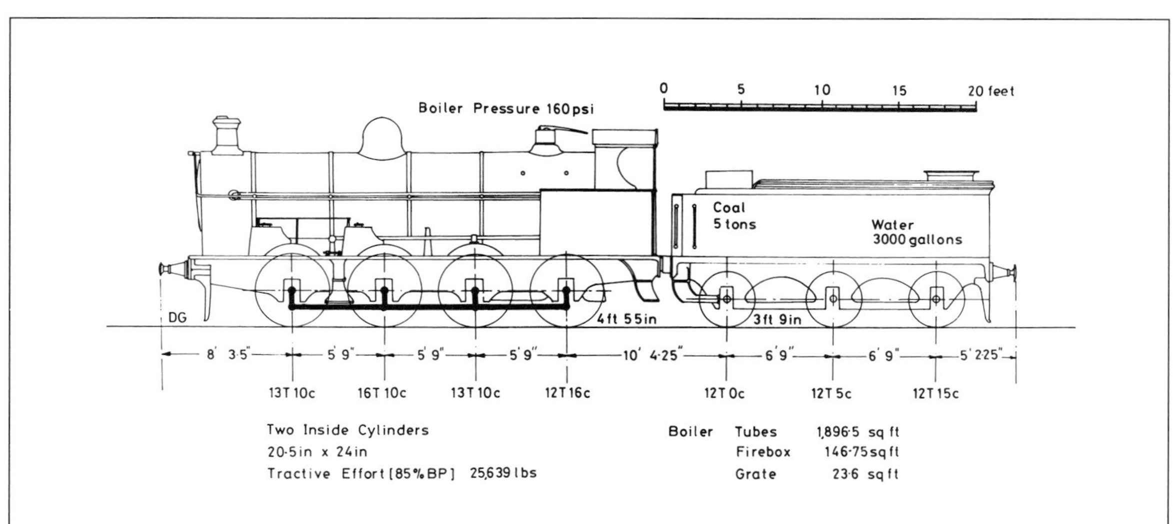

Whale G1 class 0-8-0 locomotive No 1889 with a G1 derivative behind. (Author's Collection)

converted G engines were the same although there were points which allowed identification to be made. Most obvious of these was the piano front which had formerly covered the valve gear rocking lever. Before deciding upon widespread 'simplifying' of the four-cylinder compounds Whale converted a single engine and put it to work on heavy mineral traffic in the Colwick and Northampton districts.[26] Results here justified conversion of 32 B class engines to G class and prompted building of the new batch.

When Whale retired Cooke continued the work and applied superheating. What were already useful engines became even better but, apart from the

Cooke G2 class design 0-8-0 for the LNWR.

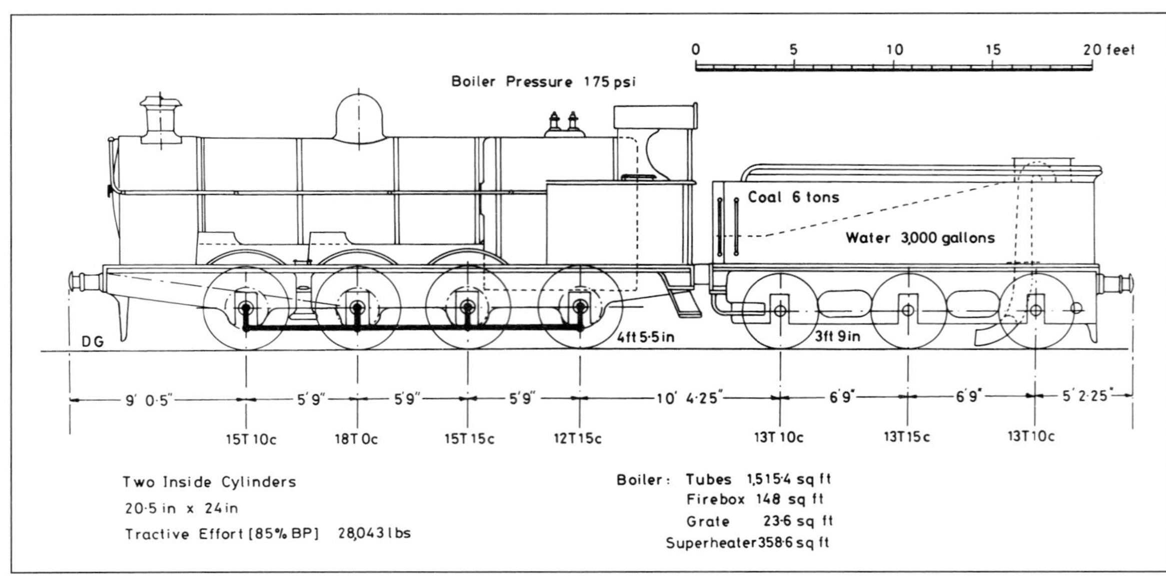

G2 class 0-8-0 No 49419 at Mirfield in 1954. (D.K. Jones Collection)

compounding, there still remained the basic arrangement as devised by Webb many years earlier. Trials with passenger engines had convinced Cooke that superheating had advantages and the concept was transferred to the 0-8-0s. By 1910 it was obvious that the G was going to remain the standard LNWR heavy freight for many years to come and Cooke made a decision to construct more engines of this type but with superheated boilers. Whilst other CMEs devised their own forms of superheater in order to avoid royalty payments Cooke adopted the Schmidt type without any hesitation; it was convenient, efficient and the Schmidt company would do all necessary work in adapting it to the boilers concerned. That approach may have lacked the intellectual engineering approach of Webb but it was far less effort and produced results immediately.

Whilst batches of superheated 0-8-0s, designated G1, were under construction a number of G class engines were given superheat boilers. A few other modifications had to be made in order to suit superheating and these included replacing slide valves by inside admission piston valves. A superheater damper also had to be fitted and this was controlled through a lever on the smokebox, the lever being operated from the cab by the boiler handrail. Over the years all 0-8-0s, apart from those scrapped, were converted to G1 class including Webb's original No 2524. As with all classes there were a number of variations, including the fitting of steam heating to some locomotives which allowed operation of banana specials from Garston Docks. Temperature is a critical factor in the carriage of bananas and it is likely that Fyffe's insisted upon such a facility if these heavy freight engines and not steam heat fitted passenger locomotives were to be used.

A final variation on Webb's original 0-8-0 theme was the G2 introduced in 1921. Needless to say there was little change from the G1 and nothing to distinguish them externally. The boiler pressure was increased to 175psi from the 160psi pressure decided upon following Whale's conversion over a decade earlier and it does seem strange that so low a pressure was tolerated for so long. A vacuum brake replaced the steam brake, a Webb introduction, and screw couplers were fitted. Vacuum braking had become something of an essential as the effectiveness of steam brakes had not improved since the days of Webb despite the fact that power and tractive effort had increased as a consequence of conversion from compound to simple. Cooke made much of the fact that an additional five loaded wagons could be taken by the G class engines but he makes no mention of the need to increase brake performance in order to cope with the extra load.

E.S. Cox considers it something of a mystery how the LNWR worked its unfitted freights during that second decade of the 20th century. In *Locomotive Panorama Vol. 1* he mentions a series of comparative trials between a LYR 0-8-0 and representative G1 and G2 engines. With a set load and running down a 1 in 100 gradient at 20mph (32km per hour) No 1369 of the LYR brought its train to rest in 1,520 yards (1.340km). With the same load under identical conditions G1 No 1585 suffered a speed increase to 25mph (40km/hr) after running 3,055 yards (2.793km) with the steam brake fully applied. Vacuum braked G2 No 2182 was also tested under the same conditions and load but fared no better, accelerating to 22.5mph (36km/lhr) after covering 3,860 yards (3.530km) with the brake fully applied. The train was brought to rest using another locomotive which had been inserted in the train for that very purpose; obviously somebody had reason to doubt the effectiveness of LNWR brakes.[27]

Subsequent development of the G class engine design to give the LMS a standard Class 7 0-8-0 will be discussed in a later chapter, however, it is worth considering two tank engine variants here. In 1911 Cooke introduced an eight-coupled shunter which was essentially a tank version of the G class. Being a shunting locomotive it does not fit into the brief for this book but mention of this 0-8-2 tank is made to indicate how well used the basic design was. Coupled wheelbase, driving wheel diameter, flangeless wheels on the third axle, and many other features were common to the main line engines although certain changes were made with respect to the boiler and valve gear.

The second variant, also a tank locomotive but of 0-8-4 wheel arrangement, was designed by H.P.M. Beames for main line freight operations. Being of tank form adhesive weight was higher than that for the G class engines and they were to be found mainly on colliery lines in South Wales. Essentially a tank version of the G2 with a higher boiler pressure of 185psi they proved themselves to be useful engines if somewhat difficult to maintain. That was probably due to the nature of work and their operating conditions more than problems with design for they differed little from the 0-8-0s in a mechanical sense. Compared with the 0-8-2 tanks they had a greater water and coal capacity to suit main line running, water capacity being 2,030 gallons (9,280 litres) and coal capacity 3 tons (3.56 tonnes). Load bearing surfaces at axleboxes, slidebars and hornblocks were greater than for the G class engines, all journals being mechanically lubricated by means of a pump, whilst cylinder lubrication was by a Detroit displacement lubricator. A novel introduction was an arrangement whereby the reversing gear could be operated by a lever or screw arrangement but standard features such as Joy valve

Beames 0-8-4T design intended for use in South Wales.

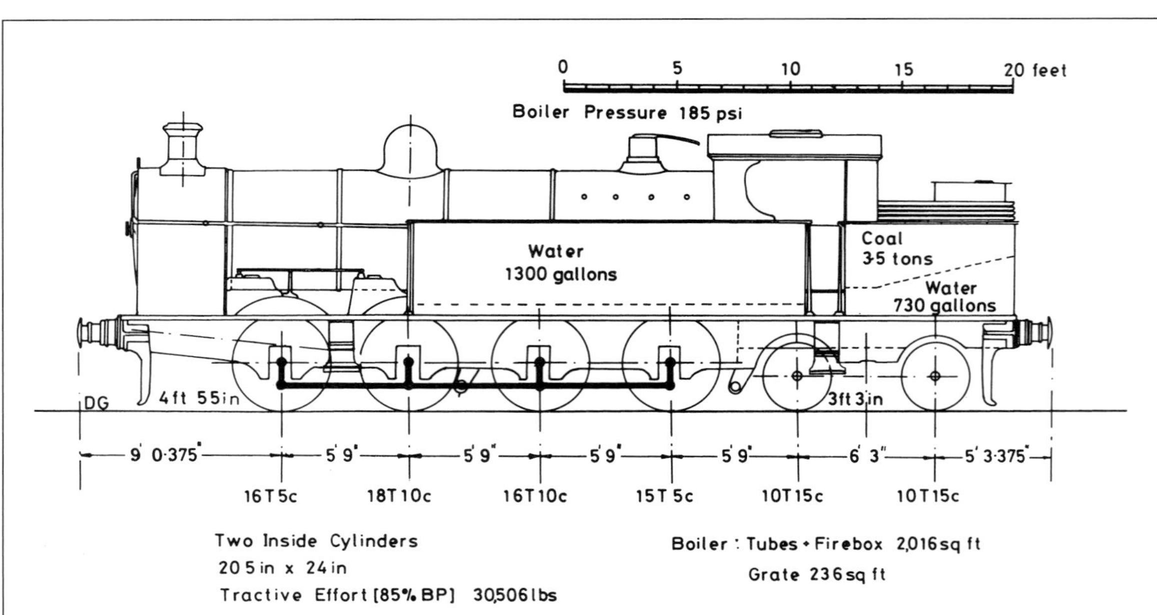

Beames 0-8-4T No 7932 at Edge Hill during 1947. (D.K. Jones Collection)

gear were retained.

Tests were carried out in South Wales with the first of the engines with large loads being hauled on severe gradients. During these tests a load of 209 tons (213 tonnes) was started from rest on a gradient of 1 in 37, whilst on another occasion a load of 392 tons (399 tonnes) could be started when the gradient was 1 in 40. Passenger train tests were undertaken and on the most severely graded section of the lines, 1 in 34, 14 coaches amounting to some 184 tons could be handled with ease. This was the longest possible train allowed due to the length of platforms in the region. In service on coal trains 19 locomotives did the work of the 30 coal tanks previously employed.[28]

Somerset & Dorset Joint Railway

The Somerset & Dorset Railway began life as an independent concern but financial problems soon forced the directors to face economic reality. By 1875 the situation had become so serious that only two options were open, bankruptcy or a sale of the line. Despite the fact that it had considerable interests in the area the GWR did not express any desire to make a firm offer which allowed the London & South Western and Midland railways to formulate a bid. This was accepted and on 1 November 1875 the line was leased to the LSWR and MR for a period of 999 years; thus the Somerset & Dorset Joint Railway came into being. Under the terms of agreement between the two sponsoring railways the Midland assumed responsibility for motive power and Derby took control of design matters from then on. The S&DJR had its own locomotive works at Highbridge and its own locomotive superintendent who, although allowed a degree of autonomy, was still subordinate to Derby.

Traffic levels increased following the take-over as both railways put considerable effort into directing their own traffic along the route and to developing local traffic, particularly coal. During the early years of the century the success of this goods traffic growth became almost embarrassing and round the clock working proved to be essential at times. Standard MR 0-6-0 goods engines were the mainstay of the freight department but they could not cope with the traffic and this prompted A.H. Whitaker, the then locomotive superintendent, to advocate the provision of an increased number of more powerful locomotives. In January 1907 Derby responded by offering a choice of two 0-8-0 designs, certainly a departure from accepted Midland practice and somewhat enlightening in view of Derby's reluctance to adopt anything larger than an 0-6-0 for its own goods work. Both were tender designs having outside cylinders and the usual array of Midland features, including undersized axleboxes. However the LSWR's Civil Engineer would not accept an 0-8-0 on weight grounds as one weighed $61\frac{1}{2}$ tons (62.6 tonnes) and the other $59\frac{1}{2}$ tons (60.6 tonnes), unless a considerable amount was spent on strengthening measures for the existing route. These proposed designs were inspired by the Midland's

CME, R.M. Deeley, who was intent on dragging that railway's locomotives firmly into the 20th century but who, it appears, was fighting a losing battle against a firmly entrenched small engine policy. A weight diagram for the heavier 0-8-0 indicates a rather attractive looking locomotive with a 17ft 6in (5.36m) wheelbase, drive being on the third pair of 4ft 7in (1.4m) diameter coupled wheels. Maximum axle loading, on the third axle, was 16 tons (16.3 tonnes).[29] With no money forthcoming for civil engineering works proposals for use of large locomotives died.

M.F. Ryan became resident locomotive superintendent in 1911 and he decided to look further into the large locomotive proposal as difficulties were still being experienced with freight traffic. Careful analysis indicated to him that a weight reduction on the coupled wheels of some 6 tons (6.11 tonnes) could be obtained by fitting a pony truck and that would allow for a reduction in the amount which needed to be spent on civil engineering work. Other ideas such as the use of a tender cab would avoid the need for larger turntables as the locomotive could work tender first without causing undue problems for the footplate crew. Ryan's final convincing argument was that an estimated annual saving of some £8,650 could be made by replacing eight older engines with six new larger ones. The LSWR Civil Engineer accepted the weights and Derby approved construction of six 2-8-0 freight engines for the S&DJR at a cost of £3,500 each.[30]

James Clayton, then Chief Draughtsman at Derby, was primarily responsible for the design so it is not surprising that a number of the standard Midland features were included. However, the fundamental design was so radically different from accepted Derby freight locomotive practice that it does indicate a desire to break free from the restrictions imposed by the Operating Department. The fact that this design was produced serves to confirm that it was not the design office which shackled Midland locomotive development. Two outside cylinders 21in (53.3cm) diameter by 28in (71.1cm) stroke drove four coupled wheels 4ft 7½in (1.41m) diameter, the coupled wheelbase being 17ft 6in (5.36m). Cylinders had an inclination of 1 in 12 in order to allow clearance at platform faces. Outside Walschaerts gear actuated the 10in (25.4cm) diameter piston valves. Surprisingly, in view of the long coupled wheelbase and the sharp curvature of some S&DJR track, all coupled wheels had full width flanges. The boiler provided a heating surface of 1,182 sq ft (109.8 sq m) from the tubes, 151 sq ft (14 sq m) from the firebox and 385 sq ft (35.8 sq m) from the superheater. Grate area was 28.4 sq ft (2.6 sq m) and the boiler operated at a pressure of 190psi.

S&DJR 2-8-0 Heavy Freight locomotive design.

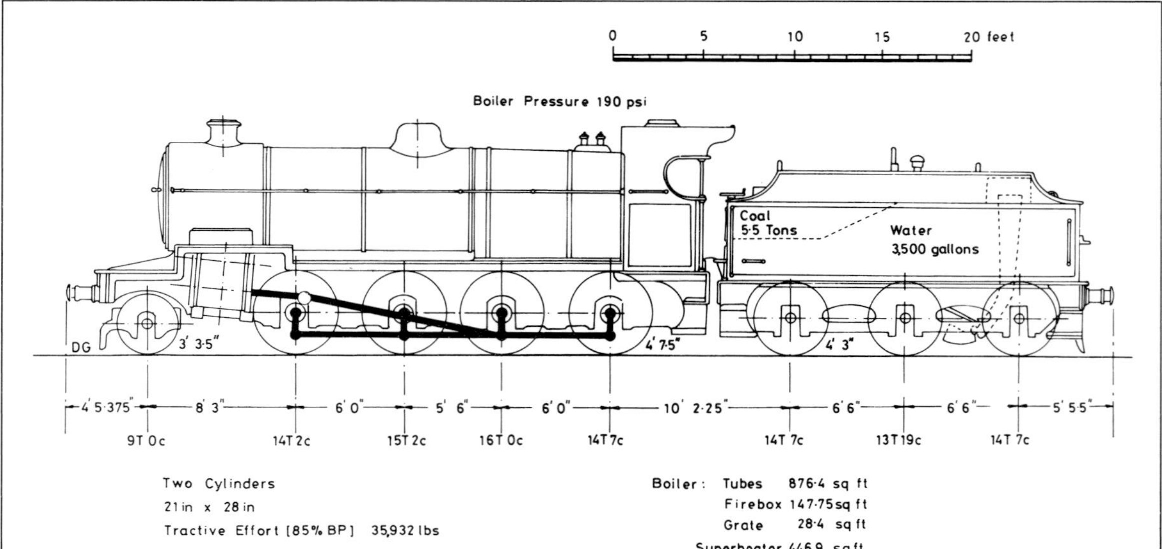

S&DJR 2-8-0 No 53806 in BR days at Swindon. (D.K. Jones Collection)

Total engine weight was 64.75 tons (65.9 tonnes) with the highest axle loading of 15.8 tons (16.1 tonnes) being on the driving axle: 54 tons (55 tonnes) adhesive weight was provided.

The boiler was a standard Midland G9AS type as fitted to the superheated compound 4-4-0, there being slight modifications in order to allow it to suit the 2-8-0 smokebox. Springs for coupled wheels were positioned below the standard Midland axle-boxes with equalizing beams connecting the front pair together and the rear pair together. High loads on severe gradients would require effective braking and the Derby team provided this in the form of two main cylinders working in tandem, for operating brakes on the three rear sets of coupled wheels; a third cylinder operated brakes on the leading coupled wheels as well as the clasp type brakes on the pony truck. Such an arrangement compares most favourably with that fitted to the LNWR 0-8-0s. Steam sanding gear was also provided for forward and reverse running, but the arrangement was subsequently altered to a gravity sanding system. Over the years a number of modifications were made to these engines and the figures given for boiler surface areas only represent one condition, values changing frequently as this was a standard boiler only in terms of external dimensions.

The standard Deeley tender was provided with a cab which proved to be of great advantage when running tender first in poor conditions but this did retain smoke and fumes whilst running through tunnels, and the overall view of footplate crew was that it had more against it than for. The low factor of adhesion, only 3.5, indicates that these 2-8-0s should have been prone to slipping on the severe gradients but that was far from the case and they proved to be very sure footed engines on all trains given to them. The initial six locomotives, constructed at Derby, were followed in 1925 by a further batch of five constructed by Robert Stephenson & Co. Ltd, these being needed to deal with additional traffic on the line. The engine unit remained as for the initial batch but a new, non-standard boiler was provided. This, designated G9BS, had a larger heating surface area and was of greater diameter. Because the overall height of the engine could not be increased and the centre line had to be pitched at the same point as on the original engines it was necessary to use a new saddle which provided a lower seating for the smokebox. The heavier boiler resulted in a slightly heavier locomotive.

Over subsequent years several changes were made including removal of pony truck brakes, fitting of wet sanding gear, increasing coupled wheel diameter by the fitting of thicker tyres, removal of the cylinder by-pass valves and replacement of the larger boiler with the smaller type. This latter arrangement required a distance piece to be inserted in the smokebox saddle. Several of the changes also applied to the earlier batch and all locomotives were

Newly constructed No 86, subsequently No 53806, with larger boiler on display at the Stockton & Darlington Centenary Celebrations in 1925. (D.K. Jones Collection)

Second batch 2-8-0 No 53809 as fitted with smaller boiler. The distance piece on the boiler saddle can be seen. (D.K. Jones Collection)

provided with vacuum brake gear for operating passenger trains. Due to weight restrictions on a bridge at the entrance to Bath shed the original batch of engines had to be shedded at Radstock but even there problems existed as they were too tall for the shed roof. Removal of the chimney lip, flattening of the dome and removal of cab roof ventilators allowed them to gain access.

Over the years these locomotives performed well and did all that was asked of them. Until the arrival of the BR Standard 9Fs no other heavy freight locomotive could match their suitability for the services they were called upon to perform. They were ideal horses for the S&DJR course. That line was not typical of main routes but it did test any heavy freight engine severely apart from the need for high speed running. Midland features had been included in the design but the nature of operations on this route did not test the more restrictive of these features to the extent that operations elsewhere might have done. Trials were carried out in LMS days in order to test suitability for operations throughout the system and these did show the problems which existed with aspects of the design. Short travel, short lap valves were standard for the Midland but by the time the second batch were constructed long travel valves having large lap had proven their worth. Performance of the S&DJR 2-8-0s suffered due to the use of short travel short lap valves, however, compared with the LNWR G2 and the LMS Garratts in their original form the S&DJR locomotives were relatively efficient in terms of coal per ton mile at similar speeds and with similar loads, but compared with the LMS standard Class 7 0-8-0 they were inferior. During dynamometer car test runs between Toton and Brent the following figures were obtained.[31]

	LMS Garratt 2-6-6-2		S&DJR 7F 2-8-0	LNWR G2 0-8-0	LMS Class 7 0-8-0
	Orig.	New valves			
Av. Train Load. tons	1,423	1,452	927	940	900
Av. speed, mph	16.0	16.0	17.5	17.6	17.3
Coal Consumption					
lbs per ton mile	0.082	0.71	0.078	0.076	0.055
lbs per DBHP/hr	4.09	3.61	4.37	4.02	2.8
Water consumption					
Galls per mile	88.3	84.6	60.8	50.0	46.1
Evaporation: lbs of water/ lb of coal	6.87	7.51	7.54	6.32	8.57

The reader can best judge how the S&DJR 2-8-0 compared with other locomotives on these main line runs but it should be borne in mind that they were not designed for this type of operation even though many of the parts were standard to trunk route engine. These runs illustrated the defectiveness of the small Midland design of axlebox. For the slow speed and short distance operations of the S&DJR few problems had been experienced but on these trials axleboxes became overheated. Apart from this problem with regard to axleboxes they were considered to be first class locomotives mechanically.[32] Greater route availability would have been open to them but for their width at the cylinders. They were good heavy freight engines but minor defects in design prevented them from being outstanding for their time.

4

Pre-Grouping Heavy Freight Locomotives on the East Coast Lines

Freight traffic to London formed a considerable part of the revenue for any railway serving the capital and the LNER possessed three major routes into that metropolis. The main East Coast route was that constructed by the Great Northern Railway (GNR) whilst the line built by the Great Central (GCR) was, by comparison, of rather recent construction at the time of the Grouping. The Great Eastern Railway (GER) served East Anglia and although a considerable quantity of freight was carried there was no heavy mineral traffic in the form of coal originating in the area. Of the railways which formed the LNER the North Eastern (NER) conveyed by far the largest amount of coal, in fact by the commencement of World War I it was lifting from local collieries half as much again as the best carried by any other British railway; 18.3 million tons (18.6 million tonnes) compared with 12.2 million tones (12.4 million tons) for the Midland Railway.[1]

Whilst the NER had no direct line to London its onward coal traffic could be hauled by the GNR and so there was a requirement for both companies to develop heavy mineral engines; additionally the GNR transported a fair quantity of coal from local pits in its own wagons. Through traffic from Scotland also presented cargo as did other smaller railways in the area. Most notable of the latter was the Hull & Barnsley Railway which operated across the region and possessed its own docks at Hull. This port, and the railway, would also handle export coal from other areas whilst other lines would convey cargo, including large quantities of pit props, imported through Hull.

Although of major importance coal was not the only commodity carried by these railways as significant quantities of fish had to be conveyed in fast trains from Hull and Grimsby as well as Scottish fishing ports. Development of heavy industry produced a demand for steel giving a boost to iron and steel making with a consequent requirement for raw materials. Coke came from coal which could be mined locally but iron ore had to be transported to the blast furnaces. Steel making developed in those areas possessing the raw materials such as coal or iron stone, unfortunately no region possessed large quantities of both resulting in the need for movement of one or other of the commodities by the most convenient means, which was rail. The development of Britain's heavy industry is a fascinating subject but has only been mentioned here to illustrate the demands placed on the railways for movement of minerals in large quantities. General freight, including iron and steel from the steel making areas, also had to be moved about the region and country and efficiency demanded heavy trains be used. This region produced a varied stock of heavy freight locomotives which served a common purpose and were of similar form but differed in detail because of the inclinations of particular designers.

Great Central Railway

The first eight-coupled locomotives appeared on the GCR during 1902 and were of 0-8-0 form designed by J.G. Robinson who had been appointed Locomotive Engineer to the railway in 1900; in 1902 he

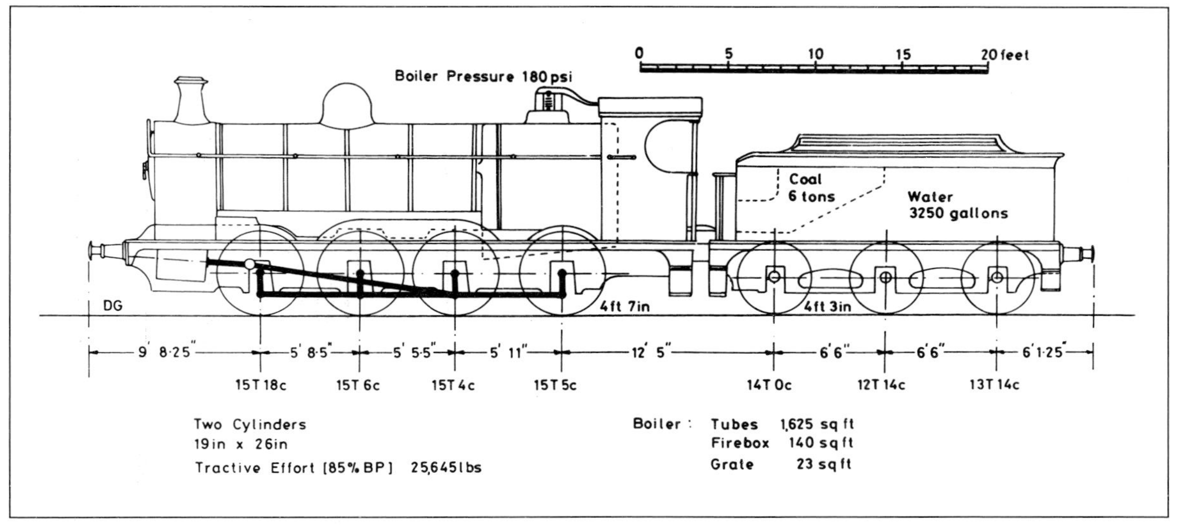

Robinson's first Heavy Freight design, the GCR 8A class 0-8-0.

became CME when the Carriage & Wagon Department fell under his control. The first class produced by Robinson for the GCR was an 0-6-0 freight engine which was constructed in large numbers and proved to be so successful that train loadings were actually increased.[2] It quickly became obvious that more powerful locomtives could do even better and Robinson commenced work on the design for a heavy freight engine which proved to be a turning point for GCR motive power. At the same time as the 0-8-0 was being schemed design work was being undertaken on the Class 8 4-6-0 for express goods duties and it is not surprising that the two classes had a number of features in common. Initial batches of both classes were constructed at Neilson, Reid & Co. and that was probably intended at the design stage in order to allow use of common parts or systems.

Similar boilers were used for both classes but the 0-8-0, designated Class 8A on the GCR and Q4 on the LNER, had a deeper firebox giving it a slightly larger heating surface area. Cylinders, placed outside the frames, were of a common size, 19in (48.3cm) diameter by 26in (66cm) stroke, and in the case of the 0-8-0 they drove the third axle. Stephenson gear, also driven by the third axle, operated vertically positioned balanced slide valves placed between the frames. The wheelbase of 17ft 1in (5.2m) and the rather long boiler gave the 0-8-0 an overhang of 8ft (2.4m) at the front and 7ft 6in

GCR 8A class No 1137. (Courtesy NRM, York)

(2.3m) at the cab end. Coupled wheels of 4ft 7in (1.4m) and boiler pressure of 180psi produced a tractive effort of 25,645lbs, very reasonable for the 61.65 ton (62.8 tonne) adhesive weight; an adhesion factor of 5.4.

Construction of the first three engines by Neilson in 1902 was followed by other batches from Kitson & Co. over the years to 1907; further locomotives were built at the GCR's Gorton Works between 1909 and 1911 bringing the total class strength to 89. Initially saturated boilers were supplied but in 1914 the fitting of superheaters, normally of the Robinson type, commenced. This conversion was never completed as the fitting of superheated boilers took place over many years and in the meantime a number of the engines actually converted were refitted with saturated boilers. Designed for working coal trains these engines found employment with allocations to Grimsby, Sheffield and Gorton sheds, amongst others. During WWI 15 of the class were taken by the Railway Operating Division (ROD) of the Royal Engineers and between 1917 and 1919 served the allied cause in France.[3]

With the Grouping the 'Tinies', by which nick-name the class was known, still operated its traditional routes on former GCR metals but they did find employment in other areas including Ardsley where they replaced the LNER 04s (formerly GCR 2-8-0 8K class), which were too long for the turntable. During the 1920s and 1930s reduction in freight traffic and the large number of 2-8-0s available caused their relegation to lighter duties but many still hauled heavy coal trains on former GCR lines. Scrapping commenced in the late 1930s but some remained in service until 1951. During WWII 13 members of the class were subject to drastic conversion into tank form to meet a demand for heavy freight tank locomotives.[4] Thompson had devised a standardization scheme shortly after he succeeded Gresley but there was no mention of an 0-8-0T design. However, the proposal for rebuilding some of the former GCR 0-8-0s into tank form appeared soon after so it would appear that the new CME was aware of the need. Wartime conditions with consequent shortage of materials did not allow for new construction when perfectly serviceable machines were still available, but sufficient steel could be obtained for the necessary conversion work.

An order for a batch of J50 class 0-6-0T engines was cancelled thus releasing material required for tanks, bunker and other parts. Initially the original frames were used but it was soon discovered that there was insufficient water capacity and the phase 2 conversions had frames extended at the rear by 6in (15.2cm). This allowed for a longer bunker but the depth was reduced as the lower portion was taken up by a supplementary water tank. Coal capacity fell by ½ ton (0.51 tonnes) from 4½ tons (4.58 tonnes) whilst water capacity increased by 500 gallons (2,286 litres) to 2,000 gallons (9,143 litres). In order to accommodate the cab and bunker it was necessary to fit a shorter boiler barrel but the original firebox was retained, however, in order to clear the driving axle boiler pitch had to be increased slightly. Whilst cylinders continued to drive the third axle because of the new firebox position valve gear was relocated on the second axle. Both versions were identical apart from the longer frames and bunker/tank capacities. That change in capacity did alter axle loadings slightly and did increase the weight on the drive axle but it was still lower than that on the leading axle.[5]

A majority of the class, designated Q1 by the LNER, remained in the central area but two were allocated to the Scottish region and two initially to the North Eastern area. They were considered so useful around Tyneside that others were transferred there over the following few years. Main line coal trains were hauled but much of their time was spent on shunting duties in yards, around docks near steel making plants and even in collieries. Their high tractive effort and high adhesion factor made them extremely useful for such duties but limited water capacity meant that they could not stray far from home. As a piece of conversion work with restricted resources the Q1s were a limited success and fulfilled a need of the time. It is easy to make judgements with hindsight but it must be rememberd that Thompson had to deal with the situation as it existed during wartime when materials were in short supply. Conversion of a class of engine which was being displaced by more powerful austerity locomotive was a much more economic solution than scrapping followed by new building. No conversion is ever a complete success as it must be something of a compromise but rebuilding did extend the lives of these 1902 designed locomotives, in many cases until 1959.

The GCR 8A design was a useful engine if limited in its application but it was a product of the times and should be judged as such. Tractive effort was moderate but acceptable for the needs of 1902 and low axle loading allowed it to venture onto most of

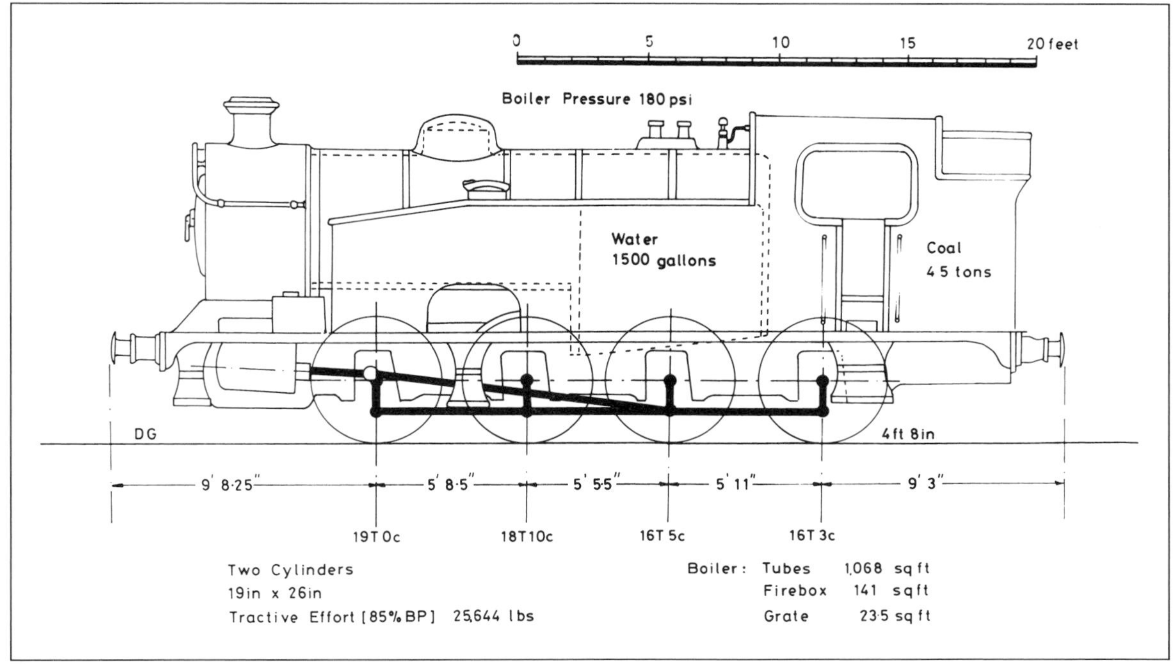

Robinson 0-8-0 converted to tank form and designated Q1 by the LNER.

the GCR's metals. The converted tanks do not really come under this section as that work was undertaken during LNER days but between the tanks and bunker it remained very much a Robinson engine and so inclusion here is justified. Useful though the 0-8-0s were in their day a later development soon put them in the shade as far as heavy freight haulage was concerned. However, the fact that they successfully performed the work for which they were constructed prompted those in charge to consider heavier trains and enabled Robinson to develop an even more useful machine. Their glory lay not in what they did but in the ideas they conceived.

Construction of the new GCR port at Immingham was expected to increase coal exports and thus a number of heavy engines would be required.

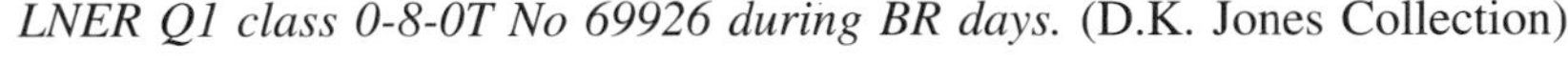
LNER Q1 class 0-8-0T No 69926 during BR days. (D.K. Jones Collection)

Heavier and longer trains could make use of the new facilities and so a more powerful freight engine was needed. After considering several possibilities Robinson decided upon a 2-8-0 configuration using the same driving wheel spacing as the earlier 0-8-0. Naturally a more powerful locomotive would require larger cylinders and a bigger boiler, which in turn dictated that additional carrying wheels were required. From the start superheating was applied to the boiler which had a greater heating area than that fitted to the 0-8-0. First of the new class appeared from the GCR's own works at Gorton in September 1911, part of an initial order for 20 engines.

In view of their widespread use by the Railway Operating Division (ROD) of the Royal Engineers it is often considered that these engines, designated Class '8K' by the GCR, were something rather different but they were nothing of the sort. The choice for service with the ROD probably owed much to the design being available and relatively proven at the time it was needed. Certainly their relative simplicity was important but so probably was the fact that Sir Sam Fay, General Manager of the GCR, was Director General of War Transport and that G.S. Lynde, who had served his apprenticeship at Gorton, was chief of the ROD workshops at Audruic.[6] Whatever the reason it was an admirable choice anyway as the GCR 2-8-0s proved their worth.

The use of superheated steam dictated that piston valves be fitted and 10in (25.4cm) diameter valves, driven by Stephenson gear, were positioned between the frames. Cylinder diameter increased to 21in (53.3cm) compared with the 0-8-0 but the stroke remained the same as did boiler pressure. Robinson always attempted to provide his locomotives with ample boiler capacity and the 8K was no exception, the unit fitted being similar in size to that of the Robinson Atlantics. Such a large boiler imposed additional weight on the driving wheels and maximum axle loading increased to 17.05 tons (17.4 tonnes) compared with the 8A but this high weight was actually on the driven axle not on the leading axle.[7] The greater adhesive weight and increased tractive effort produced an adhesion factor of 4.7, lower than the 0-8-0 but the new engine was certainly more useful. So useful in fact that by August 1914 some 126 of the class were in service. Gorton could not build at the rate required and a number of batches had been constructed by Kitson and the North British Locomotive Company.

The work of these engines on the GCR is often overlooked due to their use by the military but they did the work for which they were designed with

Robinson GCR 8K class 2-8-0.

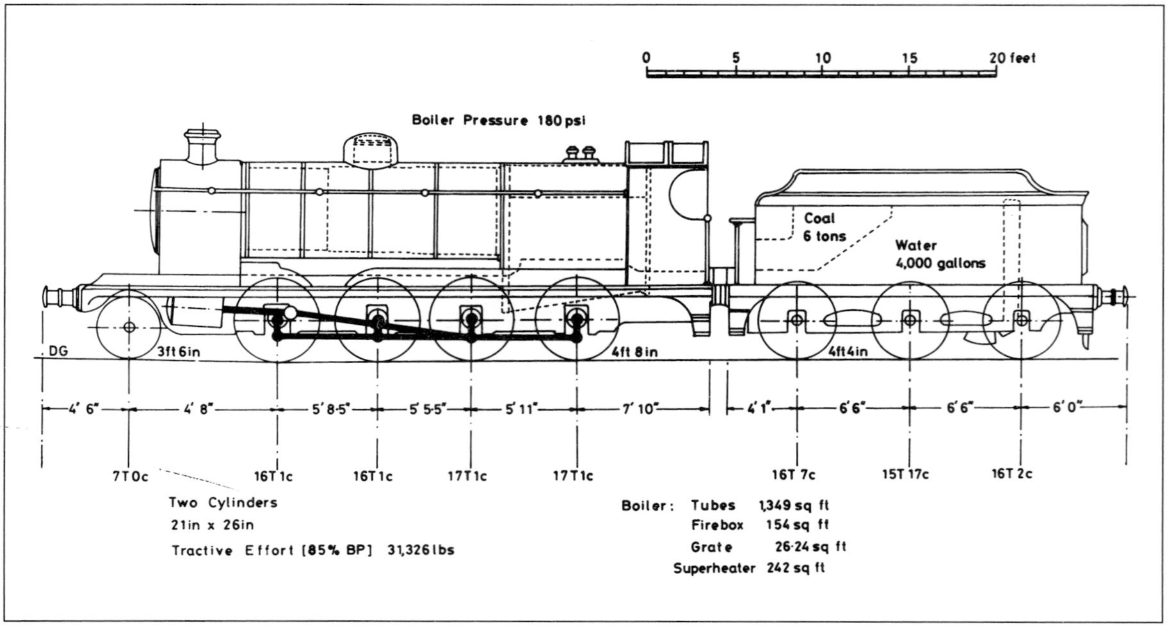

ease, hauling heavy coal trains to the docks at Immingham and throughout the GCR system, although they rarely ran south of Nottingham. As with all locomotive classes variations did occur in detail and there were differences in the batches produced by North British and Kitson compared with each other and with the Gorton engines; even the second batch from Gorton differed in boiler heating areas compared with the initial batch. Other factors remained common, however, including cylinders, valve gear, wheels, and the all important framing. Robinson built robust freight engines and the 1.24in (3.18cm) thick frames were some 25 per cent thicker than was normal in Britain. Frames were joggled, inwards towards the front end, by some 1½in (3.8cm) between the first and second coupled axles in order to ensure that the width over the cylinders remained within the maximum width of 8ft 10½in (2.7m) whilst still allowing the cylinders to be bolted directly to the frames. Due to a reduced distance between the frames at the leading coupled wheels differences in design of the wheel centres and tyre fastening arrangements were required. Because of this leading coupled wheel centres were not interchangeable wth other axles. This situation also existed with the 0-8-0s.

At the joggling, frames were heavily braced by means of the cast steel motion stay which extended the full depth of the frame, at other locations part-depth stretchers were used. At the front end the cast steel valve chest provided substantial rigidity whilst at the rear the drag box offered similar strength. These frames may have been over engineered compared with those offered by some designers but Robinson knew what he wanted in a heavy freight engine and the way in which they lasted in UK and overseas service is ample proof that he knew what he was doing.

To allow negotiation of relatively tight curves down to 462ft (141m) radius the centre coupled wheels were given flanges of reduced thickness whilst the front coupled axle had 0.25in (0.64cm) side play. No compensation was made in the springing even though much of the track around the Nottinghamshire and Yorkshire coalfields at that time made use of ash ballast. Springing was, however, made rather flexible in order to take up imperfections. About two-thirds of the reciprocating mass was balanced by means of weights fitted to all coupled wheels, thus evening out the axle loading.[8]

With the outbreak of World War I it became necessary to maintain supplies of food and ammunition to British troops operating in Europe and the only way that could be done with any certainty was by means of the railways. The Railway Operating Division initially took an assortment of 0-6-0 and 0-8-0 engines from the railways of Britain but the diversity of design and idiosyncrasies of operation did not lend itself to efficient operation. During 1916 the Ministry of Munitions decided that a single standard engine was required and after due consideration selected the existing GCR 2-8-0 rather than devise a completely new design. That Fay and others might have been influential in the choice is no matter for Robinson's heavy freight engine proved itself to be ideal for the job. Its attributes lay in that rugged simplicity of construction which allowed for ease of maintenance and enabled it to operate under extremely rough wartime conditions.

Gorton could not construct at the required rate and so contracts were placed with the North British Locomotive Company and several other builders, the GCR providing necessary drawings. Operation of these ROD 2-8-0s does not strictly come within the remit of this book which is only concerned with British railways, however, some consideration of design is warranted as many of the engines found their way into service in the UK. The specification followed closely that for the GCR being altered only slightly to suit operational needs of the forces. Provision of air brake equipment was necessary as was the need to modify tyre profiles to suit the slightly wider gauge of the French railway system. Steam heating had to be provided as the ROD 2-8-0s were required to haul troop trains, no water pick-up apparatus was fitted to the tenders but each locomotive was provided with two screw jacks on the front end of the running plate in order to enable a derailed engine to be returned to the track, poor quality track being anticipated. A major design change lay in the use of steel instead of copper for construction of the inner firebox, this situation being forced on the builders due to the difficulty in obtaining supplies of copper.

In all 521 Robinson 2-8-0 locomotives were constructed for the ROD at a price slightly in excess of £6,000 each for the initial batches and over £8,000 each for later orders. Operations of these locomotives is detailed in a number of publications[9] and need not be repeated here save to state that performance was up to expectation. With the end of hostilities the Government had a great many locomotives on its hands, a number never having been

Former GCR design 8K as rebuilt to LNER O4/7 class No 63588 at Wakefield in 1955.
(D.K. Jones Collection)

used. Following the armistice there appeared to be no defined policy concerning these engines, a number being sold and others placed on hire to various railway companies. For the unused locomotives sold to the GWR and LNWR the Government received an average price just in excess of £10,000 per engine. Hired machines went to most railways including many who had never operated eight-coupled locomotives of their own. Of the major companies only the Midland Railway and London, Brighton & South Coast Railway decided against taking any. The Caledonian Railway put its ROD 2-8-0s on the coal and steel trains for which its own 0-8-0s had been built, whilst the LYR used the ROD engines for coal trains across the Pennines. So useful were the ROD engines that several railways experienced difficulties when the Government called them in at the end of 1921. Why this action was taken is difficult to understand for the engines were simply placed in dumps to deteriorate. Eventually, in 1923 sales commenced but the asking price of around £10,000 was considered excessive. Over the follow-

Former Robinson ROD 2-8-0 as bought by the GWR. No 3017 at St Philip's Marsh October 1955.
(D.K. Jones Collection)

ing years the price fell and many railways took advantage of the situation to increase stock of heavy freight engines. The real bargain was obtained by the LNER when in 1927 it purchased 100 for only £340 each. Work was required and expenditure needed to replace the steel inner firebox with one of copper but by any estimation it was a bargain buy.[10]

Grouping brought the GCR engines within the wider frame of the LNER and developments there will be discussed in the next chapter. However, for the former ROD 2-8-0s which operated on other lines it is worth completing the discussion here. On the many railways which purchased or hired these engines few changes were made and they remained very much as they had been built, that in itself being a testimony to their original design. Apart from providing Swindon superheaters, a typical safety valve cover and top feed arrangements the GWR left its ROD engines much as they were but they found use throughout the system, handling trains similar to those hauled by the 2800 class. Many were withdrawn after less than five years service but a number survived until the late 1950s. Locomotives purchased by the LNWR and the LMS after Grouping found use on typical coal train services operated by those railways, ultimately they were designated Class 7F. Their operating life was not as long as elsewhere, and it appears that the LMS had greater need for tenders than locomotives; 75 engines had been purchased for £340 each and only 20 of these were given overhauls, the remainder ran until fireboxes were worn out and they were then scrapped but the tenders retained.[11]

Though other railways treated them very much in a utilitarian way the LNER had greater respect for them and there the former ROD and GCR 2-8-0s came into their own being used extensively for traffic throughout the system. The design proved so effective and robust that many lasted until the 1960s in original form but that same design was also adaptable in that it allowed several rebuildings without major structural alteration. These will be considered in the next chapter.

With the 8K class 2-8-0 safely in mass construction for war duties Robinson set his mind to extending their capabilities by fitting larger boilers. In 1918 the first of what was to be the 8M class 2-8-0 heavy freight engine appeared from Gorton, essentially an 8K with larger diameter boiler. That 5ft 6in (1.68m) diameter boiler was similar to the type fitted to the 4-6-0 'Sir Sam Fay' class of express passenger engine; the 8K boiler was 5ft (1.52m) diameter. Apart from the boiler the only significant difference between the classes was in terms of weight and that resulted from the fitting of the larger boiler. The 8K weighed 73.2 tons (74.5 tonnes) whilst the 8M was heavier at 75.2 tons (76.6 tonnes), of which 67.9 tons (69.1 tonnes) was available for adhesion.[12] Only 19 8M engines were constructed it soon being evident that no advantage was to be gained from the larger boiler which was non-standard compared with the other 2-8-0s. Rebuilding with smaller boilers commenced as early

GCR 8K 2-8-0 as rebuilt to LNER O4/8 class by Thompson. No 63613 at New England during May 1958. (D.K. Jones Collection)

as 1922 but the process was not completed for many years, the final rebuild taking place in 1943. There was obviously no hurry and the larger boiler cannot have been a disadvantage – it was just non-standard.

Robinson was aware of the problems wartime presented in obtaining adequate stocks of reasonable quality coal and conducted several experiments into the use of alternatives. Coal still presented the main option although several engineers had undertaken trials with various systems of oil firing. However, reasonable quality coal in large enough sized pieces was becoming more difficult to obtain and prices were increasing. Coal dust was available to any railway in appreciable quantities as the mere act of transporting and moving coal turned a certain amount into dust. Similar situations existed at the mines where screening took place. Stationary industrial plants had made use of such dust for a considerable time but use in transport applications presented problems with regard to the obtaining of a combustible mixture and variation in the firing rate. For locomotive purposes it was necessary to construct a firebox capable of burning coal dust and to provide a means of supplying the dust in variable quantities to the fire.

Robinson devised a system whereby coal dust was mixed with air and blown into the modified firebox which no longer had the traditional grate. The firebox was lined with firebrick and an enlarged brick arch was fitted at the front. The mixture of air and coal dust was supplied through two circular holes at the rear of the firebox and a second arch positioned above these holes in order to direct the coal dust towards the front. Secondary air was supplied to the fire through a number of entry ports around the firebox and this mixed with the incoming coal dust to give a highly combustible mixture. When flashing-up initially a flame had to be inserted to ignite the coal dust but once in operation a supply of dust was maintained in order to keep the flame alight. Even if the supply of dust to the firebox was interrupted heat in the brickwork would allow for re-ignition provided that the brickwork had not cooled down too much.

Fuel was contained in a special hopper in the tender and supplied by means of two conveyor screws to the air ducting where it would meet air under pressure, the blast being sufficient to convey the air into the firebox. A small reciprocating steam

Robinson design firebox for the 2-8-0 experiments, using pulverized coal.

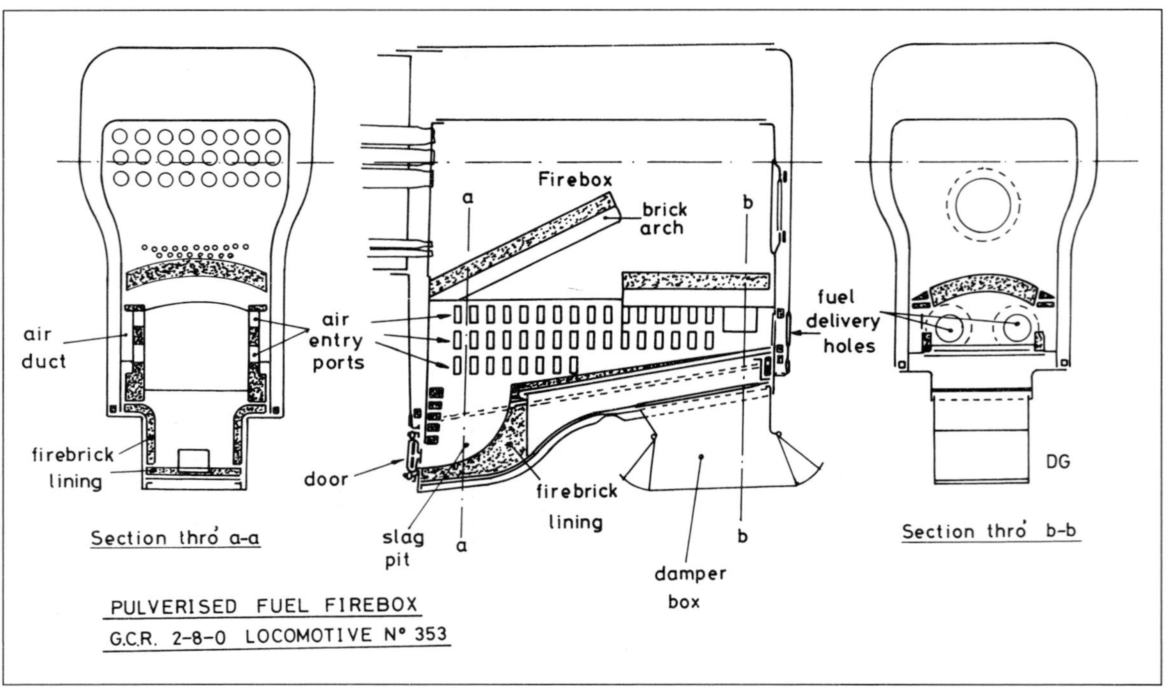

engine was used to drive the feed screws via gearing whilst the air supply came from a fan operated by a steam turbine, steam from both units condensing in the tender. Under normal conditions the de Laval turbine driven fan provided air for moving the coal dust to the firebox and also for supply to the entry ports, but in the event of turbine failure it was possible to drive the fan from the small reciprocating engine via a clutch. This would enable the locomotive to continue steaming but at reduced rate. At all times the fireman had control of steam supply to engine and turbine thus enabling firing rate to be adjusted.

Engine No 353 was fitted with this equipment during 1917, a petrol driven engine originally being used to drive the fan. Trials were conducted over the following three years and the system appeared to perform well. A series of comparative tests with a conventionally fired locomotive was arranged on the line between Manchester and Sheffield, the actual section used being from Ashburys to Woodhead. Both trains hauled loads of 545 tons (555 tonnes), the maximum for the section, up the severe gradient, the power requirement being in the order of 1,000 horsepower (746kW). These tests indicated that for every pound (0.45kg) of coal dust fuel the locomotive burnt 0.25lb (0.114kg) more water was evaporated than the conventionally fired engine. In the light of this apparent success Robinson converted one of the 8M class engines to pulverized fuel burning with No 422 having a slightly modified system. The main difference lay in the arrangement for feeding the mixture of coal and air to the firebox which, in this case, was below the footplate and boiler foundation ring. The tender was specially designed for the purpose and was carried on two four-wheeled bogies.[13]

In 1920, the year after No 422 was converted, another of the 8M class, No 420, was provided with equipment for burning a mixture of coal dust and oil. A triple nozzle burner was provided which allowed for control over the firing rate at three levels. The system was similar to a straight oil burning system except that a mixture of coal dust and oil was supplied to the burner nozzle unit. Problems appear to have existed in maintaining a consistent mixture and compressed air bubbling up through the fuel tank was used for agitation. Again Robinson

8M class 2-8-0, as fitted for burning colloidal fuel. No 420 at Gorton & Openshaw circa 1920.
(Courtesy NRM, York)

arranged for trials but this time with three 8M class locomotives, each having a different form of fuel; No 420 with its colloidal fuel, No 422 burning pulverized fuel and No 419 as the normally fired engine for comparison. Tests were conducted on the Woodhead route between Guide Bridge and Dunford Sidings with loads approximately the same at 540 tons (550 tonnes). Results were inconclusive although the colloidal fuel did produce a higher superheat temperature than either of the other engines and that locomotive completed the run in a shorter time.[14]

In 1921 the original 2-8-0, No 966, was given a pulverized fuel fired boiler and tests conducted over the following three years. No evidence was found to support further conversion and when Robinson retired at the Grouping in 1923 experimentation ceased. All locomotives were quickly converted to conventional firing and resumed their places in the stud of very useful LNER 2-8-0 heavy freight engines.

Great Eastern Railway

The ubiquitous 0-6-0 sufficed for freight duties in East Anglia and the fairly restrictive loading gauge limited developments anyway. With the outbreak of the First World War and the demand for locomotives to serve the military the Great Eastern Railway supplied over forty of its Y14 class six-coupled tender engines but on their return major overhauls were required to fit them for peacetime duties. In order to maintain freight services 40 ROD 2-8-0s were taken on hire but they could only be employed on the Great Northern & Great Eastern Joint Line between March and Doncaster due to loading gauge restrictions. So restrictive was the GER gauge that the chimneys of these 2-8-0s had to be removed for the journey to Stratford if repairs became necessary.[15]

It is no surprise, therefore, that the GER did not indulge in design and construction of its own heavy freight eight-coupled engines. However, the railway did build one 0-8-0 of its own, indeed before it became an eight-coupled engine it was of ten-coupled form. In 1902 James Holden, CME of the Great Eastern Railway, set about constructing a large 0-10-0 tank engine, subsequently known as the 'Decapod', in order to test the ability of a steam locomotive to compete with electric traction on stopping suburban services. The ability to accelerate from a station stop and reach 30mph (48km/hr) within 30 seconds gave the electric train an advantage and Holden firmly believed that steam could compete. This is not the place to discuss what was a very interesting experiment but it is sufficient to say that 'Decapod' proved Holden's point. Exactly what the purpose of the whole exercise was is now shrouded in the mists of history but it is evident that attempts were being made to scupper a proposed new electric railway which intended to invade GER

GER 0-8-0 as rebuilt from the 'Decapod'.

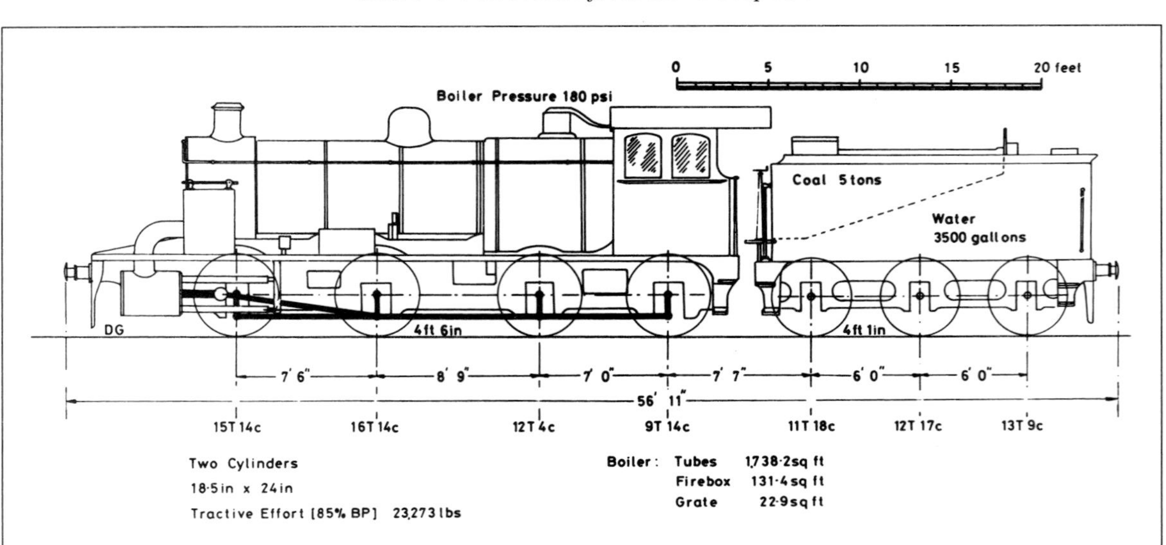

The GER's only 0-8-0, No 20. (Author's Collection)

territory. Success of the steam locomotive had the desired effect and backers for the electric scheme were not forthcoming in sufficient numbers so it was dropped.

That 'Decapod' was too heavy for much of the GER system is beyond doubt and Holden knew as much, but it was never intended for actual service. When the electric scheme failed Holden had a relatively new but practically useless engine on his hands. The locomotive had been expensive to construct and complete scrapping would have been difficult to contemplate for financially cautious directors. The solution was to make use of as many parts as possible in a new engine, thus the only GER 0-8-0 locomotive was born.

'Decapod' had three 18½in (47cm) by 24in (61cm) cylinders but only the two outside units were retained for the new engine. A new Belpaire boiler of more modest proportions had to be constructed and this operated at 200psi, also a reduction from the ten-coupled engine. Four pairs of the 4ft 6in (1.37m) diameter coupled wheels were retained but new frames had to be provided in order to accommodate their much wider spacing. Due to the rather long wheelbase, 23ft 3in (7.1m) a large degree of flexibility had to be provided by means of radial axleboxes at the leading and trailing wheels. The grouping together of the axles in pairs with a larger distance between second and third was probably an attempt to minimize difficulties when negotiating curves, certainly provision of the radial axleboxes would have assisted in that. The cab was to a standard design then being fitted to all newly constructed GER locomotives.[16]

As a single member of its class there can have been little defined work for the engine but the expectation was that it would be capable of hauling 50 of the new 20-ton (20.34-tonne) coal wagons and the 5.2 factor of adhesion should certainly have allowed for that.[17]

Whatever the claims there was no real use for this strange looking 0-8-0 and it was scrapped in 1913, only seven years after introduction. The Great Eastern was obviously not suited to eight- or ten-coupled engines but for a locomotive to have been both, and then the sole example of each on a single railway must be something of a record.

Great Northern Railway

Considerable freight traffic used Great Northern metals to reach London, and the route between Peterborough and the capital consisted of four running lines. The centre lines, working on an absolute block system, were reserved for passenger trains and fast freight traffic, whilst the two outer lines worked on the permissive system for heavy freight and mineral trains. During WWI the arrangements actually changed as the emphasis was on the shipment of war materials, including troops, in large quantities. Fast traffic ceased and all trains were run at a standard speed allowing for an increased tonnage of each train. The resultant slower speed was compensated by a reduction in delays because trains were run at fixed intervals and there was no need to give any train preference. This arrangement was only possible because of the GNR's four-track route and its extensive freight sidings at New England (Peterborough) and Ferme Park (London). The attention given to freight working in the pre-war years certainly helped during the conflict.[18]

Not only had the operating system been given careful consideration but attention had been paid to the development of heavy goods engines which would serve the system. In 1901 H.A. Ivatt introduced a new coal engine to the system, this being of 0-8-0 wheel arrangement but it was not the first eight-coupled engine possessed by the GNR. In 1866 Archibald Sturrock had contracted the Avonside Engine Company of Bristol to construct two tank engines of that form for working goods trains through the Metropolitan Railway tunnels between King's Cross and Blackfriars. They were of condensing form with exhaust steam from the two outside 18½in (47cm) by 24in (61cm) cylinders being directed to the side water tanks. With steam at 150psi and driving wheels of 4ft 6in (1.37m) diameter a tractive effort of 19,327 lbs could be developed which for a loaded weight of 56 tons (57 tonnes) gave an adhesion factor of 6.49, a necessity for working tunnel inclines.[19] These engines were not designed for main line service and so do not fall within the topic of this book but mention has been made in order to allow comparison with subsequent GNR eight-coupled types.

Ivatt and J.A.F. Aspinall of the LYR were close friends and something of a friendly rivalry built up between them. Ivatt was first of the pair to construct an 'Atlantic' but Aspinall had an eight-coupled engine in service during 1900. It is highly likely that the two locomotive engineers discussed the relative merits of different designs and reached similar conclusions as to the usefulness of eight driving wheels for mineral traffic. Engineers, and particularly those who were close friends, helped each other with their problems but the final solutions were in the hands of the CME of a particular railway.

As with many other designs, both on the GNR and elsewhere, ideas were borrowed from other locomotives and the boiler for No 401 was very similar to that fitted to the 'Klondyke' 4-4-2 engines apart from being pitched higher and having a shorter dome. For his 0-8-0s Aspinall had also made use of a boiler similar to the type he had fitted to his 'Atlantics'. An inside cylinder arrangement had been chosen with Richardson balanced slide valves being positioned above the cylinders with exhaust steam being directed into pipes which joined just below the blast pipe. Stephenson link motion actuated the valves by means of rocking levers, valves and cylinders having the same 1 in 6.5 inclination, this being necessary in order to gain the required space. A cylinder diameter of 19¾in (50cm) and stroke of 26in (66cm) were selected for the initial engine but variations in diameter existed with production batches until by 1913 a standardized cylinder diameter of 20in (51cm) was selected. Diameter of wheels with 3in (7.6cm) tyres was 4ft 8in (1.4m) whilst the 17ft 8in (5.38m) wheelbase was quite moderate and did not require any of the tyres to be flangeless.

Upon entry into service No 401 was put to trial running on the work for which she had been designed. This consisted of hauling coal trains from Peterborough to London, one such round trip being operated each day with a load to London of some 748 tons (762 tonnes) behind the tender. That load consisted of 52 fully laden 10 ton (10.2 tonne) trucks plus a 20-ton (20.4-tonne) brake van, whilst on the return trip 60 empty coal wagons would be hauled. A representative from the respected journal *The*

Ivatt original 0-8-0 Heavy Freight design, Class K1, later LNER Q1 class.

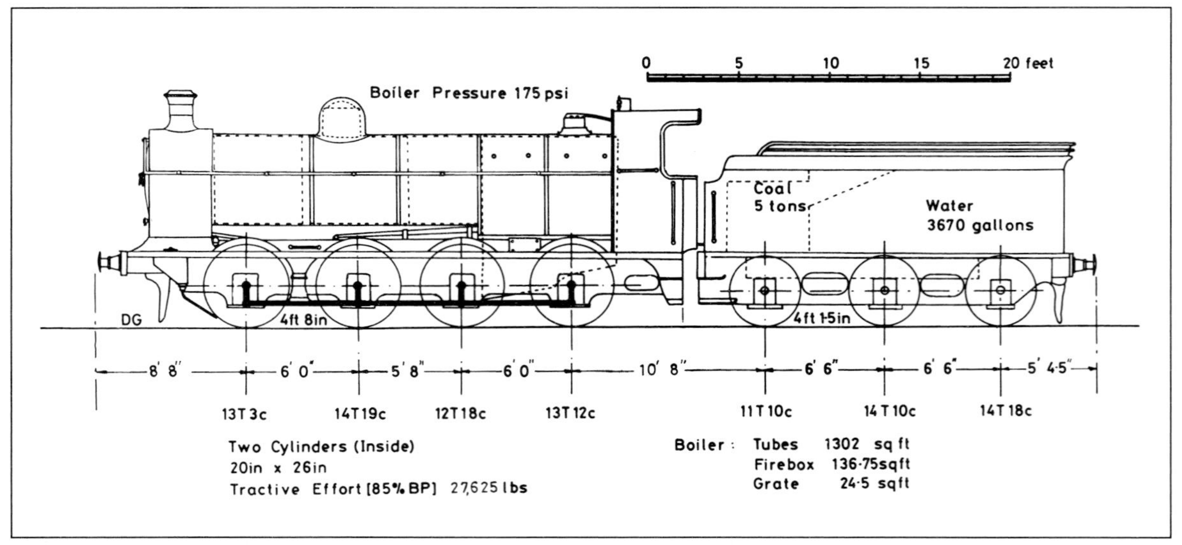

Engineer was invited to join one of the trial trips and gave a most favourable report on the working of the locomotive. Comments were made upon the ability of No 401 to maintain steam pressure of 175psi and to deal with the heavy train load on the 1 in 200 gradients, these being taken at speeds of between 17mph (27.2km per hr) and 20mph (32km per hr). Over a series of trial runs coal consumption averaged 78lb per mile (22.2kg per km) or 0.93lb per ton mile (0.27kg per tonne km).[20]

Such figures were certainly encouraging and prompted Ivatt to order more of these 0-8-0s for heavy freight duties. Ten engines were ordered in June 1901 for delivery the following year whilst further batches appeared regularly until 1909 when this, the K1 class, totalled 55 locomotives. The final batch of five were given 21in (53cm) diameter cylinders, piston valves and boilers fitted with Schmidt superheaters. The benefits of superheating had been under consideration following a study of its application elsewhere and in 1908 Ivatt fitted No 417 with a Schmidt type superheater. Boiler pressure was reduced by 15psi to 160psi, that practice being common amongst engineers when adopting superheating, and inside admission piston valves replaced the slide valves. To compensate for the reduction in steam pressure cylinder diameter was increased to 20in (51cm) and that required the casting of new cylinder blocks. The new cast steel pistons had extended tailrods and it became necessary to lengthen the frames by 9in (23cm) in order to accommodate them. Due to the change to inside admission valves the eccentrics had to be transposed in relation to the cranks but otherwise the Stephenson gear remained the same as before.

Ivatt does not appear to have waited for the trial results from No 417 before deciding upon construction of the final batch of K1s with superheaters. Gresley wanted more evidence on the performance of superheaters and when he took over from Ivatt at the end of 1911 further conversions of non-superheated K1s were undertaken. One retained its slide valves whilst others were fitted with piston valves. The success of No 415 with superheating and slide valves prompted the conversion of a further ten engines to that form using Schmidt type superheaters. Over the years to Grouping Gresley carried out trials with alternative forms of superheater and several members of the class received different types. Boiler pressure for all superheated engines was raised from 160psi to 170psi. As a group, however, the Ivatt 0-8-0s were referred to as 'Long Toms' and the class designation K1 applied during GNR days. With formation of the LNER a different classification was assigned on the basis of wheel arrangement and cylinder size; the 20in cylinder diameter version with slide valves becoming Q1, whilst those with 21in diameter cylinders and piston valves were classified Q2.

A single locomotive formed the LNER Q3 class,

GNR K1 class locomotive No 429 with a heavy coal train. (Courtesy NRM, York)

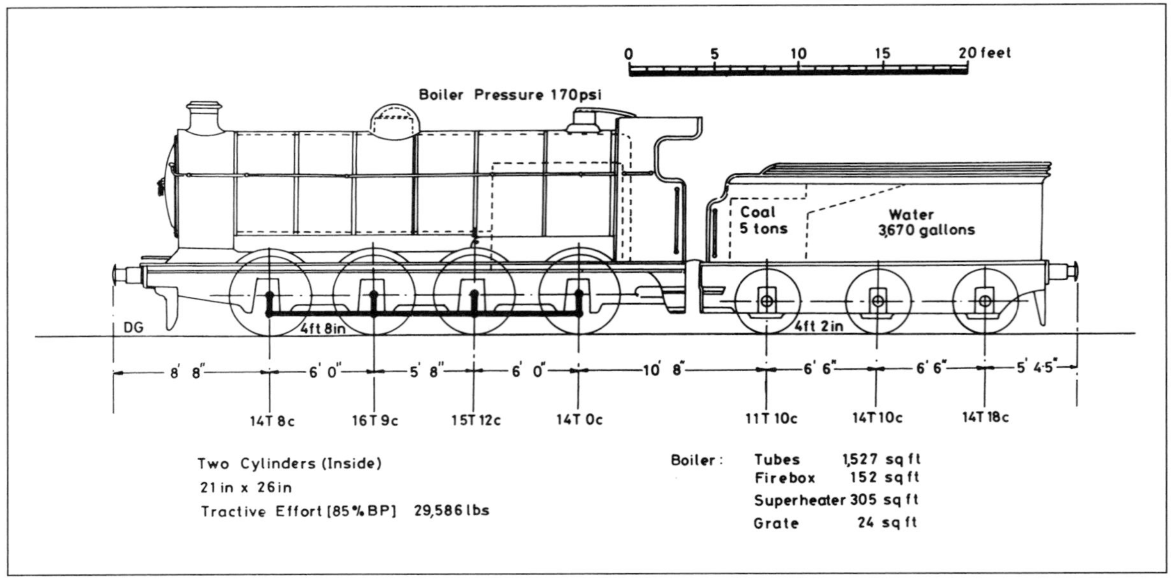

Ivatt 0-8-0 with larger boiler and cylinders. LNER Q2 class.

this also resulting from a Gresley conversion during GNR days. No 420, one of the superheated engines fitted with piston valves, was selected to receive a larger boiler with Robinson superheater. Apart from the fitting of the new boiler the only alterations required were a deepening of the frames at the rear where the firebox was supported and the provision of a new wider cab to improve forward visibility. Tractive effort did not increase as there was no change in boiler pressure but adhesion did, due to increased weight on the driving wheels. The maximum axle loading increased to 16.45 tons (16.75 tonnes) which was still within GNR limits.[21]

From the start the 'Long Toms' were used on heavy coal trains on the main line to London and there was no separation of duties for superheated and non-superheated engines. A number of regular brick trains operated between Yaxley and London, duty on these also falling to the K1 engines. The introduction of Gresley 2-8-0s gradually moved them to mineral traffic feeding the main lines and a number were loaned to the North Eastern Railway to cover for some of its engines which had been sent abroad for war duties. With the LNER acquisition of the bargain ROD 2-8-0s further use for the 'Long Toms' was limited on main line duties, but they were still valuable engines and could perform useful service around collieries. Such relegation was often the lot of former express passenger engines and although scrapping commenced in 1927 many survived until the early 1930s working pick-up freight duties in Yorkshire. The solitary Q3 class locomotive was also pushed off main line duties by more powerful engines and was assigned to Ardsley where it worked regularly on local goods trains. Its larger boiler and reduced cab working space made disposal difficult but it remained at that shed until withdrawal in 1937, principally because the turntable was too small to accommodate an ex-ROD 2-8-0.

Whilst the operating life of some 20 years may be considered short in comparison to other heavy freight classes they were not necessarily inferior. Circumstances conspired against them not least being the availability of relatively simple but powerful ROD engines which were comparatively new and cheap. For heavier traffic Gresley's 2-8-0s pushed them off main line duties and the ROD engines took over elsewhere. In total there were only 55 'Long Toms', arranged in three LNER subclasses, thus they could be considered as non-standard and dispensable.

Ivatt also made use of the eight-coupled wheel arrangement in constructing a condensing tank locomotive for working the tunnels of the Metropolitan Railway. The design was, in effect, a tank version of the K1 but its appearance looked different because the cab, chimney and dome had to be lowered in order to allow for clearance in the tunnels. Side tanks carried 2,000 gallons (9,143 litres) whilst the coal bunker contained 4 tons (4.07 tonnes). Such additions increased the weight to 79 tons (80.4 tonnes), of which 66 tons (67.2 tonnes) was on the driving wheels and the remainder on the trailing wheels which were provided with a radial axlebox.[22]

No sooner had the first of this L1 class, No 116, entered service in June 1903 than it was withdrawn on the instructions of the Civil Engineer as being too heavy. The boiler was immediately replaced by a smaller diameter unit, side tanks shortened to reduce water capacity and weight, and instructions issued that the coal bunker was not to be loaded to full capacity. These measures reduced maximum axle loading from 17 tons (17.3 tonnes) to 15¼ tons (15.5 tonnes). A further 40 engines of the modified design were constructed between 1904 and 1906 but the final 30 members of the class were sent directly to Colwick and Yorkshire for use on goods trains. It had become apparent that the design was not suitable for the purposes intended, hence the redirecting to freight duties. They were soon joined in that service by the earlier examples which had worked in London, the condensing apparatus being removed on that transfer.[23]

As with the tender versions superheating was applied in a number of cases but most of the class, designated R1 by the LNER, remained in saturated form, although they had all been provided with larger boilers during the Gresley GNR years. Use at Colwick on coal train working in and around Nottinghamshire occupied most of the class and the ten engines initially assigned to duties in Yorkshire had migrated to Colwick by 1913. On these short mineral duties these 0-8-2 tanks proved their worth and it was not unusual for a member of the class to haul a special miners' train when the need arose. Whilst never outstanding the class was useful, although not on the work for which the design had been originally produced. They were withdrawn at about the same time as the Ivatt 0-8-0 tender engines, again victims of the ROD 2-8-0s.

Gresley had his own ideas regarding locomotive stock for goods work and was not slow to see the limitations of Ivatt's 0-8-0s. One area of concern lay in the expanding coal traffic and the benefits which would accrue from hauling coal in larger wagons. However, little would be gained if existing locomotives were used in double-headed form. This is not the place to discuss Gresley's wagon designs nor his extensive testing arrangements but it is worth mentioning that he was well aware of the economic

Condensing tank 0-8-2T, GNR L1 class.

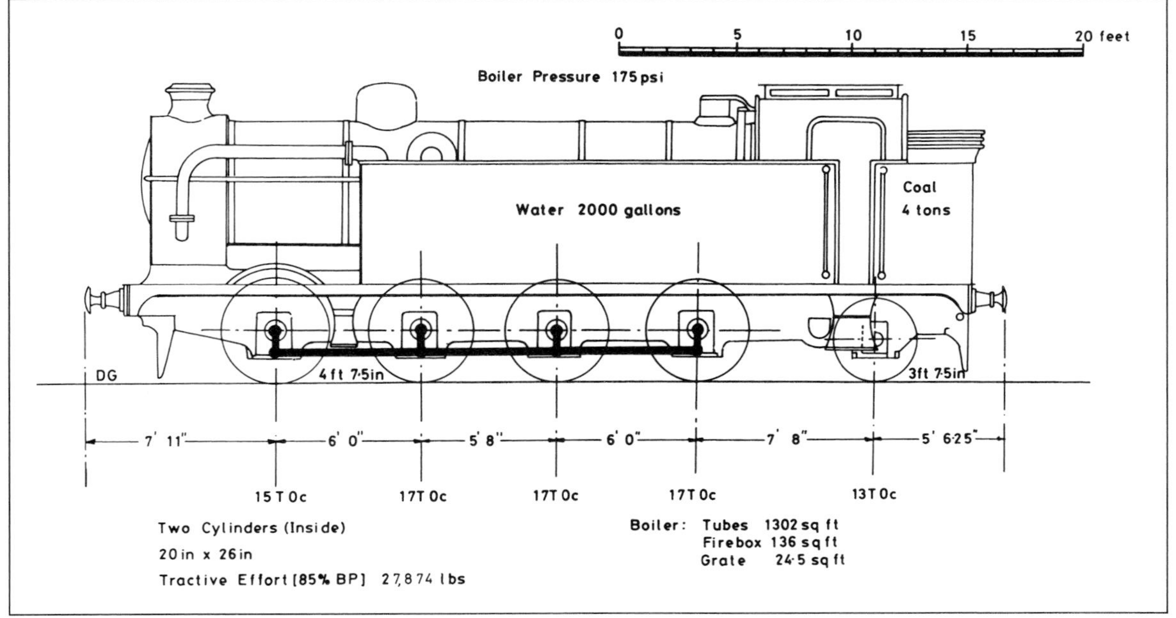

LNER R1 class; Ivatt's 0-8-2T as modified for working freight services. (D.K. Jones Collection)

advantages to be gained from the use of large wagons in vacuum braked trains. During his early years as CME he investigated the problems and organized trials with different designs. The war interrupted design and experimental work in that area but during 1922 more extensive train resistance trials were conducted in conjunction wtih Sir Henry Fowler of the Midland Railway. It was Gresley's view that wagons should be as large as possible and trains as long as possible in order to minimize the net cost per ton of freight hauled.[24]

One of the problems in operating freight on the Great Northern main line was the necessity for frequent crossing over between running track and refuge sidings to allow the passage of other trains. Gresley believed that a leading pony truck would make such operations easier whilst subjecting the track and locomotive structure to reduced loading, thus his design for a heavy mineral engine would be of 2-8-0 form. In order to haul heavy loads adhesion needed to be high and so careful calculation was required to ensure that the pony truck did not take

Gresley's first Heavy Freight design, the two-cylinder O1 class 2-8-0.

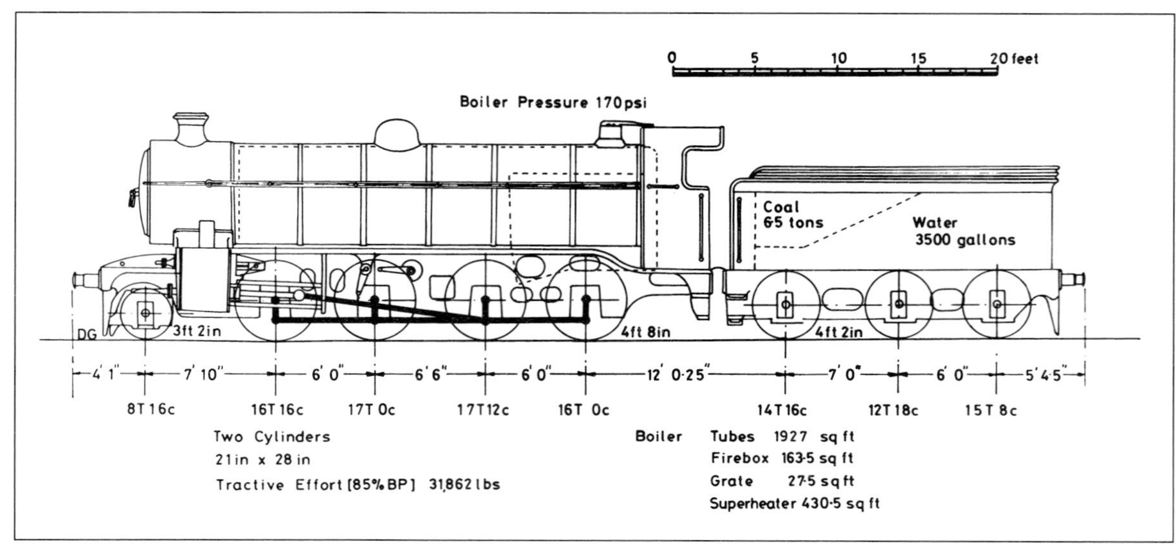

too much of the engine weight. Gresley's patented pony truck had double bolsters carried on swing links which equalized loading on the two wheels whether the locomotive was on a straight track or a curve.

The first of the Gresley 2-8-0s, Nos 456–460, appeared in 1913; the initial order being for five locomotives intended to haul coal trains comprising 80 loaded 10-ton wagons plus one 20-ton brake van, between Peterborough and Ferme Park, London. That loading represented 1,300 tons (1,324 tonnes) behind the tender which had to be hauled along rising track with some prolonged continuous gradients of 1 in 200. Only that initial order for five locomotives had been put in service before the outbreak of the First World War, but their performance did illustrate how useful the design was.

Two 21in (53cm) diameter by 28in (71cm) stroke outside cylinders, inclined at 1 in 40, took steam at 170psi from the large boiler fitted with Robinson superheater. Inside admission 10in (25.4cm) diameter piston valves, actuated by means of Walschaerts gear, provided for an easy steam flow and the large exhaust port area allowed full exhaust opening even when working at cut-off down to 15 per cent. This was achieved by means of double or trick ports which gave the locomotives very free steaming and exhausting conditions, this paying dividends in terms of power developed. Driving wheels of 4ft 8in (1.42m) diameter enabled a tractive effort of 31,862lbs to be developed for an adhesion factor of 4.7, ideal for the traffic envisaged. When the second batch of these O1 class engines (also class O1 in LNER days), were built boiler pressure was increased to 180psi thus altering the tractive effort and factor of adhesion values.

All wheels had full width tyres and laminated bearing springs were fitted at all axles. In order to provide for some compensation equalizing beams connected springing on leading and second axles, with another set connecting the third, or driving axle, and the fourth axle. A mechanical lubrication system supplied oil to cylinders, valve chests and all axleboxes, two running board-mounted Wakefield lubricators being provided for this purpose.

Gresley was very much an early enthusiast for boiler feed water heating and carried out trials with several forms of heater over the years. The first five O1s were fitted with Weir feed pumps and heaters, pumps being carried vertically between the frames in front of the driving axle whilst the heater unit, fed with exhaust steam, was fitted longitudinally below the boiler above the leading and second coupled axles. During 1916 No 459 had its heater blanked off and cold feed was supplied directly to the top of the boiler where an additional dome had been fitted behind the steam dome. Cold feed was pumped onto a collection tray in the additional dome where it

O1 class locomotive (LNER No 3459) with double dome cover, the second dome being for feed heating. (Author's Collection)

would be preheated before entering the main boiler and also deposit scale on the tray which could be removed at regular intervals. How effective these arrangements were is unknown and all were subsequently removed but Gresley persisted in his trials with feed heating. During the first three years of service the O1s averaged a coal consumption of 97lbs per mile (27.6kg per km), a very creditable performance considering the loads they hauled and many more would have been constructed had not WWI intervened.[25]

Further O1s were built by the North British Locomotive Company during 1919 thus bringing the strength of the class to 20 machines, but by this time Gresley had developed a belief in the superiority of three cylinders and turned his attention in that direction.

One of the problems relating to three-cylinder locomotives was the additional set of valve gear required and Gresley was opposed to such form of complication, and in 1915 he devised an arrangement whereby two sets of gear could be made to operate the valves for three cylinders. As a good engineer, Gresley determined on a trial of the three-cylinder engine and his conjugated valve gear, thus a prototype locomotive was constructed. No 461 was almost identical to the two-cylinder 2-8-0s and its 18in (46cm) by 26in (66cm) cylinders were sized to give a similar power output. Boiler, wheels and all other aspects were the same but the cylinder drive was to the second axle and not the third as it had been with the earlier 2-8-0s; all connecting rods were the same length. The inside cylinder had to drive the second axle as there was insufficient clearance for the connecting rod to be attached to the third axle. In order for the connecting rod to clear the first axle the inside cylinder had to be inclined 1 in 8, and because cranks were positioned at 120° to each other the outside cylinders also had to be inclined. Because of the inclination and the desire to use connecting rods of the same length, axle spacing differed slightly from that of the two-cylinder engines.[26]

The conjugated valve gear made use of a 2 to 1 lever arrangement to produce a drive for the inside valve but difficulties existed because inclination prevented the valve from being positioned above the middle cylinder. The alternative form of conjugated valve gear had to be adopted and the number of pin joints it contained caused comment in the technical press, but it did work however. This mechanism was fitted behind the cylinders and made the area around the crosshead rather cluttered. An earlier patent for a conjugated valve gear had been taken out by Harold Holcroft and the similarity between the two also drew much comment, but the systems were sufficiently different to avoid patent infringement.

Gresley considered that the three-cylinder arrangement would provide for easier starting of loads and smoother running, whilst at the same time avoiding excessive hammer blow on the track. The latter was due to the inherent better balance of three-

Gresley's first three-cylinder design, GNR No 461.

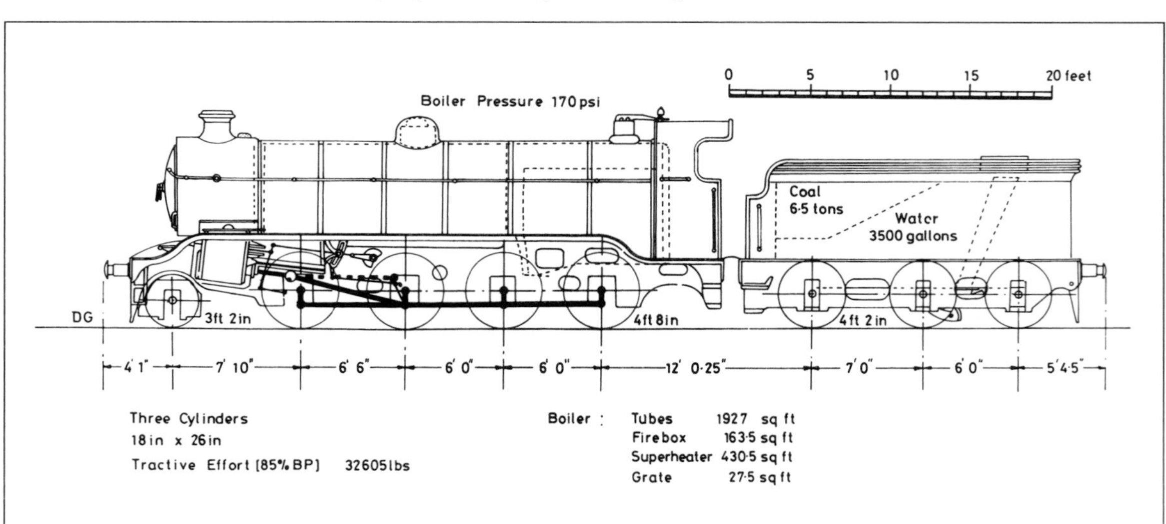

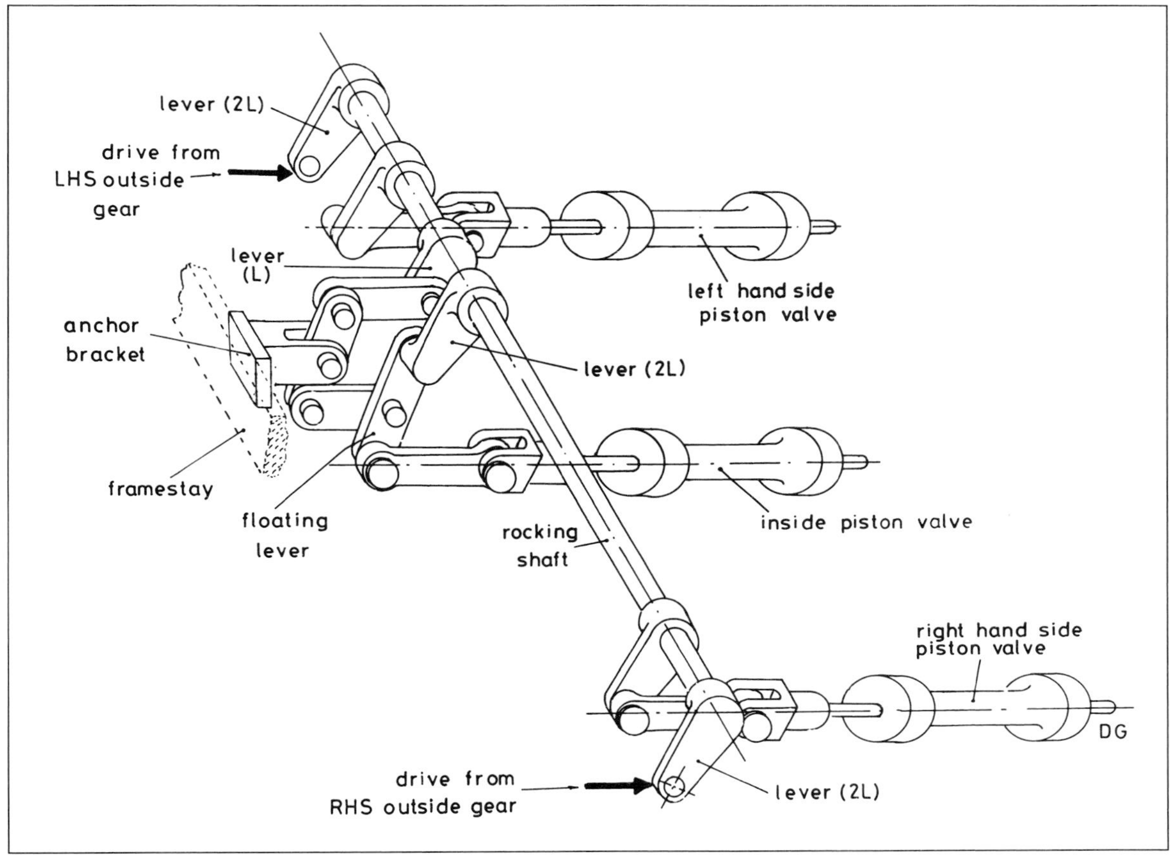

Conjugated valve gear as fitted to No 461.

cylinder design compared with one having two cylinders, thus avoiding the need for balance weights which resulted in hammer blow. An even starting torque was important when working with fitted freights as there was no slackness in the couplings which would allow the train load to increase gradually. It is likely that Gresley had this fact in mind when considering the suitability of three cylinders for freight engines, coaching stock already being close coupled with continuous brakes.

In order to test the effectiveness of the three-cylinder design Gresley borrowed the Great Western dynamometer car and made several trial runs with the No 461 and a two-cylinder 2-8-0, No 456. As both locomotives worked at the same boiler pressure and had comparable cylinder volumes the desire was more to test operation rather than performance. The GNR test track was on the main line to London and the 1 in 200 incline near Cambridge Junction presented the opportunity for a 'hill start'. Dynamometer car charts published by *The Engineer*[27] indicate how easily the three-cylinder locomotive started its train compared with the two-cylinder version. Wide fluctuations in drawbar pull which occurred with No 456, peaking at over 18 tons (18.3 tonnes), were absent with No 461. The three-cylinder arrangement proved itself to be effective at starting heavy loads without undue strain on the locomotive.

Successful trials with No 461 during 1918 enabled an order to be placed for ten similar three-cylinder engines to be constructed at Doncaster but this was soon transferred to the North British Locomotive Company. Although still fundamentally the same design there were differences between the prototype and these production engines, most notably in the cylinder arrangements and valve gear. Cylinder diameter was increased to 18½in (47cm) but the stroke and size of piston valves remained the same. A suggestion by Holcroft was acted upon with respect to cylinder inclination which, for the reasons stated, had been the same for inside and outside cylinders on the prototype, and in order to maintain even turning forces from the cylinders with cranks set at 120° to each other. Holcroft indicated that the outside cylinders could be made nearly horizontal whilst crank turning moments remained fairly equal if the middle cylinder crank was displaced by an amount equal to the former outside cylinder inclination. This produced the same crank effect as in the prototype but allowed valve centres to be placed in the same horizontal line, and that enabled the simple form of conjugated valve gear to be used. The new form of valve gear was tried on a 2-6-0 and when proved effective was stipulated in the design specification for the production batch of O2s.

North British undertook most of the detailed design work and agreed with Gresley that inclination of the inside cylinder would remain at 1 in 8 with outside cylinders and all three valve chests being inclined at 1 in 40. An increase in cylinder diameter was possible because the inside valve chest no longer occupied space alongside the inside cylinder. The three-bar crosshead guide, introduced with No 461, remained as there was still need for the centre crosshead to clear the leading axle. This arrangement consisted of an upper wide slide bar and two narrow lower slide bars, the gap between these allowing connection between the crosshead and the crosshead shoe running between the upper and lower slide bars. For standardization purposes the same system of slide bars was fitted to the outside cylinders and to other three-cylinder locomotives.

A penalty had to be paid for the reduction in outside cylinder inclination and that was the fitting of smaller diameter wheels to the pony truck which also had to be moved forward. The main frames also had to be increased in length by 7in (18cm) to accommodate this. In other major respects the production batch built by North British was the same as No 461.[28]

Despite the fact that he had almost certainly decided to build no more two-cylinder 2-8-0s Gresley continued testing both types in order to obtain comparative figures. A series of trials was run during February 1925 with No 3422 representing the two-cylinder O1 class and No 3479 the three-cylinder O2 class. Both locomotives were in a similar condition with respect to mileage since last shopping and the same footplate crew was used for all runs. These consisted of two loaded and two empty stock workings between Peterborough and London for each locomotive. Loaded trains weighed 1,300 tons (1,324 tonnes), including dynamometer car whilst empty trains weighed 420 tons (428 tonnes). Gresley provided full details of the runs and results in his paper on three-cylinder locomotives presented to the Institution of Mechanical Engineers

Three-cylinder Class O2.

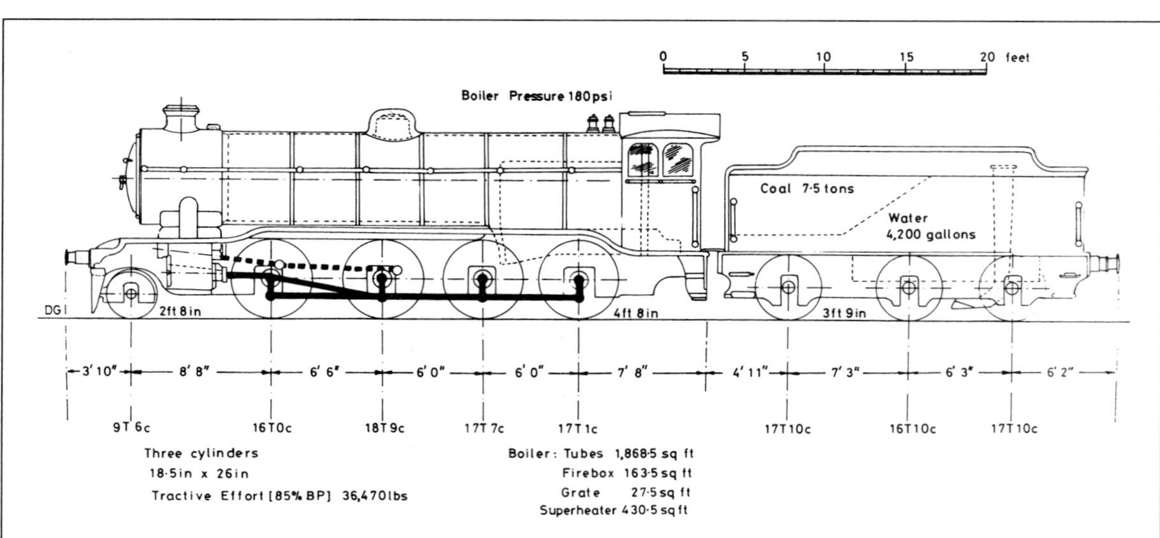

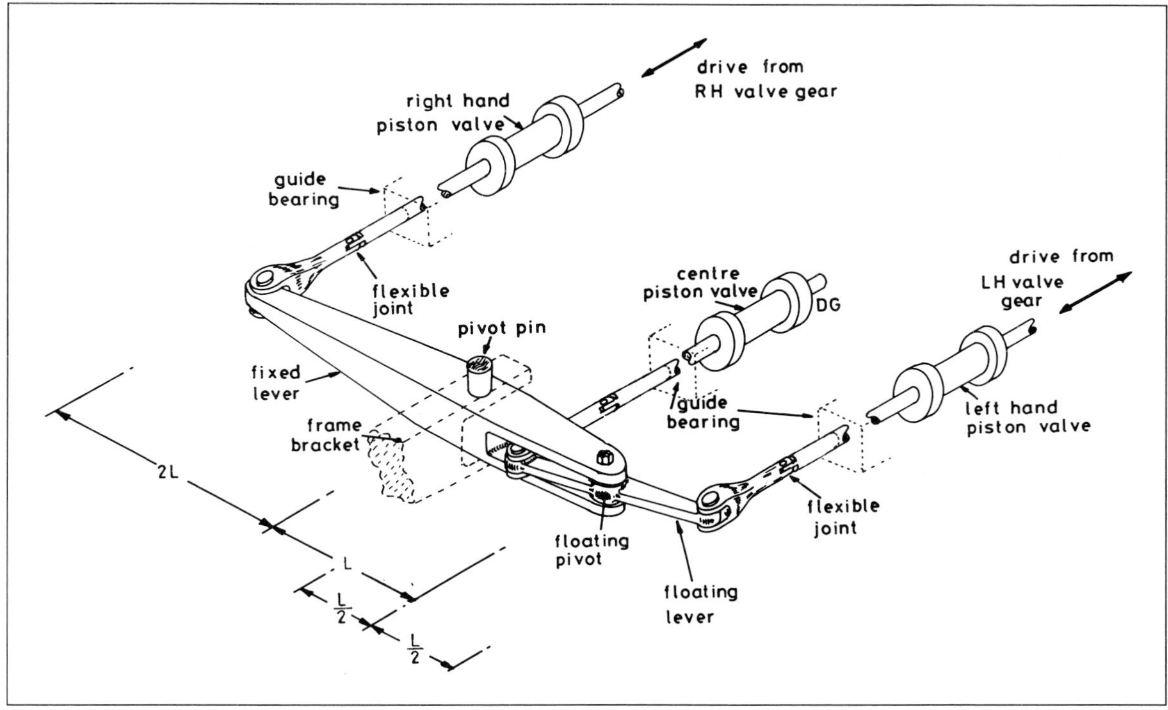

Simplified conjugated valve gear as fitted to the O2 class locomotives.

during July 1925.[29] Results with respect to consumption were most favourable to the three-cylinder type, whilst comment was also made regarding the steady operation of three cylinders compared with two.

Figures given were:

	2-cylinder	3-cylinder
Coal Consumption:		
lb per DBHP	5.19	4.76
kg per kW	3.16	2.9
lb per 1,000 ton train miles	144.1	123.9
Water Consumption:		
Gallons per DBHP	3.51	3.2
Litres per kW	21.5	19.6
Gallons per 1,000 ton train miles	100.0	84.9
Litres per 1,000 tonne train km	280.5	238.2

In conclusion Gresley stated the advantages of a three-cylinder form over the two-cylinder type to include, lower coal and water consumption, increased mileage between repairs, less tyre wear, less hammer blow, more uniform starting effort and lower permissible factor of adhesion. He also considered that the three-cylinder type was cheaper to build and maintain than one with four cylinders.

Additional members of the class were constructed shortly after grouping and these had to be constructed to the composite LNER gauge which was slightly more restrictive than that of the GNR. This resulted in a shorter chimney, repositioned whistle and reduced radius of curvature for the cab roof. In other respects the design was the same. A further batch appeared during the early 1930s whilst a final batch was constructed in 1942/3, bringing the class strength to 66, not including No 461. It is fairly obvious that Gresley would have built more of these engines had the need arose but the availability of inexpensive ROD 2-8-0s allowed most freight traffic needs to be met without resorting to construction. As with other classes of locomotives already considered there were a number of variations in the different batches and several modifications were made to individual engines, but nothing which could be considered as a major alteration apart from the fact

O2 class locomotive No 3500 fitted with Dabeg feed heater and pump units on the running plate. (D.K. Jones Collection)

that the final batch was constructed without equalizing beams. In effect the locomotives finished their days very much as they had started them.

Gresley's pursuit of improvements in thermal efficiency resulted in several O2s being fitted with feed heaters of assorted designs. Perhaps the most successful arrangement tried was the Dabeg which was fitted to No 3500 in January 1925 and not removed until December 1942 — and that was to comply with Thompson's directive concerning the removal of all 'gadgets'. The Dabeg device employed exhaust steam for heating purposes, that steam first passing through an oil separator before entering the condenser chamber where it mixed with cold water from the tender. One plunger of the pump unit drew water from the tender and forced it as a spray into the condenser chamber whilst the other plunger pumped the heated water, mixed with condensate, into the boiler. Plungers were mounted horizontally back-to-back and driven by a return crank on the rear axle using a linkage. A three-way cock regulator on the water outlet from the cold water pump was attached to a lever connected to the reversing arm, thus when the cut-off was changed the position of the cock was altered. By this means cold water supply to the heater, and hence hot water supply to the boiler, was regulated according to the cylinder steam consumption. Excess water from the three-way cock returned to the tender. No attention was required by the fireman as the unit supplied water to meet boiler requirements, but an injector was needed for auxiliary purposes. This type of heater would raise water temperature to 100°C thus causing most carbonates to be precipitated in the heater and not the boiler, a drain cock allowed sludge to be removed from the unit. This device would, therefore, allow removal of scale forming salts from the water before it entered the boiler and would also de-aerate the water thereby minimizing the risk of corrosion due to the presence of oxygen.[30]

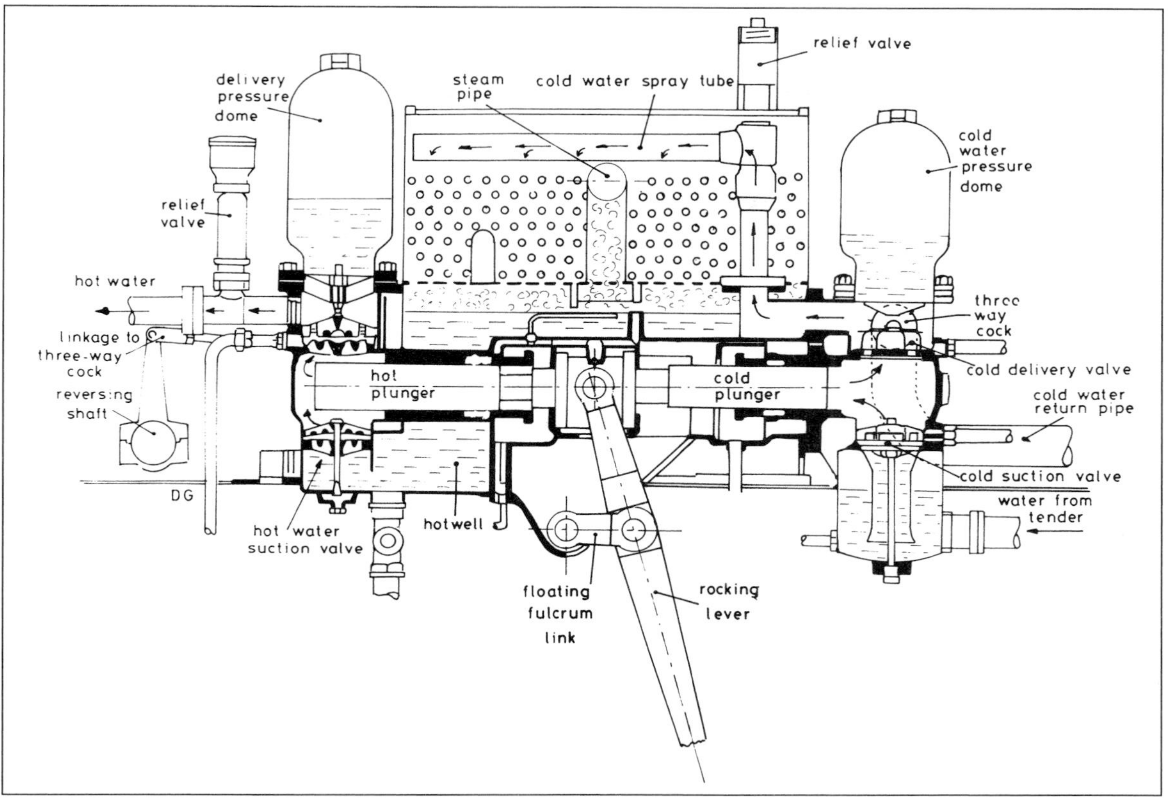

Diagram of the Dabeg feed heater and pump system.

The advantages of the device must have been recognized as it remained on No 3500 for so many years. A disadvantage of other forms was the need to control the steam driven pump in order to regulate the quantity of water being pumped to the boiler. As the Dabeg device had mechanical drive with control to suit the cylinder cut-off the footplate crew could ignore its operation and only needed to ensure that boiler water level was maintained.

The O2s worked main line coal trains between Peterborough and London during GNR days and continued on that traffic following Grouping. With additional engines constructed to the standard loading gauge they were able to be used on other sections of the LNER. During the 1930s a number were allocated to the former GER depot at March in order to work coal trains between Whitemoor Yard and Stratford. In fact they were too powerful for the size of train that could initially be operated due to the length of refuge sidings and it was not until 1937 that the load could be increased from 70 to 80 wagons. The wartime constructed O2s were allocated to Doncaster and worked heavy freights to Manchester and Hull as well as on the North to South route. Subsequent wartime duties found other members of the class at various LNER sheds and following Nationalization they mainly worked the southern part of the Eastern Region. Withdrawals commenced in 1960 with the final member of the class being withdrawn in 1963.

Hull & Barnsley Railway

In railway terms the Hull & Barnsley was quite small but it did move significant quantities of coal between the Yorkshire pits and the docks at Hull. Growth in coal exports and the opening of new mines during the early years of the 20th century prompted the railway's directors to make moves towards capturing a share of that increased trade. Success was achieved and the quantity of coal loaded into trucks for shipment on the Hull & Barnsley system rose from about one million tons at the turn of the century to some three million tons six years later. Even in 1913 in excess of 2½ million tons of coal commenced its journey on Hull & Barnsley metals. With this increase it became evident that the railway's 0-6-0 engines would not be able to cope and the locomotive engineer, Matthew Stirling, was instructed to design a class of locomotive capable of hauling heavier trains on the steeply graded lines from the South Yorkshire pits to the company's Alexandra Dock on the River Humber.

Stirling was responsible for design work but construction lay in the hands of the Yorkshire Engine Company of Sheffield. Fifteen of these 0-8-0 locomotives were ordered in two batches, all being delivered during 1908. A typical domeless Stirling boiler was fitted, this having a Belpaire firebox and operated at 200psi, quite high for that time. Two inside 19in (48cm) by 26in (66cm) cylinders developed ample power for the heaviest of trains anticipated. Cast bronze balanced type slide valves positioned above the cylinders were actuated from Allan straight link motion via rocking shafts. Driving wheels 4ft 6in (1.37m) diameter allowed a tractive effort of 29,549lbs to be developed, which for the fully loaded adhesive weight of 65.55 tons (66.74 tonnes) produced a useful adhesion factor of 4.97. In later years the operating boiler pressure was reduced to 175psi which resulted in a fall in power and tractive effort.

Gresham & Craven steam sanding gear was provided at four points, in front of each leading wheel and behind each trailing wheel. That certainly assisted in moving the heavy loads but the 16ft 6in (5m) coupled wheelbase does appear to have been rather short for negotiating tight curves. The fitting of two 20-ton (20.4-tonne) re-railing jacks on the footplate indicates the belief that derailment might be a problem. Frames, constructed from solid rolled mild steel were rigidly stayed together by means of buffer plate, cast iron drag box, and transverse stays positioned in front of the firebox casing, motion plate, footplate and cylinders. Cylinders had removable covers at each end, the rear covers carrying the slide bars.

On the route from Stairfoot and Cudworth, exchange points of the Great Central and Midland railways respectively, to Alexandra Dock at Hull these locomotives would take 45 10-ton (10.2-tonne) wagons and a 20-ton (20.4-tonne) brake van, the gross weight being 780 tons (794 tonnes). This was a significant improvement on the 0-6-0 engines which could only take 30 loaded wagons. Such loads presented a real trial for the locomotives as the starting point at Cudworth was on an incline of 1 in 300, whilst a 7-mile (11.2km) section shortly after leaving Newport was at 1 in 150.[31]

With the Grouping these engines became LNER

Hull & Barnsley Railway 0-8-0 Heavy Freight design.

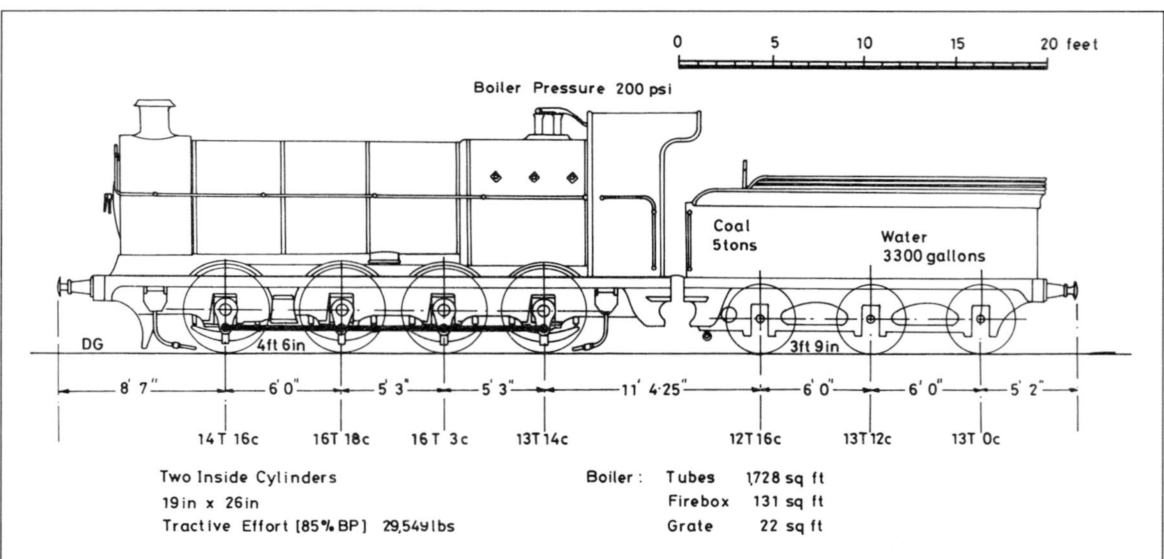

Class Q10 and were soon displaced from their traditional routes by ROD 2-8-0s. The opportunity was taken to fit new boilers from 1925 onwards and these had to be specially designed as the standard unit fitted to the Q6 class (former NER T2) would have required expensive frame alterations. Trade depression and the surfeit of heavy mineral engines due to the purchase of former ROD locomotives resulted in early demise despite the expense of new boilers. All were withdrawn in 1931, some within three years of having the new boilers fitted. Despite the rather short lives of these locomotives they were well designed with ample capacity for hauling loads. Circumstances and their non-standard form conspired against them but such is frequently the case when 'Big Brother' swallows the minnows. Corporate plans and ideas of efficiency through size leave little scope for the 'small guy' to survive.

North Eastern Railway

In terms of coal loaded into wagons on its system the North Eastern Railway was by far the most productive of any railway in Britain during the great days of heavy mineral traffic before World War I. During 1913 some 41 million tons (42.25 million tonnes) of coal commenced its journey on NER metals, which was half as much again as the nearest rival, the Midland Railway.[32] Coal was, however, only one mineral commodity with which the railway had to deal for the blast furnaces of the North East required supplies of iron ore and limestone. Just like the coking coal, limestone could be obtained locally, but iron ore, then not imported in any real quantities, came from Cumbria over some severely graded lines. Mineral traffic was also available in the opposite direction as coke from the region fed the blast furnaces of Barrow. In order to deal with such quantities an extensive fleet of powerful freight locomotives was required and in 1900 the then CME, Wilson Worsdell, decided that the 0-8-0 wheel arrangement had good potential.

Building upon experience gained from the introduction of the large 4-6-0 express passenger engines Worsdell made use of a similar boiler and cylinders for the heavy freight engine. Unlike fellow CMEs elsewhere Worsdell decided upon outside cylinders as they were more accessible for maintenance and history was to prove him correct. These cylinders were of 20in (50.8cm) diameter and 26in (66cm) stroke but despite their size consistently available power was limited somewhat by the rather small boiler which operated at 175psi. The pulling capacity was not, however, in doubt as one of these T class engines could draw 72 loaded coal wagons and a 10-ton (10.2-tonne) brake van; a gross load of some 1,180 tons (1,200 tonnes). Aware of the need

T class NER Heavy Freight 0-8-0 locomotive No 83, operating as LNER Class Q5 No 3274. (Herbert Collection/NRM, York)

LNER Class Q5 No 3271 at Tyne Dock in August 1947. Formerly NER T class piston valved 0-8-0.
(D.K. Jones Collection)

for effective braking Worsdell provided a steam brake on the locomotive which also operated brake blocks on the tender wheels. A disadvantage of this arrangement was that failure of the linkage between engine and tender brakes left the entire unit without a means of braking. The fitting of outside cylinders imposed no restrictions on which axle could take the drive as it did with inside cylinders, there being no axle in the way of the connecting rod, and Worsdell selected the third axle as being the most suitable for taking the drive. A further feature distinguished the T class engines from many others of the period and that was the provision of a very commodious cab.[33]

The first ten members of the class were constructed at Gateshead and had 8$\frac{3}{4}$in (22.2cm) diameter piston valves although why piston valves were specified is unknown. Subsequent construction makes it appear as though Worsdell was attempting to discover if there was any economic or operating advantage between the two forms of valve, for in 1902, a year after the T class appeared, ten more engines were produced but these had slide valves. In all other respects the two types were identical but the slide valve engines had the designation T1. Certainly they must have been successful in both forms for further construction of both types quickly followed with 30 T class being built at Gateshead between 1902 and 1904 and an additional 40 T1 engines at Darlington between 1907 and 1911.

The wheelbase for the engines was only 17ft 2in (5.23m) and that gave them access to sections of tightly curved track whilst the maximum axle loading of 16.9 tons (17.2 tonnes) was not too restrictive in terms of route availability. In order to allow for working special duties three engines were provided with Westinghouse air brakes but the equipment was soon removed from two, although in the remaining case it stayed on the locomotive until 1930. Four of the class had vacuum ejectors fitted so that they could be used with the continuously braked trains of 40-ton mineral hopper wagons. When the slide valve engines were introduced a representative from *The Engineer* was invited to observe the performance on coal hauling duties between Stella Gill, a collection point for lines from a number of collieries, and Tyne Dock, the distance being about 11 miles (17.6km). Initially on this sharply curved and steeply graded section the locomotive would take 60 trucks and a brake van, a load of some 985 tons (1,003 tonnes), but this was later increased to 72 trucks, representing a load behind the tender of 1,180 tons (1,200 tonnes). During the visit of *The Engineer*'s representative 81 trucks were hauled giving a total load of 1,326 tons (1,350 tonnes); the train length of 569.3 yards (520.6m) being the longest the NER had dealt with to that time.[34]

Up until the outbreak of WWI the class was stationed in the Durham and Tyneside areas in order to serve the local pits. The needs of the military required the use of all 50 T1 engines for duties with the ROD in France and there they found considerable employment on the heavy stone trains from the Marquise quarries, situated between Calais and

Slide valve fitted T1 class 0-8-0, running as LNER Class Q5 No 939. (D.K. Jones Collection)

Boulogne. Their high adhesion, ample tender capacity and reliability made them popular with both footplate crew and the operating department.[35] Upon return to the NER the engines were overhauled and resumed normal duties, but a brass replica of a bursting grenade, the Royal Engineer's insignia, and three service stripes were fitted, originally to the cab side but later to the leading combined sandbox and splasher.

Normal duties had changed somewhat with those of the pre-war days as electrification of the Shildon to Newport line removed one duty to which they were previously assigned, but some 44 T and T1 engines were stationed at the ends of the electrified section. At Shildon they were basically used for shunting and gathering in the coal wagons to form trains, whilst at Newport they were employed on hauling those trains to the docks and steelworks. Grouping brought the two variants together as the Q5 class but their duties remained very much in former NER territory. Throughout the LNER period there was little change in the engines apart from the fitting of the relatively new boilers from the scrapped former Hull & Barnsley engines between 1932 and 1934. These boilers were larger than the originals and required some structural alterations to be made including the fitting of a new cab. When these boilers were eventually condemned boilers of original size, but slightly modified heating surface were provided.

Mineral traffic was the reason for construction of the T and T1 engines and it was on that traffic they were primarily engaged. As necessary they would deputize for other locomotives on local and pick-up goods but the Traffic Department needed reliable mineral engines and they were ideal. Work in isolated locations was not beyond them and before the outbreak of WW1 they worked on the line to Tebay. Subsequent weight restriction on the viaducts between Barnard Castle and Kirkby Stephen resulted in their being banned from the line but a relaxation of the restriction allowed them to return in 1929. They were allowed to work between Kirkby Stephen and Tebay and in order to reach the shed at Kirkby Stephen they had to negotiate the viaducts. That was allowed only with boiler and tender empty and with the motion partially dismantled.

Arrival of the bargain ROD 2-8-0s heralded a bleak future for the class and they were spread further throughout the North Eastern division of the LNER system. The Second World War probably saved the class from an early demise and the engines served Britain again during that second world conflict, this time on home metals. With the armistice and a reduction in heavy freight traffic the end came. Withdrawals commenced in December 1946 and the final member of the Q5 class, a former T1 engine was condemned in 1951.

Vincent Raven became CME when Worsdell retired in 1910 and three years later introduced the T2 class. This was essentially an improved version of the T and T1 engines with larger boiler and superheating; because of the latter all T2 engines had $8\frac{3}{4}$in (22cm) diameter piston valves. Although the locomotive remained much the same as the earlier classes a number of features were changed

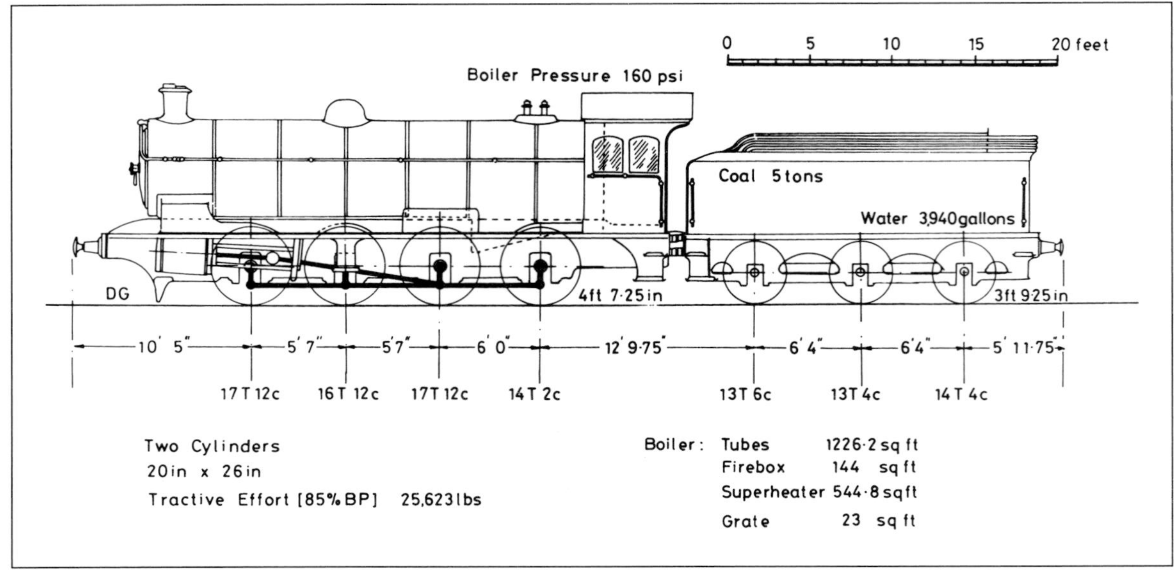

Raven NER T2 class Heavy Freight 0-8-0 design.

including the provision of a saddle for mounting the smokebox. Initially boiler pressure was set at 160psi, many designers adopting lower pressure with the introduction of superheating, but this was raised initially to 175psi and by the time the final members of the class were delivered in 1921 boilers were operating at 180psi. That certainly improved on tractive effort, raising the value to 28,800lbs.

Two batches, amounting to 30 engines, were constructed during 1913 but no further members of the class were built until 1917 and over the following four years further construction raised the class strength to 120. Apart from boiler replacement and modification to the tenders all members of the class remained virtually in original form until they were withdrawn during the 1960s; a number were still in service as late as 1967. That longevity is an indication of the usefulness of a class which was but a minor improvement on an earlier design, if superheating could ever be classed as minor.

During LNER days the T2s were classed as Q6 whilst Raven's final 0-8-0 design, the T3 was designated Q7. Raven had a firm belief in three-cylinder locomotives, earlier passenger and tank classes proving that his faith was not unfounded. Just like Gresley he was of the opinion that the smooth starting torque would be ideally suited to heavy freight operation and convinced his superiors of the fact. Approval was given for construction of five high powered three-cylinder engines even though there was no defined need and despite the fact that production of the T2 class was in full swing. These T3 locomotives were constructed at Darlington in 1919 and caused much comment in the railway and technical press. When much of the design work was being undertaken Raven, by 1917 Sir Vincent Raven, was assisting with the war effort as Controller of Armament Production for the Admiralty and so will have had little direct influence, but as CME he will certainly have been consulted.

Cylinders were in three castings, two for the outside consisting of cylinders only and a central unit comprising inside cylinder and common steam chest. Piston valves were of the same diameter as those employed for the T2, each valve being worked by its own independent Stephenson gear positioned between the frames. The piston diameter of 18½in (47cm) was smaller than that employed for the two-cylinder engines but with three such units ample power would be available, as subsequent trials were to prove. With a working boiler pressure of 180psi the tractive effort at 85 per cent boiler pressure amounted to a staggering 36,909lbs making the class the most powerful 0-8-0 in Britain. Engine weight in working order amounted to 71.6 tons (72.9 tonnes) giving an adhesive factor of 4.34 which might be considered low for other 0-8-0s but it must be

LNER Q6 class No 2254, formerly NER T2 class. (Stephenson Collection/NRM, York)

remembered that this was a three-cylinder engine with smoother starting torque making it less liable to slipping.

The boiler provided 1,573 sq ft (146 sq metre) of heating surface with an additional 530 sq ft (49 sq metre) in the superheater; the grate area amounted to 27 sq ft (2.5 sq metre). These figures were for the first members of the class but the additional ten engines constructed during 1924 had some variations. Locomotives were provided with steam reversers but gravity application of sand was employed, this being in front of the second pair of wheels for running ahead and behind the trailing wheels for running in reverse. Driving wheels were the same diameter as the T2, all cylinders driving the second axle, but wheel spacing differed and the wheelbase was longer at 18ft 6in (5.64m). In order to allow the negotiation of relatively tight curves the trailing axleboxes were given sideplay and the coupling rods were knuckle jointed. Tenders were of the self trimming type with space for 5¼ tons (5.6 tonnes) of coal and 4,125 gallons (18,851 litres) of water. As designed they were intended to handle loads of 1,400 tons (1,425 tonnes) on inclines of 1 in 200 without assistance, work of this nature primarily being found in the Newcastle area.[36]

Figures derived from cylinder and other dimensions give an indication of potential power but only service can indicate actual power and the dynamometer car trip described by the journal *Engineering* indicates how useful these engines were. On 10 November No 901, a relatively new engine which only left Darlington Works the previous month, hauled a loaded test train over the line between Newcastle and Carlisle. The 1,402 tons (1,427 tonnes) load, consisting of 60 coal wagons, brake van and dynamometer car, was handled with ease throughout the trip. The dynamometer car chart indicates the high power ability of the engine and the steady acceleration even with such heavy loads. From a dead stop at Haydon Bridge no problems were experienced in starting the load on the 1 in 298 gradient, the drawbar pull being 12 tons. In order to determine maximum pull three of the 30-ton wagons and ten of the 20-ton wagons had their brakes pinned down, but the locomotive started the train without difficulty, the dynamometer car spring being extended to its maximum amount indicating a pull in excess of 16.3 tons. On the return trip the load was approximately 787 tons (801 tonnes) and again no problems were experienced with starting on gradients as severe as 1 in 107.[37]

Following its experience with the Great Western's 2-8-0 (related in Chapter 2) the North British Railway was keen to test other heavy freight locomotives on its line and approached the NER to see if a T3 could be borrowed for that purpose. No 903 went north and ran three trials on the Glenfarg

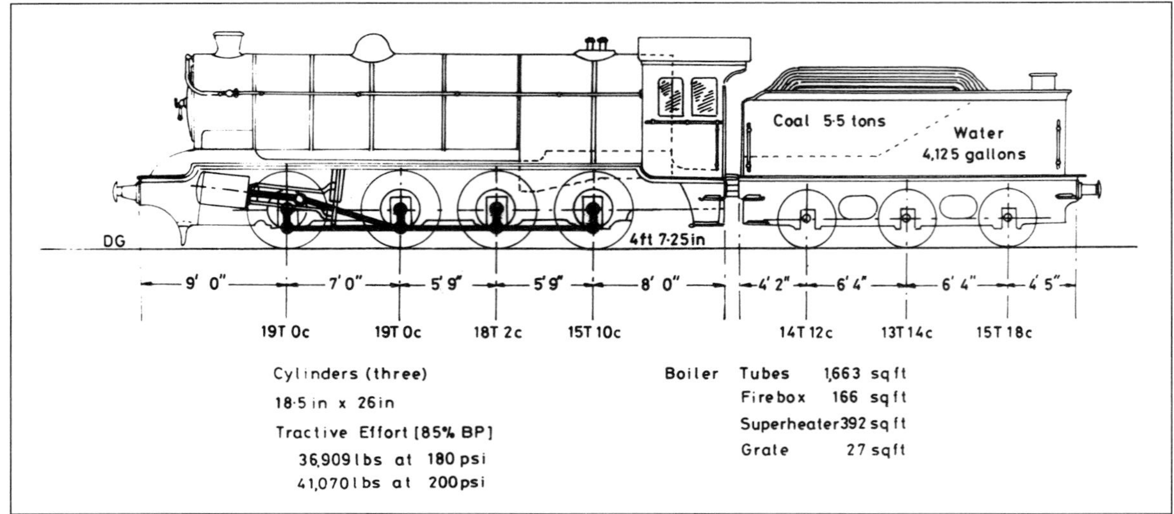

Raven three-cylinder 0-8-0 T3 design.

Bank on 28 August 1921. Each of the trials up the 6.66 mile (10.66km) incline was conducted with a different load and the time for each run monitored. The North British had no intention of checking power or economy, the only question was ability to haul a heavy load in an allotted period of time up the 1 in 75 incline. The first run with a load of 617.25 tons (628 tonnes) took 35½ minutes but with a load of 702.95 tons (726 tonnes) the locomotive only required 30 minutes. Even for the third run it only took 33 minutes to haul a load of 754.95 tons (769 tonnes). The reason for the higher time on the first run was put down to the cautious approach of the driver who set the engine to a 53 per cent cut-off and full regulator. The second run was at 75 per cent cut-off with full regulator opening for the first half of the distance and then cut-off was reduced to 65 per cent. During the final and most heavily loaded run cut-off remained at 75 per cent throughout.[38]

Although the T3 was officially designed for a boiler pressure of 180psi during the Glenfarg trials the operating pressure was increased to 200psi. It has been considered that the increase in pressure was required in order to ensure that the locomotive provided sufficient power to haul the train up the bank, however, later tests on the Newport to Shildon electrified line were also undertaken at the higher boiler pressure. It is possible, therefore, that the boilers were designed for 200psi but sufficient power could be obtained at reduced pressure and the lower pressure was adopted in order to restrict boiler maintenance requirements.

Impressed with the running of his T3 in Scotland Raven undertook further haulage trials on his own steeply graded line between Newport and Shildon, this line having been electrified. No 903 was again selected and in October 1921 competed against one of the electric locomotives specifically constructed for the line. Identical loads, including a dynamometer car were attached to each engine in turn for a series of three runs. The first was a non-stop through run over the 17½-mile (28km) lines, the second had stops at the bottom of the three steepest gradients whilst the third required stops with the entire train on each of these three gradients. Information gathered produced the following results.

	Time (Mins)		Average DBHP (kW)	
	Steam	Electric	Steam	Electric
1st test	56.5	54	862 (643)	870 (649)
2nd Test	77	53	602 (449)	883 (659)
3rd Test	68	66	682 (509)	716 (534)

Again a steam pressure of 200psi was employed so nobody could accuse Raven of loading the trials in favour of electric traction, with which he was totally in agreement on specific lines. He would, however, always present the best case for favoured projects and in the same paper which described the Newport-Shildon trials he compared the performance of an electric propulsion unit with the T2 engines, claiming that three of these 0-8-0s would be required to do identical work. He also produced the outline scheme for a two-cylinder 0-8-2 which could do the same work as an electric unit then under consideration. This was not a serious attempt at design but was intended to illustrate how much more effective electric traction could be. The projected steam locomotive was way out of gauge and excessively heavy but it served Raven's comparison purpose.[39]

It can be argued that the electric units designed for hauling freight trains on the Newport-Shildon line should be covered in this book but interesting as they are the author has decided not to do so, giving two reasons to defend his actions. A strict dictionary definition of locomotive is that of a self-propelling machine and as such devices require an external power supply they are not self-propelling. As the line was short and isolated the units were not for general use throughout the system and so were limited in application; for the same reason eight-coupled shunting engines are not given any detailed coverage.

Only five T3s were constructed by Raven for the NER but Gresley ordered a further ten in 1924 for the newly formed LNER. Why this order was placed is difficult to understand; despite the obvious success and abilities of the class there was no real need for essentially non-standard heavy freight engines, particularly as a large number of former ROD 2-8-0s were then available. These had been purchased for about £2,000 apiece whilst the new T3s cost considerably more. The first batch cost £7,609 each in 1919 and so 1924 construction will have been more expensive; 1919-built T2s cost £6,026 each whilst those in 1920 cost £8,000 each.[40]

Grouping saw the T3s reclassified Q7 by the LNER, the original engines and the 1924 batch remaining on heavy freight duties throughout the North Eastern division. During the Second World War some engines operated as far north as Edinburgh but the entire class eventually gravitated to the Tyne Dock area. In order to allow working of iron ore trains comprising large capacity hopper bogie wagons between the River Tyne and Consett five Q7s were fitted with Westinghouse air pumps, this being necessary as these wagons had air-operated bottom doors. Allocation of BR Standard 9F 2-10-0s to this duty meant removal of the Westinghouse equipment but the class still worked heavy freights out of Tyne Dock. Withdrawal of the entire class took place in 1962 but fortunately, No 63460, the first member of the class and originally NER No 901, was set aside for preservation.

5

Heavy Freight Locomotives of the Inter-war Years

For many the period between the two world wars represented the golden years of railways as the Grouped companies settled down to provide the services for which they had been formed. Post-Grouping rationalization caused each of the companies to expand its express services thus requiring larger and more powerful locomotives, as well as improved coaching stock. Fads such as streamlining and special train sets were indulged, usually to satisfy directors rather than the travelling public, but it all added to the glamour of the railways. GWR 'Kings' and 'Castles' dominated express services from Paddington and the Southern constructed what it considered the most powerful British express steam locomotive, in the shape of its 'Lord Nelson' class. On the East Coast Route to Scotland Gresley's Pacifics drew praise from all, whilst after a nervous start, the LMS replied with its 'Royal Scots' and Stanier Pacifics running northwards from Euston. The 1920s and '30s were certainly glorious for the express passenger locomotives but little was heard of freight, which still provided the largest share of any railway's revenue.

In pre-Grouping days no company which formed the Southern Railway had constructed an eight-coupled main line freight locomotive and that situation did not change after 1922. Schemes were proposed for such a wheel arrangement, but quickly dropped when it was realized that refuge sidings could not cope with trains of the length which could be hauled by a heavy freight locomotive of this power. The GWR was well stocked with eight-coupled locomotives, tender and tank types, and as these designs had served the railway well there was no need for any change.

On the other two railways the situation was less clear but a period of consolidation was required following Grouping in order to assess the situation. The LNER did not appear to suffer from the infighting which afflicted the LMS and its birth pains were certainly less traumatic. In fact the LNER had it quite easy, the constituent railways bringing many fairly recent heavy freight engines into the new company and the government providing a bargain by way of surplus ROD locomotives which were essentially standard with one of those used by one of the constituent companies. At Euston things were less easy and everything seemed to hinge on the needs of the former Midland Railway, this causing problems with locomotive design and application.

LMS Heavy Freight Locomotives

On the Midland line between Toton and Brent coal traffic had to be dealt with in large train loads due to the problem of line occupation. The use of two Midland 0-6-0 locomotives was traditional and continued into early LMS days. However, the use of two crews was seen by some as an unnecessary economic burden. A large engine solution appeared to be the easy option but there were restrictions on the line with respect to axle loading and locomotive dimensions, to upgrade the line was considered to be prohibitively expensive. Midland Railway ideas caused the problem and imposed restrictions on the solution.

Several proposals were considered, including the use of a booster on conventional locomotives and a Mallett type locomotive, but George Hughes, then CME of the LMS, favoured a Garratt design. With a 2-6-0 + 0-6-2 arrangement in mind he approached Beyer, Peacock during March 1925 who responded with a design of 2-6-2 + 2-6-2 form. Hughes considered the proposal to be ideal and requested estimates but as he retired towards the latter part of that year no further progress was made. When Sir Henry Fowler became CME thoughts again returned to a conventional locomotive of 2-8-2 wheel arrangement but it would appear that Fowler was not complete master of his own locomotive house. Unbeknown to him and to Hughes an independent approach had been made to Beyer, Peacock by J.E. Anderson, the LMS Motive Power Superintendent, also in March 1925. How such a situation can have been allowed to happen is difficult to understand but during its first decade the LMS can hardly be classed as a well run organization.

Most railways allowed Beyer, Peacock a fairly free hand in the design of Garratt locomotives, simply indicating power requirements and applicable restrictions, then letting the designers get on with the work. That was very much the way in which Hughes approached the matter but Anderson had other ideas and insisted upon certain Midland practices being followed. Naturally, Beyer, Peacock would construct locomotives to the purchaser's requirements but there must have been some raised eyebrows when the LMS order was placed. Anderson had been Chief Draughtsman at Derby and so was responsible for many of the Midland ideas which were incorporated in the Garratt design, but he does not appear to have been concerned with the possible implications of using small engine ideas for large locomotives. It was Anderson and not the CME or representatives from his department who discussed technicalities with the builders, and it was even Anderson who signed the contract for construction of three Garratt 2-6-0 + 0-6-2 locomotives.[1]

From such events it would appear that the Motive Power Superintendent considered his department as a separate entity and able to order locomotives from wheresoever it wished. Such an attitude may even have been reasonable if the LMS design staff and workshops could not meet requirements but why higher management allowed the situation to develop to that extent is indicative of incompetence. The three Garratts were delivered in 1927 and to some people they appeared to be the answer to the double heading problem, which they were. However, many other factors had to be considered before they could be classed as the real solution to the problem.

The design specification called for an ability to haul coal trains of 1,200 tons (1,222 tonnes) but the journal *Railway Engineer* reported that during their first six months of operation the Garratts had been hauling loads of 1,500 tons (1,527 tonnes) on the Toton to Brent route, a running time of 7 hours 49 minutes being allocated for the 126 mile (202km) trip. Several stops were allowed for water and general engine duties but the overall average speed of just over 16mph (25.6 km per hour) was considered very good at the time.[2] Power came from four outside cylinders, two on each power unit, these being of 18½in (47cm) diameter and 26in (66cm) stroke. With steam at 190psi a tractive effort of some 45,620lbs could be developed on a loaded adhesive weight of 155½tons (158.3 tonnes). Without a doubt the machines were powerful and the maximum axle loading of 20¼ tons (20.6 tonnes) was within line limits and they could negotiate track with a curvature of 396ft (121m) radius at normal speed or 330ft (101m) radius dead slow speed.

During the first three months of 1928 Garratt No 4998 took part in tests alongside Class 3 and 4 0-6-0 freight locomotives on coal trains between Toton and Brent with the two smaller locomotives double headed, two Class 4 and a Class 3 with a Class 4. Several runs were made in each direction for each of the three arrangements of motive power, loads being slightly different in each case to suit hauling capability; the LMS dynamometer car (formerly the Hughes L&Y car) being added to the normal train load. Enginemen were instructed to keep to time as far as possible and the footplate crew working the Garratt also manned the leading locomotive of each double headed pair. E.S. Cox had charge of the testing and detailed results were originally published in LMS report No 15 and can also be seen in *Historical Locomotive Monograph No 1* by Essery and Toms.[3]

Despite early optimism concerning introduction of the Garratts as expressed in sections of the railway press results of those tests were not over impressive, particularly as far as coal and water consumption were concerned. When working train loads of about 1,500 tons (1,527 tonnes), equal to two Class 4 freight engines, the Garratt could not keep time on gradients of 1 in 200 and its overall

LMS Garratt No 4979, as originally numbered. (Author's Collection)

coal consumption was about 4 per cent greater. For the loading of a Class 3 plus a Class 4, about 1,380 tons (1,405 tonnes), the Garratt did keep time but its coal consumption was about 2 per cent greater. Special tests trips were organized with design loadings but at accelerated speeds of 23mph (36.8km per hour) and in these the Garratt maintained time with coal consumption about 3 per cent less than two Class 4 locomotives. In all tests the Garratt showed reduction in water consumption between 6.7 and 12.4 per cent. Overall it was concluded that the Garratt could economically operate the 1,200 ton (1,222 tonne) trains for which it was designed but when forced with higher loads economy suffered.

Despite the problems with respect to firing, results were satisfactory as far as the Operating Department was concerned and after the first batch had been assessed a further 30 members of the class were ordered. There were, however, operational problems which required modifications to be made to the design. As with all designs certain problems are only evident when a machine enters service but a number of the Garratt difficulties should have been foreseen, particularly as it was the motive power people who took the lead in the project. When working at Toton it was necessary for the locomotives to pass over the hump in the marshalling yard and when this manoeuvre was first tried defectiveness in the design became evident. After the leading power unit cleared the peak of the hump its rear headstock fouled the boiler cradle, in passing over the summit there had been a tendency for the wheels of that unit to lift clear of the track. As the rear power unit reached the summit and the boiler unit moved downwards to follow the leading power unit the driving wheels of the rear power unit forced their way upwards through the cab floor. The solution was to lower the summit of the hump and cut holes in the cab floor to accommodate the wheels.

Another problem which should have been evident to the Operating Department concerned watering arrangements. At certain locations two columns had been provided to allow simultaneous filling of double headed 0-6-0 tender tanks. Had the spacing of such columns been given to Beyer, Peacock tank filling holes on the Garratts could have been positioned so that both tanks could be filled at the same time. The Garratt design did have an equalizing pipe between the tanks, its purpose being to even out weight distribution whilst on the road, but not to allow for the replenishment of both tanks by filling only one. The leading power unit tank was also provided with a water scoop which could be operated when running in either direction.

A major problem as far as the footplate crew was concerned manifested itself when running bunker first. The cab became very draughty with coal dust from the open top bunker irritating those trying to do their job. Hot bearings were also encountered with the three initial Garratts but no steps appear to have been taken to correct the defect, probably because it

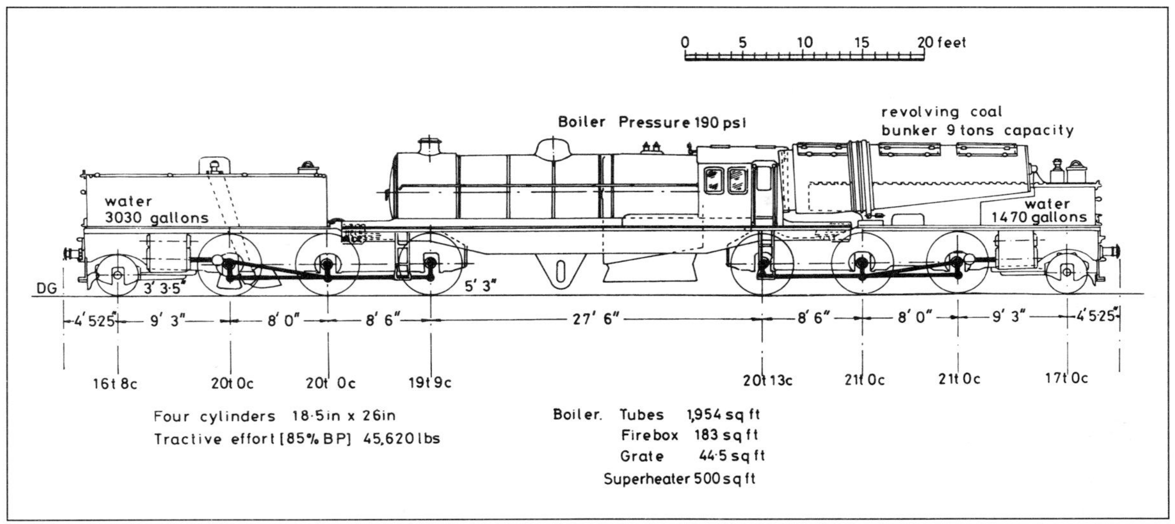

LMS Garratt design with rotary coal bunker.

was normal with Midland engines and became an accepted fact of life, at least for Midland people.

The new batch of Garratts, all delivered during 1930, perpetuated most of the defects although a number of minor changes had been incorporated. Taller chimneys and domes were fitted whilst water and coal capacities were increased. Frame cracking had been experienced with the initial batch and for the new locomotives frames were strengthened above the axlebox guides. In order to minimize the problem caused by coal dust when running bunker first a substantial tarpaulin sheet was fitted over the bunker top, this sheet running in specially provided guides. A winding apparatus was fitted and as the level in the coal bunker fell the sheet could also be moved to cover the gap and thus prevent wind rushing into the cab via the bunker. Unfortunately sharp pieces of coal soon put paid to the tarpaulin screen and the idea was abandoned.[4] Increased coal capacity caused another problem as trimming of the bunker became extremely difficult due to the new shape of the bunker floor.

No 4996 was fitted with a steam operated coal pusher but this did not prove to be really effective, however, No 4986 was provided with the Beyer, Peacock rotary bunker, designed and patented by Samuel Jackson the company's Chief Designer and Works Manager. The bunker tank was shaped in the form of a conical frustum, its axis being tilted downwards towards the cab to such an extent that the top of the tank appeared parallel with the rail. The effect of this inclination allowed coal to fall naturally towards the cab end of the bunker where a door was situated through which the fireman gained access to the coal. Three filling doors were situated along the body of the bunker. At the cab end support was provided by rollers abutting onto a cast steel ring which surrounded the bunker whilst at the rear end a spindle was located into a bearing mounted on the water tank. Rotation was produced by a reversible two-cylinder steam engine which rotated a worm mounted in a cross shaft on top of the water tank. This worm engaged with a toothed wheel incorporated in the cast steel ring. Operation of the steam engine turned the worm thus rotating the bunker via the toothed wheel. Under normal conditions three or four rotations would trim coal from the rear of the bunker to the shovel plate, the operation taking about 90 seconds.[5] The 30 newer Garratts and No 4997 of the original batch were all fitted with rotary bunkers at a cost of £320 each.[6] The arrangement also minimized entry of coal dust to the cab.

Seventeen of the new Garratts joined the original three at Toton with most of the remainder being allocated to Wellingborough, apart from two which went to Cricklewood. All were essentially used for working coal trains to London but by the mid-1930s some had been moved to Hasland shed near Chesterfield from where they covered workings over the Hope Valley line and as far north as York. It seems strange that a class specifically designed for

LMS Garratt No 7973, formerly No 4973. (Author's Collection)

the heavy coal trains between Toton and Brent should be moved away so early in their lives but production of the Stanier 8F 2-8-0 was probably responsible.

Mechanical problems appeared very quickly, the cracking of the frames with the original three already having been mentioned, and frequent shopping became essential in order to keep the locomotives operational. It may well be that the original three locomotives, being relatively new, confused the issue by producing reasonable performance with fairly good availability. However, as they and the subsequent 30 got older that availability fell off dramatically as design defects became evident. Such a situation was not the fault of Beyer, Peacock but resulted from LMS insistence upon ideas which had no credibility. At the end of their operating days in the early 1950s these machines were achieving no more than 20,000–25,000 hours between shopping.[7]

A major source of trouble was the old Midland adherence to the small axlebox bearings. Midland main line track was generally of lower standard than existed elsewhere in Britain and routes contained many sharp curves. This imposed problems with respect to locomotive design, particularly as far as axleboxes were concerned. There was a tendency with Midland locomotive design staff to allow a certain amount of straining of the frames as a locomotive negotiated a tight curve but that was only possible if bearings were kept short. Long bearings tended to overheat as journals rubbed against them but with short bearings there was less rubbing as frames were strained when negotiating curves.[8] A solution would have been to reduce track curvature but a conservative Midland Board was always reluctant to spend money and the small engine policy with short axlebox bearings sufficed for Midland traffic.

Why that situation persisted into the enlightened days of the 1920s and the larger LMS system is difficult to imagine but persist it did, and many locomotive designs suffered simply because those in command would not, or could not, comprehend the needs of the LMS were more important than those imposed by a constituent railway. The lowest common denominator dictated matters. Had the bearings fitted to the Garratts been of standard size and thus interchangeable with other classes there might just have been a glimmer of justification but that was not the case. Old ideas remained and bearings had to be short for no other reason than it suited Midland practice. Beyer, Peacock always used large sized bearings in its own designs and made a specific plea for such on the LMS machines but to little avail. Anderson had indicated that bearings 8½in (21.6cm) diameter by 8¼in (21cm) long should be used but relented somewhat and allowed the use of 8in (20.3cm) diameter by 9in (22.9cm) long bearings, hardly an improvement. Not unnaturally the axlebox bearings wore rapidly resulting in shopping at half the time interval which should have been achieved.[9] It would appear that dogma got the better of engineering sense.

The other outdated Midland practice insisted upon was the use of short travel valves, the gear being based upon that fitted to the S&D 2-8-0s which had been designed by Anderson when he was Chief Draughtsman. This gear caused losses and the Garratts, although capable of doing the work required, were much less efficient than they might have been. Further trials carried out during 1931 and 1932 illustrate this fact. The 1931 tests were aimed at assessing the improvement of the new locomotives compared with the older type and that they did, showing a reduction of some 12 per cent on coal consumption and about 5 per cent on water consumption when hauling fully loaded trains. It was also evident that steaming was not as good when using Warsop coal, that normally supplied at Toton, compared with the better quality Grimethorpe coal. Tests the following year concluded that coal consumption per unit of work done was about the same at the trial speeds of 17.5mph (28km per hour) and 20.7mph (33.1km per hour) but evaporation rate improved at the higher speed.[10]

The new Garratts were provided with double exhaust valves which to some extent compensated for short travel by providing a larger exhaust area at the valve. This enabled exhaust steam to flow more freely from the cylinder, thus reducing back pressure on the piston and allowing more power to be developed.[11] The improvement in coal consumption of the new Garratts can be seen from the table on page 59 but from this it is also evident that the contemporary standard 0-8-0 Class 7 freight locomotive was more efficient. It must, however, be borne in mind that no other locomotive had the hauling power of the Garratt and for pulling heavy loads it was in a class by itself. Double heading was avoided and if a single Class 7 0-8-0 was to be used the load hauled would have been less than that of the Garratt, thereby leading to line occupation problems. Despite their many faults these locomotives served a purpose and they avoided the additional crewing costs of double heading. That they could have been better is beyond doubt and had the builder been given a free hand they would have been.

During the Stanier era Beyer, Peacock was approached with a view to eliminating the problems and making the Garratts into the machines they should have been in the first place. The work involved new frames, axles and axleboxes, amongst other things, but when the 1938 price of £3,500 per locomotive was made known no further action was taken.[12]

In pre-World War II days the locomotives were generally based in the Midlands for working coal trains although unsuccessful attempts were made to deploy members of the class as bankers on the Lickey Incline. During the war these activities continued but, as with many other classes, they were taken for other duties as and when required.

Periods between overhauls were prolonged and the Garratts had to suffer the lack of attention which afflicted all locomotives during that conflict; efficiency of performance did not matter in those days — just the ability to perform and the high hauling power of the class, even in run down state, must have been useful. In post war years Toton and Hasland sheds retained their allocations with duties continuing much as before, but the frequent maintenance requirements were making them a rather expensive luxury despite their haulage potential. With the arrival of the Standard 9Fs on the London, Midland Region the days of the Garratts were certainly numbered and withdrawals commenced in 1955. Rapid depletion of numbers took place over the ensuing two years and the final Garratt was withdrawn in April 1958.

The Garratt name and that of Beyer, Peacock deserved better but interfering outsiders imposed ideas which the patent holders would never have countenanced themselves. However, Beyers were in business to build and sell locomotives and if the customer wanted certain features he got them.

The Garratts had been constructed for a specific purpose, namely high power coal haulage, but there was still a need for a good freight locomotive of more conventional power output. During the mid-1920s that requirement was filled by 0-8-0 designs produced by the Lancashire & Yorkshire and London & North Western railways but LMS management dictated that a new standard design should be constructed as a replacement. In order to provide the necessary power within applicable weight and other restrictions it was decided that the new locomotive would be based upon one of the existing designs. The L&Y 0-8-0 was quickly discounted on the basis of size and it appeared that the new design would be a development of the G2 but former Midland men would not give up the fight to the LNWR fraternity that easily. It was proposed that the S&D 2-8-0 design could be adapted as a standard for the entire LMS system and trials were arranged in order to test the economy and performance of both designs. The first trial with coal trains on the Toton to Brent route indicated that the G2 was the better design, but Midland men were unwilling to believe that, and called for a rematch after their champion had been put through the works. Again the G2 came out on top and a decision was made, probably reluctantly, to base the new standard 0-8-0 on the G2 but with a number of Midland 'refinements'.

A 'G2' boiler would be erected on a chassis provided with Midland style wheels, axles and assorted other gear, the work of arranging the engine diagram being given to E.A. Langridge, then a grade II draughtsman at Derby. It had been decided that Joy gear, as fitted to the G2, would not be used but, at long last, long travel valves were adopted. Outside cylinders, even of 19in (48cm) diameter as planned, could not be arranged within the loading gauge and weight restriction so inside cylinders had to be used. Stephenson valve gear presented problems and Walshaerts gear offered the only real option but there were difficulties of space. However, by increasing the spacing of the leading wheels by 12in (30.5cm) from the 5ft 9in (1.75m) of the G2 Langridge was able to fit in the gear he wanted and at the same time reduce the inclination of the cylinders.

Wheels were to be of 4ft 8½in (1.44m) diameter which, with the 200psi boiler pressure and 26in (66cm) stroke cylinders, would give a tractive effort of 29,747lbs, somewhat above the G2. Increased length due to the greater wheel spacing at the front end increased engine weight but by doing away with the crank axle centre bearing and frame stretcher, together with the use of lighter coupling rods, it was possible to keep the weight close to that of the G2. All wheels had flanges due to the intervention of the Civil Engineer, but no effort was made to deal with the large number of flangeless wheels on former LNWR locomotives and it was probably just the Civil Engineer exercising his authority. The increased wheelbase presented certain problems as it mitigated against the negotiation of tight curves, the requirement being for operation on 462ft (141m) curves at normal speed and 330ft (101m) curves running dead slow.

The running plate was positioned above the wheels hence no splashers were required, with the boiler being pitched rather high compared with the G2. Use of larger diameter wheels influenced that to some extent as did the need to provide sufficient clearance for the ashpan. The boiler itself was a good one and steamed very effectively, its ancestry in the G2 design ensured that few changes needed to be made. Three locomotives were provided with ACFI feed water heaters from new but the devices

LMS 7F class design; the 'Austin Seven'.

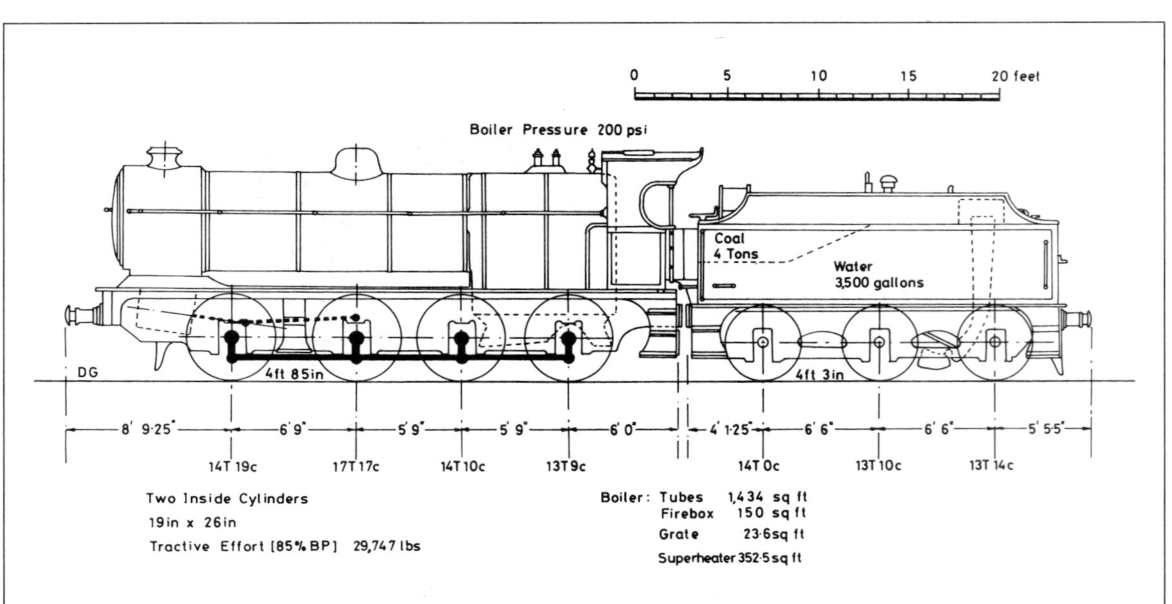

Fowler/Anderson LMS 7F class 0-8-0 No 9556. (Author's Collection)

were removed during the Second World War when life was difficult enough just keeping basic locomotives working.

Langridge's diagram was accepted and detailed design work commenced but it was here that Midland influence conspired to ruin what was potentially a good locomotive. LNWR adjustable spring links were dropped in favour of Midland style solid links and conventional laminated springs were applied to the trailing axle instead of the LNWR transverse springs. A steam brake replaced the vacuum brake but the valve gear was given back to Langridge for detailed work and so he was able to impose his own ideas. In that respect the Chief Draughtsman made a good move as larger diameter pins were fitted at links and a very effective long travel arrangement was produced. Again Midland men insisted on small bearings and that effectively undid the good work others had put in. From calculated forces based upon 19in (48cm) diameter pistons and a 200psi steam pressure it seemed that big end and axlebox bearings of the size fitted to the Class 4 0-6-0 would be sufficient. However, the nature of loading on an 0-8-0 was different from that on the smaller class and piston diameter was soon increased to 19½in (49.5cm) thus increasing the potential force on the bearings.[13]

In service the standard Class 7 0-8-0s, referred to by railwaymen as 'Austin Sevens' after the ubiquitous family car of the period, were quite popular as they could pull well and were quite economical on coal, a factor much appreciated by any fireman. Consumption figures arrived at over a series of tests were very good and compared favourably with all other freight classes then in service. It was, perhaps, natural that some former LNWR enginemen would compare these 'Midlandized' locomotives unfavourably with the G2s and that did happen, but the tractive effort was undoubtedly greater for the Class 7 engines. Pulling power may have been influenced by the slightly larger wheel diameter and the increase of cylinder diameter to 19½in (49.5cm) was undertaken to placate the Operating Department. Comparative trials were run between locomotives having different cylinder diameters and subsequent construction was to the larger size. In this form they were highly regarded as engines with good pulling power which could be slogged when necessary, and some former L&Y men considered them to be as useful as the later Stanier 2-8-0.[14]

Low coal consumption and an ability to work hard were ideal assets but the design was let down by its short axlebox bearings. Repair costs were high, some 50 per cent above that of the G2, and availability relatively low.[15] Hot boxes and bearing failure were common, resulting in that low availability, the basic cause being the short, small area bearings. Whilst such bearings might have been suitable for small Midland 0-6-0s they were not ideal for the longer wheelbase of the 0-8-0. Additionally there was higher loading on the bottom end and axlebox bearings due to the increased cylinder diameter. Bearings had been sized on the basis of the original cylinder size but the half-inch increase in diameter produced a higher force on the piston and hence on the bearings. With full boiler pressure of 200psi acting on the piston the increase in force due to the larger area would amount to some 3,020lbs, or 5 per cent of the original force. This figure relates to full boiler pressure but cylinders were never actually subjected to maximum boiler due to losses in the system. However, it does indicate how the loading on the big end, and other bearings, was increased by a relatively small increase in cylinder diameter.

During 1930, with just over 100 locomotives in service, 53 hot axleboxes were reported whilst one cranked axle had to be replaced due to fracture.[16] The mechanical record was not good from the start and deteriorated as years went by. A total of 175 Class 7 0-8-0s were constructed between 1929 and 1932 and they all suffered due to the short Midland style bearings. As heavy freight locomotives they were certainly useful and could haul the loads for which they had been designed but pulling power and fuel consumption are not enough; if a locomotive is a frequent visitor to the works for attention it is no use to the Operating Department and is a drain on the finances of the Mechanical Engineering Department.

Most of the locomotives remained unaltered throughout their working lives but five were fitted with oil burning equipment in 1947 as part of the abortive scheme to divert coal for export. Only one of these was converted back to coal firing when the experiment ceased in 1948, the other four being withdrawn the following year. That premature withdrawal of the oil burners was part of an overall scheme to rid the recently Nationalised railways of a class which had not really proved successful from a commercial point of view as a result of the heavy maintenance requirement. In 1949 61 members of the class went for scrap and others followed in each of the succeeding years, apart from 1958, until the class became extinct in 1961. They were outlived by former LNWR G2s, the locomotives they were supposed to replace, simply indicating that new is not necessarily better.

The 'Austin Sevens' occupied their time on similar work to that of the G2s and the withdrawn Hughes 0-8-0s, particularly mineral traffic on former LNWR and LYR routes. Others worked the same sort of traffic on the Midland Division of the LMS together with the usual run of mixed freights. It may fairly be said that the Class 7 0-8-0 was an

LMS 'Austin Seven' early in BR days; No 49592. (Author's Collection)

unspectacular design which could have been useful had the mechanical problem of its bearings been sorted out. That necessary modification was not considered worthwhile during the Stanier years is indicative of the new attitude which then reigned. Five locomotives were ordered in 1932 but this was cancelled by the new chief on his arrival and replaced by an order for two 2-8-0s, the prototype Stanier 8Fs. For these new engines the Derby 0-8-0 was no match and it appears that a policy existed to just let them wear out. Had World War II not intervened with the need to provide all freight power possible it is likely that some of the class could have been withdrawn earlier. Maintenance costs and availability were the new gods in terms of locomotive design and construction.

The appointment of Stanier changed many things about LMS locomotive policy and his arrival also brought about a change in attitude. Stanier was not simply a locomotive designer as many enthusiasts would wish to believe, in fact he never considered himself as a locomotive designer. Stanier was an engineer, a very good engineer. Being such he understood the benefits of team work and his initial task was to gather about him a team which would design and develop the locomotives he wished to see built. That team included R.A. Riddles, R.C. Bond and E.S. Cox, who were to play such a valuable role in developing the standard British Railways locomotives, together with Tom Coleman the Chief Draughtsman. It is no secret that much of the inspiration for the Stanier locomotives was down to Coleman and men like Cox recognized that from the start.[17]

Being an outsider Stanier was able to make a clean break from the old Crewe versus Derby infighting which so plagued the LMS and one of the early tasks was to sort out heavy freight motive power. E.J.H. Lemon, interim CME between Fowler and Stanier, recognized a problem in that area and had instructed his Locomotive Assistant, S.J. Symes, to investigate the possibility of a new design. Symes came up with a 2-8-0 based upon the successful Horwich 'Crab' 2-6-0 and at the same time H.P.M. Beames at Crewe also produced an eight-coupled freight design using the Class 7 0-8-0 boiler. Both ideas were stillborn but they illustrate how attitudes were changing and how bad the heavy freight haulage situation had become.

The first heavy freight proposal under Stanier's regime was for a three-cylinder 2-8-0 using many parts common to the 'Royal Scots', but it was soon realized that three cylinders for a freight engine were a costly indulgence which had little benefit. A two-cylinder version was schemed by Cox and approved by Stanier; Coleman then got his team involved with the detail design of what was to become the Stanier 8F 2-8-0. When No 8000 appeared in 1935 it was classified '7F', in fact the initial batch comprised twelve locomotives and these had boilers which

Stanier 8F class 2-8-0; a classic Heavy Freight design.

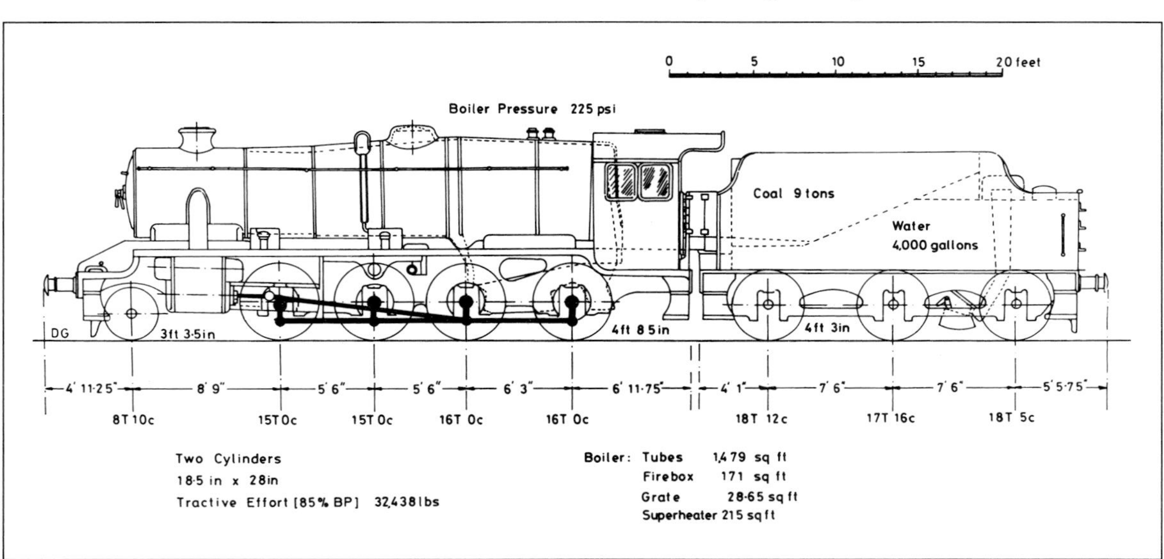

LMS 8F No 8519 at Heaton during 1946 whilst on loan to the LNER. (D.K. Jones Collection)

differed from later versions. In other respects, apart from the absence of vacuum brake equipment, they were identical to later versions classified '8F'; locomotives Nos 8000–8005 not having vacuum brake equipment. Boilers as fitted to the first twelve '8Fs' was smaller in terms of grate area, heating area and superheater area, although the working pressure was the same as subsequent members of the class at 225psi; that early boiler was also domeless.

Compared with their immediate LMS heavy freight predecessors, the Class 7 0-8-0s, the 8Fs proved to be more powerful, better riding and easier on the track. They were also much more economical on coal and enjoyed wider route availability due to lower axle loading and ability to negotiate curves of 297 feet (90.5m) radius. In effect there was no real comparison as the 8Fs were simply much superior in every way.

The Stanier 8F has been described so often that it is almost unnecessary to go over the same ground again but some details will be repeated for completeness of text. Any reader requiring further details of the class should consult volumes such as *Stanier 8Fs at Work* by Alan Wilkinson.[18]

So effective was the class from the start that, apart from the boiler changes already mentioned, there were few significant alterations in the design over the years it remained in production. With the outbreak of WW2 the War Department took the Stanier 8F as a standard and a number were requisitioned directly from the LMS whilst orders were placed for new batches. Wartime construction took place away from the LMS at the private locomotive builders North British and Beyer, Peacock, whilst the three rival home railway companies also undertook construction. By the time building of 8Fs ended in 1946 a total of 852 had been constructed, of which 133 were intended only for War Department use. The initial WD idea had been to make use of the 8Fs in Continental Europe but retreat to Dunkirk brought about a change in plans, ultimately the 'Austerity' freight locomotives being used to serve allied forces in Europe and the Stanier engines headed for the Middle East. Areas of operation included Egypt, Iran and Turkey, several remaining in service in this region long after British steam operations ceased.

8Fs constructed at Swindon served the GWR until being transferred to the LMS during 1946–7 whilst those built at the SR's Ashford, Brighton and Eastleigh works were intended for the LMS and LNER, but a number did operate on Southern metals for a short period when new. The LNER was short of heavy freight power but materials for construction of locomotives were in short supply so the company agreed to take up to 100 8Fs in the national interest.

Stanier 8F in BR days; No 48735 at Aberdare during March 1964. (D.K. Jones Collection)

Presumably the national interest was that this design was a standard for the War Department and the locomotives would be available for military duty if called upon. Gresley would have preferred his own three-cylinder design, as will be seen from his offer to transfer Robinson 2-8-0 to the War Department in return for construction of a similar number of his own O2s, (see Chapter 6) but the Stanier 8Fs must have been a good substitute. LNER Class O6 was assigned and the locomotives worked normal freight

8F No 48200 with a heavy freight train at Mirfield during July 1966. (D.K. Jones Collection)

services, if the term normal could be applied to wartime operations. They operated freights over the Woodhead route, mineral traffic from Tyne Dock, and an assortment of traffic over the East Lincolnshire line. Several were also sent to Scotland where they operated main line goods and some passenger stock trains, being highly regarded by enginemen there.

At its peak the number of 8Fs in service on the LNER, in stock and on loan was 128. With the end of the war and the allocation of 'Austerity' 2-8-0s to the LNER the Stanier engines became surplus to requirements and by the end of 1947 all but one of the O6s had been transferred to the LMS. The final locomotive moved from the Eastern Region to the London, Midland Region of the newly Nationalised British Railways in January 1948.[19]

Being of power class 8 these locomotives could be trusted with the heaviest traffic and they were, including coal and iron ore trains. Toton received an early allocation and use was made of them on traffic previously reserved for Garratt haulage. In order to minimize the risk of broken couplings a limit of 70 loaded wagons was imposed for the 8Fs but as the Garratts were also operating the same services this limit also applied to them.[20] Iron ore trains, 1,000-ton limestone trains, heavy mixed goods, and a variety of other duties fell to the 8Fs and the locomotives became very popular because of their economy and reliability. During the war similar duties were also performed, together with traffic of a more military nature including ammunition trains heading north to naval bases at Rosyth and Scapa Flow. Some were even tried on the Somerset & Dorset line but braking power was not as good as the resident 7Fs and the experiment soon ceased.

Post war duties continued much as before with the class being well dispersed throughout the London-Midland Region with work not being confined to mineral traffic. They were highly regarded by footplate crews and maintenance staff and they lasted to the end of steam on BR in 1968. On heavy trains they could be driven for long periods on full regulator and up to 45 per cent cut-off without any problems regarding steam or fall off in performance. Because of their freight classification operating speeds were expected to be low and many of the 'foreign' built engines had coupled wheels with cast-in balance weights rather than the usual LMS pattern built-up weights. At low speeds this caused few problems but at higher speeds, above about 40mph (64km per hour), large fore and aft forces were present causing uncomfortable riding. The situation became severe when coasting at speed on falling gradients as the buffing gear and springs were compressed. Conditions on the footplate became hazardous and the crew needed care when dealing with the situation. In order to distinguish locomotives which had reasonable balance, and so could operate at higher speeds, from those without, the

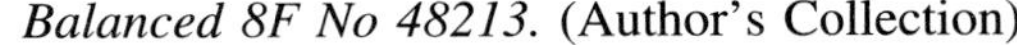

Balanced 8F No 48213. (Author's Collection)

Star painted on cab, signifying a specially balanced 8F.

balanced engines had a star painted on the cabside. These 8Fs could be used for partially fitted freights at speeds up to 50mph (80km per hour), and also on passenger trains.[21]

It would be easy to fill many pages with complimentary accounts of 8F workings as footplate biographies abound with such tales. It is left to the reader to consult such works and all that needs stating here is that the general consensus seems to be that the 8Fs were excellent locomotives to drive and fire.

From a railway point of view they also offered good service with availability being high and coal consumption reasonable compared with other freight classes available. Problems did occur but few were of major significance and none ever required the whole fleet to be modified. Cracking was experienced with the early frames but when these were increased in thickness with subsequent batches the problems ceased. Good sized Stanier bearings suffered few problems regarding overheating but axlebox thrust faces did require attention more frequently than was expected and in 1954 it was decided to fit 50 of the class with manganese steel liners to the horn faces in an attempt to reduce the problem. The nature of heavy freight operations with its movement in and out of marshalling yards or sidings tended to increase tyre wear to a level greater than that suffered by passenger or mixed traffic locomotives. Tyre wear, therefore, frequently became the deciding factor for shopping and that interval was usually shorter than that needed for axlebox attention. In 1953 R.C. Bond quoted an average mileage between periodic repairs of 50,361 (80,578km) which compared less favourably with the GWR 2-8-0, the WD 2-8-0 and the LNER O1 class 2-8-0.[22]

Despite this the 8Fs were kept in service right to the end of British steam operations, undertaking the work for which they had been designed.

LNER Heavy Freight Locomotives

Despite the amount of freight traffic on its lines the LNER developed only one original heavy freight locomotive of its own and that was the P1 class 2-8-2. Modifications were made to existing designs and the O4 was the subject of extensive rebuilding by Thompson but Gresley's two Mikado locomotives stood alone as LNER heavy freight designs.

The fact that no real need existed for further heavy freight engines is indicative of Gresley's earlier success with the O2 design and the extensive use made of the Robinson 2-8-0 purchased in large quantities from the government. Despite the satisfactory situation which existed on the LNER, Gresley had his mind firmly on the future, and a more powerful freight locomotive than that already in existence formed part of his plans. Use of parts, particularly the boiler, already standard to the Pacifics allowed work to progress rapidly and a 2-10-2 was originally schemed with 4ft 8in (1.42m) diameter wheels on the same total wheelbase as the A1 class express locomotive. However, the ten-coupled idea was dropped and a 2-8-2 version adopted with the Civil Engineer agreeing to its use on lines passed for Pacific operations. In the form

Gresley's P1 design 2-8-2.

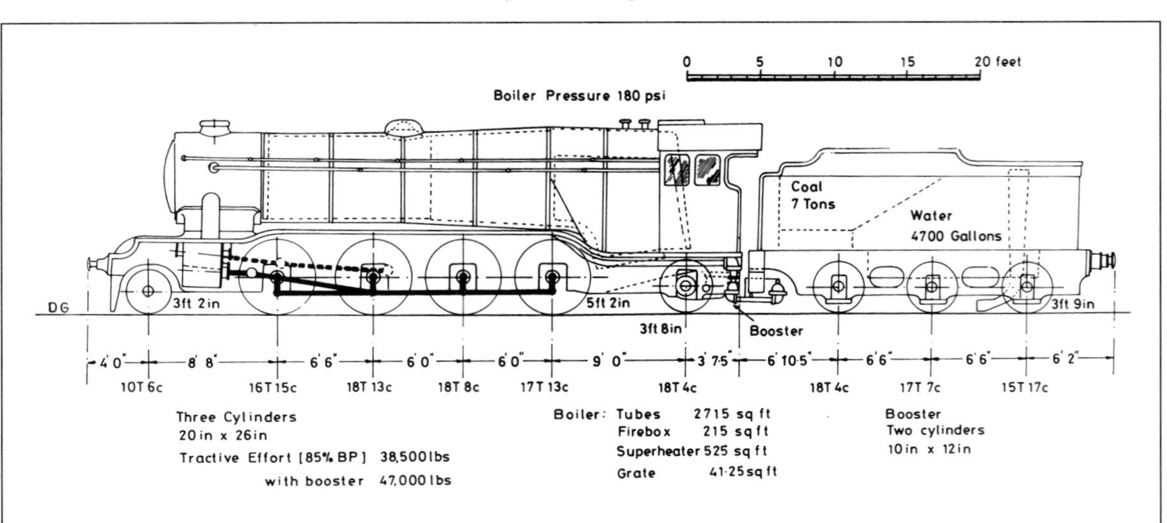

P1 class 2-8-2 No 2393. (LNER Official Photograph)

arranged the new locomotive would be capable of hauling 25 per cent more wagons than any 2-8-0 then in service on the railway although it was never actually defined where that work was and it would appear that the Operating Department never actually requested greater hauling capacity.[23]

Proposals were submitted in 1923 and the two P1s entered service during 1925, with No 2393 being available just in time to take part in the Stockton & Darlington Centenary celebrations. Gresley was well aware that freight locomotives were subjected to frequent stops due to being moved into refuge sidings and that maximum power was only required when starting away from such enforced idleness and when climbing severe gradients. For much of a journey maximum available power was not required and the owner was, in consequence, paying for a capability which was used only infrequently. There was no way around this but Gresley's view appears to have been that the basic locomotive should be operated at nearly full power under normal conditions with a supplementary device supplying the extra power needed for starting or haulage on severe gradients. Such a device was readily available in the form of the booster and it was decided to fit one to each P1.

Gresley had fitted a booster to a 4-4-2 passenger engine, No 4419, during 1923 and trials proved successful enough to encourage its adoption for the P1 locomotives. In basic terms the booster consists of a two-cylinder steam engine driving the axle of the trailing pair of wheels by means of gearing, thrust being transmitted to the main frames via a pivoted thrust block which allowed vertical and horizontal movement to take place between the booster unit and locomotive main frames. Exhaust from the booster engine passed to the main blast pipe which had to be redesigned for the P1 as that fitted to the 4-4-2 had proven unsatisfactory. The booster was engaged during periods of high tractive effort requirement, an air actuated control system being used for that purpose, thus a compressor and air reservoir were required. Design of the system was such that the booster could only be used with the locomotive in full gear and tests with the passenger locomotive indicated that whilst it was easy to engage the booster with the engine standing there were problems engaging the unit at slow speeds.[24] As boosters for the P1 class were the same design as that fitted to the 4-4-2 it is highly likely that similar problems existed thus rendering the unit less useful than it should have been when the locomotive was on severe gradients. Bulleid's paper on the booster, ref 24, gives a full description of the device and its application on the LNER.

P1s were given the same boiler as that fitted to the Gresley A1s, the working pressure being 180psi. No 2393 had a conventional Robinson superheater but, following a recommendation of the Superheater Company, No 2394 was given a type 'E' double superheater manufactured by that concern. This did not live up to expectation and was replaced by a Robinson superheater in 1931. Higher pressure,

220psi boilers of the A3 Pacific type replaced the A1 boilers in 1942–3.

Three 20in (51cm) by 26in (66cm) cylinders provided considerable tractive effort; 38,500lbs, whilst the booster could add a further 8,500lbs. With the fitting of higher pressure boilers the cylinder diameter was reduced by 1in (2.54cm) but the same 8in (20cm) diameter piston valves and Gresley derived motion, Walshaerts gear was retained.

In constructing the P1s as opposed to the 2-10-2 a driving wheel diameter of 5ft 2in (1.57m) was possible due to fewer wheels fitting within the overall wheelbase and the larger wheels also allowed for higher speed running. It is possible that Gresley believed the introduction of the P1s would indicate to the Traffic Department that an acceleration of fitted freight timings was possible, more power was a way of getting faster trains, not necessarily heavier and longer trains.[25] If freight services were accelerated more trips could be fitted in, thus giving the necessary tonnage, and there would be less disruption on main line workings as fewer movements into sidings would be needed. At the time it was stated that the locomotives were to work coal trains between Peterborough and London, such trains consisting of 100 wagons giving 1,600 tons (1,629 tonnes) behind the tender. Faster not heavier mineral trains would certainly have been of great benefit to the LNER, the existing infrastructure needing no alteration. High power for fast running was available from the basic locomotive whilst the booster provided supplementary power for starting or hauling on severe gradients.

In practice the Operating Department tended to use the class on heavier trains but problems relating to the size of refuge sidings and difficulties encountered at depots, where splitting of the trains was needed, conspired against them. As more normal loads were allocated the booster became unnecessary and they were ultimately removed; 1937 from No 2394 and 1938 from No 2393. There had been mechanical problems wtih the booster units but the fact that they were not absolutely essential for the traffic actually worked probably meant that they suffered some neglect and were not developed to the extent possible had there been a real need for them. The fact that the P1s were capable of higher speed operating is illustrated by use of No 2394 on passenger train workings between King's Cross and Peterborough, speeds of 65mph (104km per hour) being easily maintained.[26]

Following their introduction in 1925 a number of test runs were carried out but the maximum capacity of the dynamometer car draw spring was a pull of 18 tons and that limited the load which was applied. At many locations it was unnecessary to operate the booster as the load was well within the locomotive's capabilities. Trials also showed coal consumption to be high and a recommendation was made that drivers operate with a fully open regulator and vary power by means of cut-off. Care also had to be taken when running with the booster engaged as that

LNER P1 No 2394 with a heavy freight train. (Author's Collection)

influenced total operation and smokebox draught. Booster-fitted P1s were not the straight forward steam locomotives most footplate crews were familiar with.

Introduction into service resulted in a special diagram being evolved for the two-strong class with workings confined to the New England to Ferme Park route. Train lengths were approximately 670 yards (613m) and if either of the P1-hauled trains was diverted from its booked working a '100 wagon special' had to be notified to all staff likely to be involved on the route.[27]

In working their own heavy freights or normal loads the P1s were generally kept waiting in loops for passenger trains to pass, thus they never did justify their construction. Had Gresley worked more closely with the Operating Department and convinced people there of the need for the operating of 'express' style heavy freights the congested lines between Peterborough and London would certainly have reaped the benefit. With his eye on the future Gresley was correct in wishing to see faster freights operating on the already congested system and such an arrangement would probably have been more cost effective than additional operating lines. Intensive use of track and rolling stock requires powerful locomotives but other parts of the LNER did not appear to understand what the CME was hoping to achieve. With no real work to do both locomotives were withdrawn in 1945.

When Gresley died in 1941 Edward Thompson became CME and he immediately instituted a policy of standardization which was based upon simplicity. Included in his proposals was a heavy freight 2-8-0 intended as replacement for existing eight-coupled freight locomotives and certain 0-6-0 types. Wartime conditions prohibited production of an entirely new design but that did not worry Thompson who considered the numerically large O4 class ideal for modification as the new standard type. Simplicity mattered and that discounted Gresley's three-cylinder design, not as some would believe an antipathy towards anything designed by his former chief.

An initial design appeared late in 1941 showing the recently designed No 2 standard boiler, as fitted to the B1 class 4-6-0, standard B1 type cylinders and outside Walschaerts valve gear. The production design differed but slightly from the initial proposal, except for the boiler pressure being increased by 5psi to 225psi and the straight running plate being carried forward past the cylinders. It had been intended to fit a new pony truck in place of the Robinson type and to shorten the frames by 9in (23cm) at the rear end, but economy dictated otherwise. The Robinson tender was also retained.

Higher boiler pressure more than compensated for smaller diameter cylinders and the tractive effort of the rebuild, designated Class O1, was higher than that of the original Robinson design. The rebuilding of the O4s into O1s commenced during 1944 and 16 locomotives were converted that year; each of the succeeding years also saw rebuilt O1 locomotives

Thompson's LNER O1 class 2-8-0 design rebuilt from Class O4.

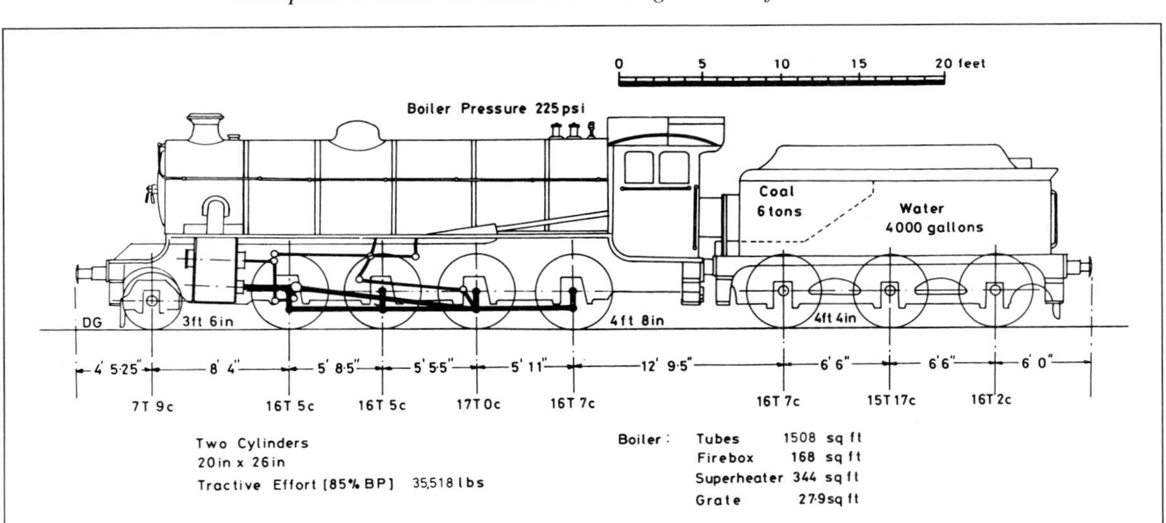

Thompson O1 No 63652 at York during June 1962. (D.K. Jones Collection)

enter service until the final five left Gorton Works in 1949. A total of 58 O1s were produced in this manner, only eight of these being after Thompson retired in 1946. Several factors mitigated against a larger number of conversions, amongst these being the fact that during the war Stanier 2-8-0s were being built by the LNER, many 'Austerity' 2-8-0s were available from 1946 and Nationalisation brought about a radical rethink on locomotive matters.

In respect of the essential features which influence performance, namely boiler and cylinders, the O1s were new machines but results obtained from the Locomotive Interchange Trials of 1948 tended to be confusing. Coal consumption per unit of power was the lowest of the freight locomotives; 3.7lbs per hp per hour (1.25kg per kW per hour), as was water consumption, 25.73lbs per hp per hour (8.72kg per kW per hour), but evaporation rate was poor, only the 'Austerity' 2-8-0 having a lower figure. Evaporation figures pointed to a low boiler efficiency as they were identical at 7.68lbs of coal per lb of water (or kg of coal per kg of water) for the O1 and B1, both of which used the same design of boiler.[28] From a mechanical point of view the O1 suffered to some extent due to it not being exactly what was originally intended. In making do with certain original parts which he had intended to replace Thompson appears to have put the class at something of a disadvantage. By the early 1950s availability was not all it should have been and in 1951 the O1s averaged only 55,616 miles (88,986km) between periodic repairs, less than the 'Austerity' 2-8-0.[29]

A number of O1s were allocated work on the former Great Central line between Annesley and Woodford where they established a reputation as good running engines. By 1950 no fewer than 40 of the class were based at Annesley. Tyne Dock had an allocation and in 1952 five were fitted with continuous vacuum brake equipment and given Westinghouse air pumps for operating hopper wagon doors. Initially they worked as train engine but with the arrival of BR 9Fs they took over banking duties and remained on that work until withdrawn for scrapping in 1962. By the mid-1950s some of the Annesley locomotives had moved to March and Colwick but a number remained at Annesley for working Nottinghamshire coal trains. At March an assortment of goods traffic was handled including local freight trains. Withdrawals commenced in 1962 and the final example went for scrap in 1965.

Thompson had, for a relatively small cost, extended the useful life of an old design, many of the rebuilds having been constructed in 1912 and one in 1911. It illustrated what could be done with some thought and in the light of subsequent Nationalisation, standard designs and elimination of steam he probably saved his employers a great deal of money.

6
Heavy Freight Locomotives of World War II

With the outbreak of the Second World War R.A. Riddles was appointed to head the Directorate of Transportation Equipment, a sub-department of the Ministry of Supply, and to him fell responsibility for procurement of railway vehicles to assist the military. Locomotives and rolling stock were needed to serve the British Expeditionary Force (BEF) in Europe but the African and Eastern theatres of war also required attention. As an immediate solution 100 'Dean Goods' 0-6-0s were taken from the GWR but Riddles was well aware that a much more powerful locomotive would ultimately be required.

The Robinson 2-8-0 which had served the nation during WWI was still available in large quantities but it had undergone many modifications since that first world conflict and could no longer be classed as standard. It became obvious that construction of new locomotives to an existing standard form would be required but which standard form presented problems. The size of the GWR 2-8-0 mitigated against it from the start as it was expected that at the end of the conflict large numbers of locomotives would be available for sale to British railway companies, as they had been at the end of the First World War.

Ultimately Riddles selected the LMS 2-8-0 design and 208 were ordered; 158 from the North British Locomotive Company and 50 from Beyer, Peacock while a further 51 were taken from the LMS. Unfortunately, just as the first of these engines were being handed over the BEF was fighting its rearguard action at Dunkirk and, far from wanting more equipment, it was frantically trying to destroy what it could not take back to Britain in order to prevent it from falling into enemy hands. The initial order from outside builders had actually been for 240 engines but the fall of France resulted in cancellation of the final 32. However, many of the LMS 2-8-0s and some Robinson 2-8-0s were sent to the Middle East. Operations there provided Riddles with valuable information for later use, including the fact that in very hot regions standard injectors did not perform well.[1]

Construction of the LMS 2-8-0s for war service resulted in a decision being made in 1941 that the design be adopted as a standard for British railway company needs, thus enabling a reserve of locomotives to be ready if required for use overseas. However, although delighted with the performance of the LMS heavy freight engine Riddles realized that use of this design had its limitations.

As the war progressed, or perhaps failed to progress as far as the allies were concerned, there were people who could foresee the days when an invasion of France would take place. Even in the darkest days of the war a degree of optimism was evident and by 1942 the need for heavy freight locomotives to support an invasion and a liberation force was evident. Riddles again considered the Robinson 2-8-0 but the lack of standardization amongst the existing engines was objectionable, despite the fact that Gresley offered all the Robinson 2-8-0s that the LNER possessed. Gresley was as patriotic as anybody but he also served his employer and the price asked was somewhat high as far as Riddles was concerned. All that Gresley asked for

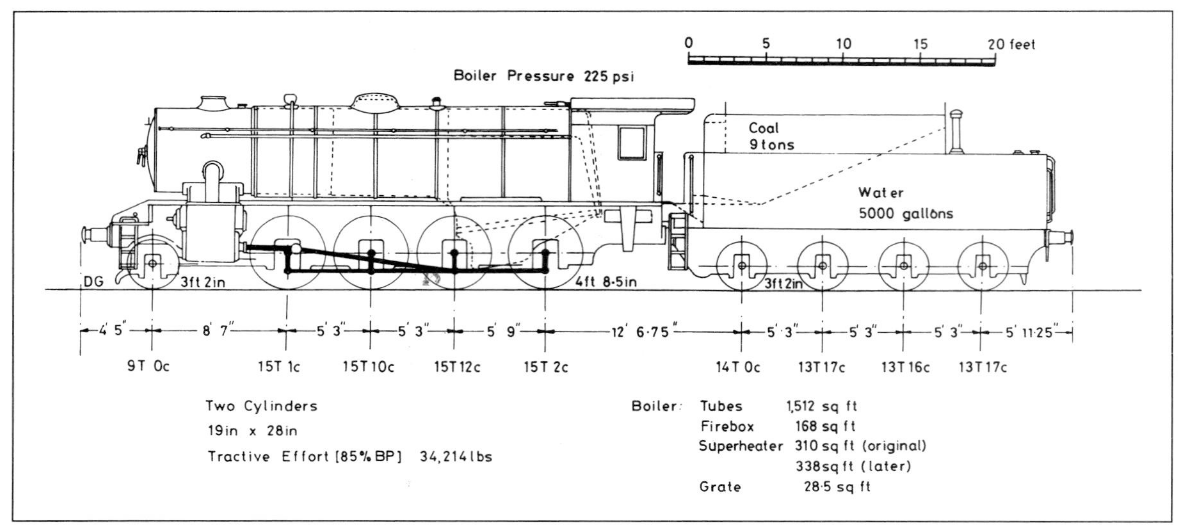

Weight diagram for Riddles 2-8-0.

his Robinson engines was replacement with an equal number of his own design three-cylinder 2-8-0s as soon as possible. It was an offer which Riddles could, and did, refuse, considering that he could construct two to two and a half of the type he had in mind for the same cost as a Gresley O2. Another

Cast steel driving wheel with cast iron coupled wheels alongside. The spoke structure and cast-in balance weights can be seen as can the absence of a flange.

fault with the Gresley scheme was procurement of materials; there was simply a shortage.

It is evident that Riddles had in mind a completely new design, one which would fit wartime needs and no other. One point about choosing an existing design was that, as with the Robinson 2-8-0s of WWI, they could be sold to British railway companies when the conflict ceased, but it was suggested that no CME would touch the engines proposed. The Riddles response was that he indicated disinterest in their fate after the war was won. His design was to suit a particular purpose and no other — winning the war was what mattered.[2]

The North British Locomotive Company was invited to co-operate with design and development work, although there would be little time for development, and large numbers of the 'Austerity' 2-8-0s were ordered directly from the drawing board. The specification was similar to that for the LMS 2-8-0 covering such matters as tractive effort, axle loading and minimum radius of track but the philosophy behind the design differed radically. Low cost, minimum time for construction and use of available materials had to be carefully woven into the design plan and it is a tribute to Riddles and the team he gathered that the eventual design worked so well. Use of steel castings for engine parts has many advantages but the cost of their production is high and could not be justified; whilst the LMS 8F made use of steel castings weighing 22 tons (22.4 tonnes) the 'Austerity' 2-8-0 only required 2$\frac{1}{2}$ tons (2.55 tonnes). Certain parts on the 'Austerity' used fabricated steel sections whilst others, including three pairs of coupled wheels, were made from cast iron. Only the main driving wheel centres were steel castings. The use of fabrication was not necessarily economic in terms of labour but its adoption did reduce the need for steel castings and forgings, manufacturing facilities for which were then fully engaged meeting other wartime requirements. Riddles did not have a free hand in all things and had to do the best he could with the facilities available. Few other locomotive designers have had to work under such restrictions.

Not only steel was in short supply, copper and other non-ferrous materials were difficult to procure and the design also had to take account of these shortages. Despite this the inner firebox of the boiler was made from copper but some of the stays were constructed from steel rather than copper. The boiler

Compensating lever arrangement for tender wheels.

was of parallel barrel form with a round top firebox thus allowing for simplicity of construction. Riddles had no real concern for the thermal efficiency of these engines, they were designed to help win a war not cut the Army's coal bill, and for this reason he decided that lagging of the boiler, except for the backplate, was unnecessary. The air space contained between boiler plate and cladding would provide sufficient insulation. As many of the locomotives would be working in regions hotter than northern Europe the need for insulation was reduced, making its incorporation a needless expense.

Usual items such as cylinder blocks, cylinder covers, smokebox saddle and blast pipe were made from cast iron but its use for driving wheels caused comment as that appeared to be a retrograde step. Riddles argued that good quality cast iron wheel centres were adequate for the purpose as the locomotive was designed to haul 1,000-ton (1,018-tonne) loads at speeds up to 40mph (64km per hour) and at these speeds the 4ft 8½in (1.44m) diameter driving wheels would not be subjected to very high centrifugal stresses. Traction stresses, divided between four axles, would also be relatively low whilst the shrunk-on steel tyres added to the wheel strength. The specification for the cast iron was a minimum tensile strength of 26 tons/in^2 (4.10 tonne/cm^2).

Balance weights for rotating forces were cast integral with the wheel centres but no allowance was made for balance of reciprocating masses, again the low design speed making this generally unnecessary. Steel and cast iron wheels were of similar patterns but a lower force was used to press the cast iron wheels onto the steel axles compared with steel wheels. Excessive force could have caused bursting of the cast iron wheel centres. The wheels for the leading truck were solid forged and then rolled. No compensating levers were provided on the locomotive, as might have been expected with the requirement for operation on indifferent wartime track, nor was there any provision for adjustment after assembly. Tender wheels were fitted with compensating levers.

A steel casting was used for the rear cylinder cover as this enabled Riddles to incorporate a support for the front end of the slidebars. This indicates the care which went into the design; the value of each item being analysed and full use made of its strength for other purposes. In order to keep cost, weight and construction time to a minimum the design had to be correct.

Axlebox guides were simply made from flanged plate strengthened with triangular ribs. Considerable use was made of strip plate for items such as brake hangers and spring-link brackets whilst the screw reversing shaft and reversing rod were constructed from tubes with welded ends.

Although essentially a special design for economy purposes a number of standard items were incorpor-

'Austerity' 2-8-0 in BR days, No 90033 at Stafford during 1961. (D.K. Jones Collection)

2-8-0 cast steel rear cylinder cover incorporating support for front end of slide bar.

ated because they were readily available, reasonably inexpensive and fitted into the design without the need for modification. Such items included a superheater from the Superheater Company, Auld cast iron cylinder packing, Davies & Metcalf injectors, Westinghouse air brake equipment, etc. Vacuum brake equipment was also provided for engine and tender whilst steam sanding gear allowed for the application of sand in front of the leading coupled wheels and both sides of the driving wheels.

Outside Walschaerts gear was provided for the two cylinders, this being of conventional form but all pin bushes were of cast iron. That reduced the need for non-ferrous material and made use of the self-lubricating properties of cast iron. Piston valves of 10in (25.4cm) diameter were used. A tractive effort of 34,214lbs could be obtained from the 19in (48.25cm) diameter by 28in (71cm) stroke cylinders with the boiler pressure at 225psi. Total weight of the locomotive in working condition was 70.25 tons (71.5 tonnes) and this was disposed to give a maximum axle loading of 15.6 tons (15.9 tonnes), on the third pair of coupled wheels.[3]

The first of the 'Austerity' 2-8-0s was formally handed over to the Ministry of Supply on 16 January 1943 and attracted considerable attention, not least because people were expecting something of a monstrosity having witnessed the Bulleid 'Austerity' 0-6-0 not many months earlier. As it turned out the design was well received being considered pleasant to look at if not attractive; beauty is always in the eye of the beholder. Riddles cared little for what people thought if the product worked but it has been said that he deliberately fitted a small dumpy chimney in order to give the detractors something to criticize. As it turned out there was little complaint and the chimney worked well anyway.[4]

The tender was a very basic affair, being essentially a coal and water container on wheels. Capacities for both were high compared with British freight locomotives but they were designed for duties away from regular supplies of both essential commodities. When fully loaded the tender weighed 55½ tons (56.5 tonnes) and required eight wheels in order to keep the axle loading reasonable, even then maximum weight on the tender axle was 14 tons (14.25 tonnes). Aware that these locomotives would probably have to operate tender first for a fair proportion of their time abroad Riddles ensured that the view over the tender was reasonable, hence the inset arrangement of the self-trimming coal bunker. Space above the water tank was then available for stowing fire irons. Within the utilitarian limits imposed the cab was comfortable, and a definite improvement on some British main line locomotives constructed immediately before the outbreak of war.

Tenders were designed to allow for easy conversion to carry oil instead of coal should that be necessary for overseas operation. Likewise the boiler was also designed for easy conversion to oil firing, the conversion being possible without lifting the boiler from frames. A false bottom had to be fitted in the ashpan whilst oil burners were located at the front of the firebox near the bottom. Replacement of the firedoor with a blanking plate, together with provision of an oil heater and suitable plumbing to carry oil to the burner completed the conversion.

Despite being produced in quantity immediately from the drawing board there were surprisingly few defects of any significance. One which did show up when a number of engines were in service related to the tender wheels which had been constructed from chilled cast iron. That material had been successfully used for heavy freight wagons in the USA but British drivers had a habit of descending banks with steam and hand brake applied thus putting considerable thermal loading on the wheels due to friction. This damaged the wheels and resulted in rolled forged wheels being used for subsequent construction and as replacements for the tenders already in service. Another problem resulted from the fore and aft motion of the engine due to the unbalanced reciprocating masses. Intermittent contact between engine and tender produced high loads which caused the buffer between these units to collapse. The solution here lay in the fitting of stronger control springs at this location to keep engine and tender more firmly coupled and hence avoided the hammering.

During the years 1943, 1944 and 1945 a total of 935 2-8-0s were turned out by the North British Locomotive Company (545) and the Vulcan Foundry (390). With both builders fully engaged the delivery rate was about five per week, twice that for LMS 2-8-0s, but at its peak locomotives were completed at a rate of seven per week. Needless to say when the first locomotives were delivered there was no military work for them to do as the invasion of Europe had not yet taken place. Some 450 were loaned to British railway companies and performed well on assorted freight duties in all regions before being taken back into military service for shipment overseas in October 1944.

Having given further consideration to the needs of the military in terms of locomotive support the War Office decided that the maximum axle loading of 15.6 tons (15.9 tonnes) might be too high for certain track conditions. A request was made for a locomotive which could provide the same tractive effort as the 2-8-0 but with an axle loading no greater than 13.5 tons (13.7 tonnes). Initially Riddles thought of a 2-8-2 arrangement but changed his mind in favour of a 2-10-0 as the former, he believed, would suffer from lack of adhesion. The problem with the ten-coupled form was the risk of derailment on curves down to the 99-yard (90.5m) radius as specified by the Ministry. However, Riddles overcame the prob-

2-8-0 No 77030 still in WD ownership whilst operating a passenger train at Wandsworth in June 1947. Air pumps may still be seen on the smokebox. (D.K. Jones Collection)

'Austerity' 2-8-0 No 90275 at Grimsby during 1960. (D.K. Jones Collection)

lem in a simple way, one with which he was familiar from his LNWR training. The centre coupled wheels had flangeless tyres whilst adjacent wheels were provided with flanges of reduced thickness.

This was the first 2-10-0 designed for operation in Britain and even North British was rather sceptical about the tyre arrangement but Riddles was convinced that he was right. In order to prove his point he had laid out a section of track to the required radius and when the first locomotive was tested it took the curve without the slightest grinding.[5]

In most respects the ten-coupled locomotive was similar to its eight-coupled sister; certainly they made use of the same cylinders, wheels, motion, tender, cab, etc, but the additional length allowed a larger boiler to be fitted. The 2-10-0 had three rings on the boiler barrel whereas the 2-8-0 had two, and to support this larger tube area a bigger firebox and grate were provided. Three arch tubes were provided in the firebox, these increasing the heating surface

Diagram for Riddles 2-10-0.

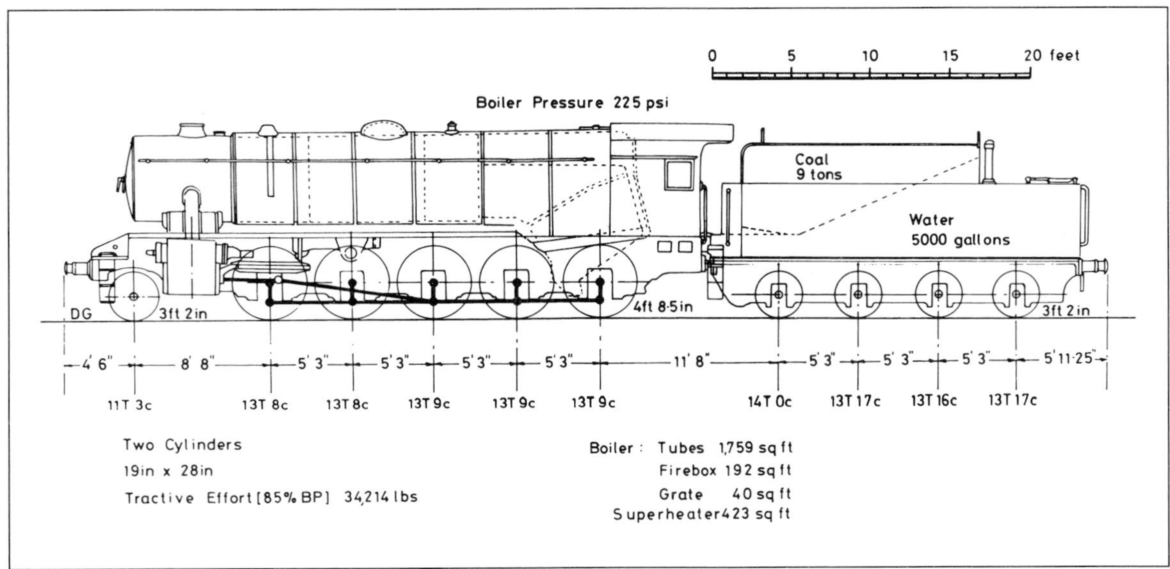

and promoting water circulation; to some extent the effect was similar to the thermic siphons fitted by Bulleid to his Pacifics. A rocking grate with Hulson firebars was provided in order to minimize the work involved in cleaning the fire. The firebox was constructed of steel and it extended into the boiler barrel to form a combustion chamber. It had been suggested that the ten-coupled locomotives were likely to work in northern Europe and because of the anticipated lower ambient temperature Riddles decided that boiler lagging should be provided. An asbestos matting was, therefore, fitted on the barrel and the firebox beneath the cladding plates.[6]

Due to the size of the firebox a number of flexible steel stays were provided but shortly after the 2-10-0s entered service in Britain during 1944 they were the cause of some distress for Riddles, who by that time had returned to the LMS. A number of locomotives were stopped at Peterborough due to broken stays and news of this circulated amongst the railway fraternity, including CMEs of the four companies. The problem was, however, with the shed staff and not the locomotive. Unaware that they were dealing with flexible stays the boilersmiths had been tapping them and expecting them to ring just like normal stays, which they would not. Their immediate reaction was to presume broken stays and the locomotive was failed when it should not have been.[7]

Because of the increased length of the boiler the frames were longer and so were slightly more flexible than those of the 2-8-0. This factor also assisted the ability of the 2-10-0 to negotiate tight curves without difficulties. Apart from these isolated examples parts were interchangeable between the two 'Austerities' and that was an advantage in wartime conditions. As cylinder dimensions, wheel diameter and boiler pressure were the same for both classes it follows that tractive effort would also be the same. However, the larger boiler could meet a higher steam demand and so the ten-coupled engine was likely to be the more useful for sustained haulage of heavy loads. The specification had called for an ability to negotiate curves down to 396ft (121m) radius at a normal maximum speed of 40mph (64km per hour) and, as mentioned above, curves down to 297ft (90.5m) radius at slow speeds; for the 2-8-0 an ability to negotiate curves down to 110yd (101m) radius was required.[8]

For both locomotives the maximum expected working speed was to be 40mph (64km per hour) and in later years criticism was made regarding the quality of riding at higher speed. This was particularly the case for the 2-8-0 but it was, however, somewhat unfair as they were not designed or constructed for high speed operations. During the locomotive exchange trials it was claimed that the 'Austerity' 2-8-0s displayed objectionable running characteristics and on the Western Region locomotive No 77000 suffered from considerable vertical movement and bumping between locomotive and tender during normal running.[9] In fact when running at speed in normal service the eight-coupled 'Austerity' engines did exhibit considerable fore and aft movement.

All 150 2-10-0s were constructed by North British, the first being completed in June 1944. Demand was such that the initial 20 members of the class were sent overseas almost immediately to serve the cause in the Middle East. Many of the 2-8-0s worked in Britain before the call came and that served two useful purposes: it provided some time for running-in and also relieved the home railways which were desperately short of heavy freight motive power. All four railway companies took allocations of 2-8-0s with by far the largest number going to the LNER. Only the LMS and LNER received any 2-10-0s for use during 1944, with 79 working on LMS metals. Several 'Austerities' were used by the military for instruction purposes in this country and a number were simply placed in store until required. Following the successful allied invasion of Normandy a demand for motive power came and regular shipments of 2-8-0s and 2-10-0s took place across the English Channel, using modified Southern Railway train ferries. This book is essentially concerned with the operation of heavy freight locomotives in Britain and so wartime duties will not be considered, and the work of these engines, together with the Robinson 2-8-0s and Stanier 8Fs, is well documented by J.W.P. Rowledge in a three-volume set.[10]

Not all locomotives actually went overseas as the arrival of the USA S160 class engines somewhat swamped the advancing forces with motive power. It actually turned out that demand was not as great as expected due to the fact that the existing locomotive stock on the European mainland was not irreparably damaged. With the end of hostilities the requirements within Europe became clearer and it was soon obvious that the 'Austerities' were not needed on a long term basis. By November 1945 repatriation had commenced and the Riddles engines could be set to work meeting a demand from the home railways for

'Austerity' 2-10-0 No 90774 at Grangemouth during 1962, following withdrawal. (D.K. Jones Collection)

heavy freight power. In general locomotives remained under Ministry of Supply ownership and were loaned out to three of the home railways, but in 1946 the LNER actually purchased 200 2-8-0s, 190 of which were already on loan, the purchase price being £4,500 per locomotive. Only the LMS did not take any of the 'Austerities' at this time preferring to take its own design of 2-8-0 from the other railways which received the 'Austerities'.

Following Nationalisation the British Transport Commission purchased more 2-8-0 and 2-10-0 locomotives and issued an instruction that they were no longer to be referred to as 'Austerities' but were to be known as WD 2-8-0 and WD 2-10-0, both types being classified as 8F. In British Railways' ownership a number of changes were made, including replacement of the 2-10-0's steel firebox by one made from copper. Fibreglass lagging was applied to the boilers of the 2-8-0s and the flexible crown stays were replaced.

During the 1948 locomotive exchange trials both 'Austerity' classes performed well considering that they were not designed for the work they were then called on to perform. In order to allow footplate crew to gain experience on a particular route a number of preliminary runs were allowed using coal from the parent region but no such runs were made with the 'Austerities', enginemen from the region in which the particular trial runs were taking place being employed. This was because all of the former pre-Nationalisation companies had operated 'Austerities' and, at least theoretically, footplate crews would have been familiar with the type. For the preliminary runs coal from the home region could be used but for actual trials all locomotives burned Blidworth Hards. The report of the trials gives full information of routes, loads and individual performances and should be consulted by anybody interested in the details.[11] The general public did not have access to freight services and so the operation of the heavy freight engines received little attention in the railway press at the time. Following publication of the report Cecil J. Allen produced a supplement to his book on the trials and this gives details as to freight locomotive performances. Entitled *New Light on the Locomotive Exchanges* it is more readily available than the official report.[12]

Both 'Austerity' classes performed well although coal and water consumptions were higher than for other heavy freight classes. They did have to suffer the disadvantage of being handled by a succession of crews in the different regions thus there was no familiarity between crew and individual locomotive which existed for other classes. On the Western Region the crew had had no previous experience of working 'Austerities'. However, despite this they did put in creditable performances with the 2-10-0 being considered the better of the two WD classes. Both of the Riddles types proved their ability to steam well and keep to time but the 2-8-0 exhibited a tendency to slipping — not surprising in view of its low design axle loading. The 1948 Interchange

Trials were conducted on normal service trains which were subject to normal operating conditions such as signal checks, thus figures need to be treated with caution. Although comparisons have been made and will continue to be made it is possible to read practically anything into the results which were inconclusive enough for all parties to be satisfied, and for Riddles to believe in the need for a series of standard classes.

Overall consumption figures for the freight engines are given on page 25, these being aggregates of all runs throughout the trial period. The reader is encouraged to avoid any urge to compare designs on the basis of these selective figures alone. It must be remembered that particular designs were evolved to suit the needs of a particular railway and the 'Austerities' were constructed for wartime duty using available materials. Many factors need to be considered in forming an opinion as to the 'best' design, water and coal consumptions being but two. Construction cost, maintenance costs, availability, and hauling capability all need to be considered.

Regarding maintenance the 'Austerities' were economical compared with most other heavy freight locomotives and their availability was also high. During the early 1950s the 2-8-0 averaged 62,624 miles (100,198km) between periodic repairs and that was only bettered by the GWR 28xxs[13] — not bad for a design constructed in a hurry to serve wartime needs.

During 1952 the 'Austerities' were involved in a series of performance and efficiency tests, No 90464 representing the 2-8-0s whilst the ten-coupled class was represented by No 90772. Both locomotives were fitted with two Monitor live steam injectors and both had the blast pipe diameter reduced to 4.875in (12.38cm). Using the London, Midland Mobile Test Plant trials were conducted on the Scottish Region between Carlisle and Hurford, a round trip distance of 178.6 miles (286km). Two grades of coal were used, Blidworth Cobbles (grade 2B hard) and Blackwell B Winning (grade 3B soft), the soft coal being used to provide a comparison with the Blidworth coal which had been used for similar tests on other locomotives. Results of the trials and details of the tests were published in BR Bulletin No 7[14] and in certain sections of the railway press.[15] Results indicated that both steamed better on the hard coal and that, as expected, the larger boiler of the 2-10-0 gave it an advantage in maintaining power and burning coal efficiently. The 2-8-0 did not steam well on the soft Blackwell coal but the larger grate of the ten-coupled engine enabled it to deal with wide variations in coal quality.

The 'front end limit', ie the point at which balance is achieved between steam production and demand, was 19,500lbs (8,864kg) of steam per hour for the 2-8-0 on Blidworth coal. With the soft Blackwell coal a maximum steaming rate of 13,000lb (5,909kg) of steam per hour could only be maintained for 45 minutes, any attempt to steam at higher

'Austerity' 2-10-0 retrieved from Greece; No 3672 at Ropley on the Mid-Hants Railway, now named Dame Vera Lynn *and since moved to the North Yorkshire Moors Railway.*

rates failing due to the formation of clinker. For the 2-10-0 much better figures were produced: 27,000lb (12,273kg) of steam per hour on Blidworth coal and 23,500lb (10,682kg) of steam per hour on Blackwell soft coal.

Riddles was already convinced as to the benefits of a wide firebox in the burning of poor quality coal and the results of these trials will have come as no surprise. At this time the Standard 9F 2-10-0 was in production and the results will have had no influence on the design, but that was not the intention anyway. In order to make the best use of the British Railways' locomotive fleet it was important to know the capabilities of individual classes and performance tests were undertaken for that purpose. Even the best figures were inferior to that obtained from 'company' heavy freight engines but Riddles had never paid much attention to thermal efficiency; it must be remembered that the 'Austerities' were designed for a particular purpose and not for general railway use. It should also be remembered that the 2-8-0 had no lagging between boiler and cladding thus heat loss was to be expected; from 1955 onwards fibreglass mattresses were fitted for boiler lagging. In commercial service other factors had to be considered and a bonus from the trials was to see how well a locomotive could perform on the cheaper soft coal; at the time Blidworth cobbles cost £2 18s 11d (£2.95p) per ton whilst Blackwell soft coal could be obtained for £2 16s 8d (£2.84p) per ton.

During May 1959 WD 2-10-0 No 601 underwent comparative trials with coal and oil firing, the intention being more towards the requirements of the military than commercial operation. For working on coal the boiler was modified slightly by removal of the arch tubes together with a reduction in blast pipe and superheater areas. Under these conditions steaming was slightly better than in unmodified form but when operating on oil firing steaming was very poor and the locomotive was unable to meet the military requirements. That remained the same as when constructed, ie a capability of hauling a 1,000-ton train at 40mph.[16]

Both War Department classes performed satisfactorily during postwar service in Britain and they underwent a number of minor modifications depending upon the region served. They were set to work on the same duties as other heavy freight locomotives but the 2-8-0 could not compete in terms of haulage potential with others of its type and in general was limited to power class 5 haulage work. A speed restriction of 40mph (64km per hour) was normally applied and that also caused operational problems. Heavy mineral traffic, general freight, pick-up goods and some occasional passenger trains fell to the 'Austerities'.

Whilst they may not have been as good as other heavy freight locomotives in terms of haulage or thermal efficiency they were cheap to construct, reliable and easy to maintain — important factors in steam locomotive operation. They were constructed for wartime use but lasted in commercial service until the final decade of British steam operations. Like their maritime counterparts, the 'Liberty' ships, the 'Austerity' locomotives were long lasting because they were useful and economic, that being justification enough for their retention.

USA Class S160

With entry of the USA into the European war it became evident that the American troops would require logistical support from the railways. However, it was equally evident that such support would not be forthcoming from the existing European locomotive stock. Although the British Ministry of Supply was engaged in a locomotive construction programme the Americans decided that they would need to produce a locomotive capable of supporting allied troops following the invasion of the European mainland. As in the case of the Riddles locomotives the American design would be to a definite power and weight specification, as simple as possible to construct and maintain, and dispensable when its purpose had been served. In terms of the latter cost was to be a minimum conducive with meeting the first two requirements. In fact there was no intention of returning the locomotives to the USA after victory was achieved, the cost would be prohibitive and the locomotives would not meet American needs anyway as most USA railways were turning to diesel traction. In meeting the other design criteria a number of features standard to American steam practice were omitted including provision of mechanical stokers, electric lighting and power reversers.

When the needs of the military were known the task of designing the support locomotive for the American forces in Europe, subsequently known as Class S160, was given to Major J.W. Marsh of the USA Corps of Engineers (Railway Branch), subsequently part of the USA Transportation Corps. In order to meet axle loading and route availability restrictions a 2-8-0 form was selected with certain details taken from the existing S200 design. Major

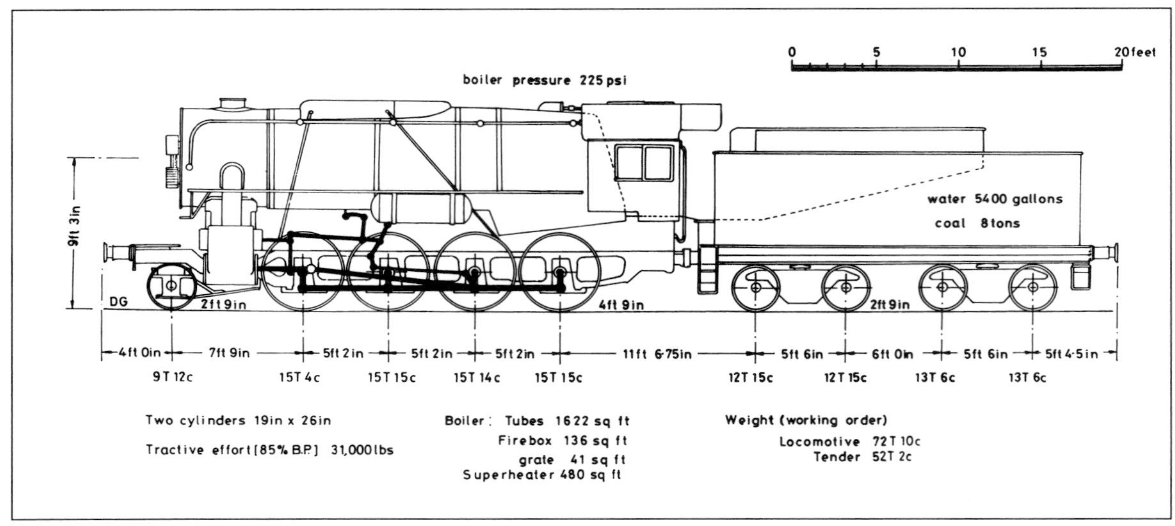

American 2-8-0 wartime locomotive as used in Britain.

Marsh supervised a design team which included representatives from the three chosen builders, American Locomotive Company (ALCO), Baldwin and Lima.

In order to haul military support trains a high tractive effort was required but the locomotive had to be capable of operating on indifferent track with fairly tight curves. So as to comply with stated restrictions only essential items were incorporated in the design but what was produced was a very effective locomotive for the job in hand. American practice made use of bar frames instead of plate frames as favoured in Britain so it is no surprise that the S160 had cast steel bar frames. Apart from

The unfussy motion arrangement of the American 2-8-0. The abundance of room for access between the frames may be seen.

cylinder blocks, wheel centres and a few other small items these were the only castings employed in the design. Cast iron cylinder blocks were formed from two identical castings bolted together, the complete unit incorporating valve chest and smokebox saddle. The entire assembly braced the frames at the front of the locomotive. Pistons were 19in (48cm) diameter and 26in (66cm) stroke whilst piston valves were of 10in (25.4cm) diameter and had a maximum stroke of 6½in (16.5cm). A lightweight Walschaerts valve gear was used with the die block working in the upper half of the radius link whilst running ahead; in British practice the die block is usually in the lower half when running ahead.

Many items were similar in dimension to the 'Austerities' including driving wheels, however, the S160 had a coupled wheelbase of 15ft 6in (4.72m) compared with 16ft 3in (4.95m) for the Riddles 2-8-0. American tyre flanges were thin by British standards thus the USA locomotives should have been capable of negotiating tighter curves than their British counterparts. The S160s were also provided with equalizing levers between first and second, and third and fourth coupled axles thus enabling them to ride easier on indifferent track. The easy nature of their riding was commented upon when the S160s operated in Britain before moving to France. Thinner flanges did, however, result in certain problems as a number of times they caused the locomotive to take the wrong turning at cross overs having sharp radii, this being more likely when running tender first.

The boiler barrel consisted of two telescopic rings, large dome and regulator valve being located in the rear ring. Safety valves, the larger a muffled type and the smaller an open type, were mounted off-centre behind the dome, the off-centre setting being used in order to clear the loading gauge height of 12ft 11in (3.94m). The crown of the round top welded steel inner firebox was supported by wrought iron stay bolts and two rows of flexible stays at the front. A number of the firebox side stays fitted above the foundation ring were hollow, this feature allowing broken stays to be detected easily but it also allowed entry for secondary air, no firebox dampers being provided. Within the firebox three 3in (7.6cm) diameter arch tubes provided support for the brick arch and added to the firebox heating surface, however, these were a source of problems and were not fitted to later examples. The wide firebox had a large grate, some 7ft (2.13m) long by 5ft 10in (1.78m) wide, and this was provided with two rocking sections, one on each side of the centre line. Features such as the rocking grate and arch tubes found their way onto the 'Austerity' 2-10-0 and it seems likely that Riddles decided upon their adoption having observed the ideas on the American locomotives.

Hollow firebox stays fitted just above the foundation ring.

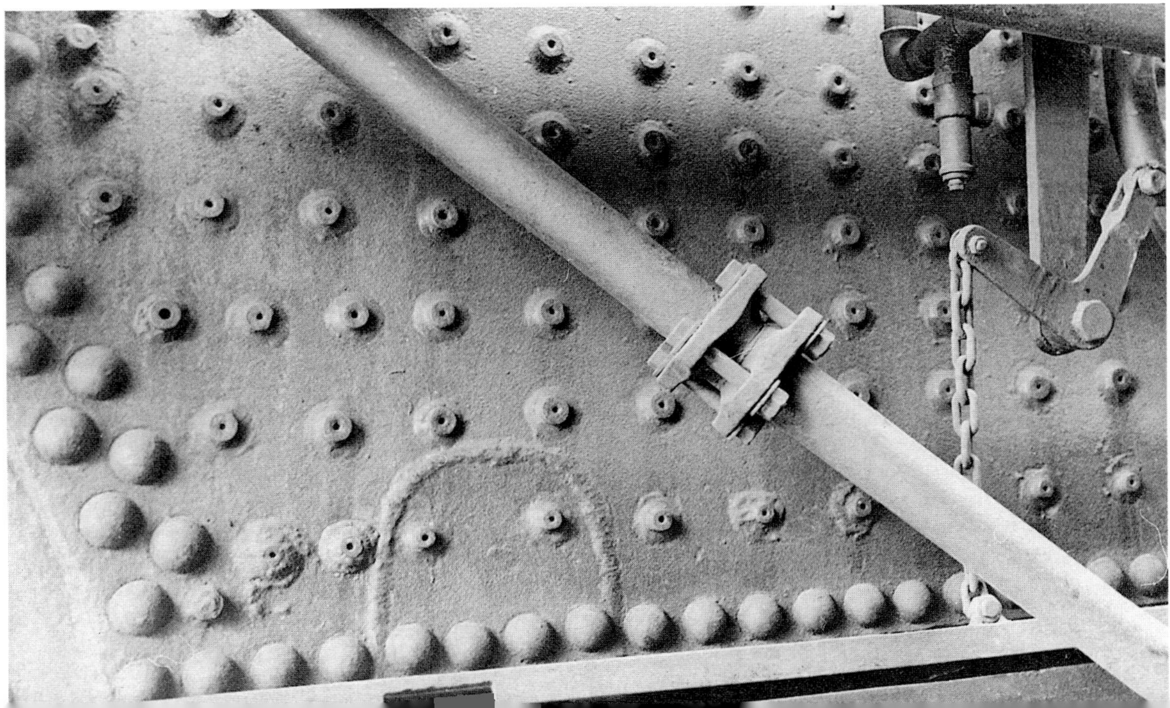

Certain American practices were adopted for constructional reasons but other ideas were included to suit expected difficult operating conditions. Use of grease-lubricated bearings had long since ended in the USA but the S160s were so fitted, presumably on the grounds that in the aftermath of war attention to lubrication might be neglected and adequate supplies of reasonable quality oil might not be available. During work in Britain there were many incidents of overheated axleboxes but this probably resulted from the higher speed running than was anticipated for work in Continental Europe. Driving axles were provided with large bearings, journals being 8in (20cm) diameter and 11in (28cm) long, so it is likely that the designers did anticipate problems through the use of grease lubrication and made some attempts to compensate.

The tender had similar coal and water capacity to that of the 'Austerities' and its basic design was also similar apart from the fact that it was supported on two bogies. The inset bunker provided a good rear view when running tender first and also allowed for storage of fire irons and tools.

The first S160s arrived in Britain towards the end of 1942 and altogether some 756 were landed as a prelude to shipping to Continental Europe. At that time the British railway companies were in a parlous state with respect to freight locomotives. It was not necessarily their fault as a considerable portion of railway company workshops had been turned over to assisting with the war effort and many skilled men were similarly employed. New construction was severely limited and routine maintenance also suffered. With a view to alleviating the problem 398 of the 'Yankee' locomotives were loaned to British companies, the exercise also serving the purpose of running in. Even those locomotives not on loan went through British workshops in order to fit them for service, items of running gear not being fitted for the Atlantic crossing.

As the design was within the British loading gauge there were no problems with respect to operations, apart from route restrictions due to axle loading and track curvature. Initially the S160s were concentrated in the South Wales area but the LNER also took a fair proportion and by January 1944 there were 174 on loan to the GWR, 50 to the LMS, 168 to the LNER and six to the Southern. Two locomotives were also placed with the military for crew training purposes. The 'Yankee' engines served throughout Britain covering most main line freight operations although service on Southern metals was limited due to the small allocation. Wartime freight traffic was similar to that of peacetime except that there was more of it and the operation of a normal timetable could not be guaranteed because of the very nature of military requirements. Mineral traffic was still heavy but so was the movement of armaments for both British and American forces, Britain being the staging post for the Allied invasion of Normandy. Even Scotland played host to the American engines when St Margaret's depot was allocated 22.

In general footplate crew were happy with the S160s although there were certain reservations. Because of their military application on trains of unknown formation a variety of braking systems had to be provided in order to cover most eventualities. Steam brakes were fitted to engine and tender whilst Westinghouse air brake systems and ejectors for vacuum brakes were also provided. Braking capability had been based upon the anticipated needs of a 1,000-ton (1,018-tonne) train operating on fairly level track, military expectation being that the S160s would support the forces operating in the European low countries. Many areas of Britain, Scotland in particular, were not so flat and difficulties were experienced with the braking of trains, however, crews did become accustomed to the idiosyncrasies of the brakes and worked within their limitations.

Sand boxes positioned on top of the boiler were difficult to reach for filling, British facilities being geared to the filling of running plate-mounted sand boxes. The cab was spacious but tended to be rather cold during winter months compared with the British type, principally because of the absence of steam pipes in the cab. Despite the large firebox few firemen experienced much difficulty in getting the boiler to steam and, because of the firebox design, practically any coal would burn reasonably freely. This free burning capability related to the size of the grate as Riddles was to discover with his 2-10-0s.

One aspect of the design which resulted in problems, unfortunately fatal in a number of instances, was the gauge glass. British practice made use of the glass tube type of gauge with steam cock at the top and water cock at the bottom. American practice used the stronger reflex type of gauge which, because of the prizmatic glass it contained, showed water as a black region whilst the space above the water level showed as silver. Instead of cocks valves were used for steam, water and drain, the steam valve being operated by means of an extension spindle and valve handle. A full turn of a valve handwheel moved the valve from fully closed to fully open or vice versa. If a steam valve was not fully open partial condensation of steam took place in the top of the gauge and water rose, thus giving a higher level than actually existed. Three boiler explosions occurred within the period of nine months on the S160s due to the firebox crown becoming overheated due to the water level being too low.

The first was at Honeybourne on the GWR during the morning of 17 November 1943 when the firebox crown of No 2403 fell in, slightly scalding the driver but fatally injuring the fireman. The crown sheet was torn away from its roof stays pulling in the firebox front and sides. At the enquiry the cause was put down to overheating due to low water level which resulted from the top gauge valve being partially closed. Plates had been positioned near the valve handle stating that the valve must be in the open position but following the accident these plates were amended to read, 'This valve must be full open'. The footplate crew of No 2403 did believe that the gauge glass steam valve was fully open but a bent valve spindle binding on the gland nut caused the valve to become tight and appear fully open.

The second accident occurred with No 2363 at 12.40am on 12 January 1944. This locomotive was hauling a freight from Ipswich to Whitemoor when the crown sheet gave way as the train approached Thurston, near Bury St Edmunds. The explosion was due to the same cause but was more severe than the Honeybourne incident, although both fireman and driver escaped serious injury.

With the experience of two incidents it appeared that the problem had been overcome but on 30 August No 1707 suffered a similar fate whilst it was hauling a freight through South Harrow Tunnel on the former GCR line between Neasden and Woodford. Both enginemen were killed and the cause was the same as for the previous occurrences. However, inspection showed that gauge valves were fully open and the conclusion was drawn that the footplate crew had misread the water level in the darkness of the tunnel.

Despite these problems the 'Yankee' engines were popular with footplate crews and many were unhappy to see them go when they were recalled for military duties. Shed staff had slightly different views about them for although they were more accessible than most British locomotives many of the nuts were non-standard for the available British spanners. At a time when the railways of Britain were desperate for heavy freight motive power the S160s were a Godsend and for the British engine crews not familiar with 'foreign' locomotives they turned out to be something of an eye opener.[17]

All of the S160s eventually left British shores for service on Continental Europe but one was returned

USA Transportation Corps 2-8-0 No 2356 on a wartime freight train. This was one of only six such locomotives allocated to the Southern Railway. (D.K. Jones Collection)

in 1946, No 3257 being presented to the Longmoor Military Railway. Unfortunately this locomotive was scrapped during 1957 but by the efforts of the enthusiast fraternity four of the class are now preserved in Britain. The Keighley & Worth Valley and North Yorkshire Moors railways' examples came via Poland, another undergoing restoration is from Hungary, whilst that operating on the Mid-Hants Railway was purchased from Greece. It is easy to appreciate the contribution that these 'Yankee' engines made to the war effort and to the movement of freight throughout Britain but it is not so easy to judge the contribution that they had on British locomotive design. Without a doubt the Ivatt designed locomotives for service on the LMS illustrated a number of features common to American practice which were employed on the S160s.

These included the self-cleaning smokebox, rocking grate, hopper ashpan and high running plate, but many other ideas were not used. Locomotive designs evolve from the experience gained by the design team and through contact with other designs and designers. Whilst it would be wrong to say that Ivatt, or the Riddles team responsible for the BR Standards, copied ideas directly from the S160, or any other design for that matter, circumstantial evidence would suggest that the influence was there.

7

BR Standard Class 9F

The original BR locomotive standardization plan called for a dedicated heavy freight locomotive of 2-8-2 form, but no immediate steps were taken for its construction as sufficient former War Department and railway company freight locomotives still existed. The design made use of the boiler fitted to the 'Britannia' class 4-6-2 locomotive and many other standard parts. Riddles was unhappy with the idea of a pair of trailing wheels because of the reduction in adhesive weight they would cause. The wheel diameter had been chosen in order to allow for a higher operating speed than existing heavy freight locomotives managed but if the standard 'Britannia' boiler was to be used there was no alternative to a 2-8-2 wheel arrangement. It is clear that with the new order of the Nationalised British Railways thinking was towards the operation of fast fitted freights and mineral trains, not the traditional heavy goods trains.

In support of their proposal for a 2-8-2 the Chief Draughtsmen's Committee produced a memorandum outlining ten reasons why a 2-10-0 would not

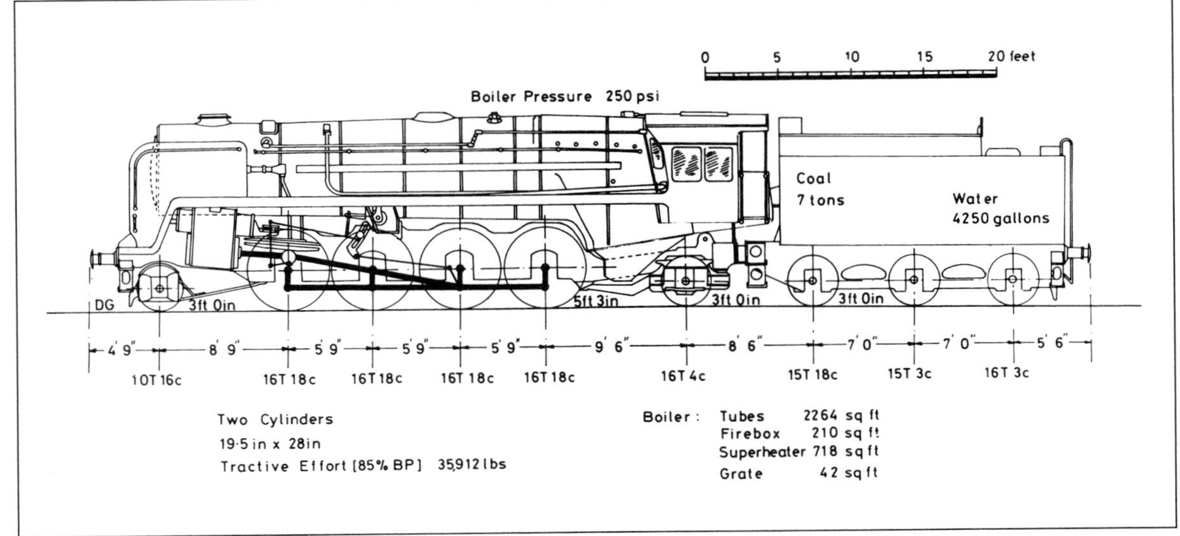

Original scheme for a 2-8-2 standard Heavy Freight locomotive.

be suitable for future needs. One main objection concerned the limitations imposed by loading gauge on the size of boiler which could reasonably be used as a wide firebox placed above trailing coupled wheels would seriously restrict boiler diameter and firebox volume. Conversely if the boiler was to be of reasonable size driving wheel diameter needed to be no greater than 4ft 10in (1.47m) and the team considered that 5ft 3in (1.6m) diameter driving wheels were necessary for working fast freights. Riddles asked the design team to think again as he was convinced that a loss of adhesive weight due to the use of trailing wheels would severely impair hauling ability. Riddles well understood that when starting or hauling up a gradient the 'sitting down' effect placed additional load on those trailing wheels and so some adhesive weight would be lost. Others, including R.C. Bond, still believed that the advantages to be derived from the use of standard parts had much in its favour and that the loss of adhesion due to 'sitting down' would not be significant.[2]

By the time the need arose for a heavy freight locomotive to be included in the standard scheme a design for a 2-10-0 wheel arrangement was acceptable, but its boiler was not standard with any other in the range. By using coupled wheels of 5ft (1.52m) diameter an increased running speed could be obtained and it was also still possible to fit a boiler of reasonable diameter with a wide firebox. Few compromises ever produce the desired results but the 9F 2-10-0 was certainly an exception; for many it was the most successful of the Standard designs and the best heavy freight steam locomotive to operate in Britain.

After the basic engine diagram had been worked out at Derby responsibility for detailed design work was passed to the Brighton drawing office. As was usual for BR locomotives instructions were given to incorporate as many standard components as possible, thus the design work did not entail any particular problems other than with the boiler. Two outside 'Britannia' class cylinders of 20in (50.8cm) diameter and 28in (71cm) stroke were incorporated and as the boiler pressure of 250psi was the same for both designs it followed that the 9F and 'Britannia' would be capable of developing the same power. However, in view of the freight locomotive's smaller wheel diameter its tractive effort was much higher.

Skilful design work also minimized axle loading, the load on each set of coupled wheels being the same at 15.5 tons (15.9 tonnes); when fully laden the tender had a higher axle loading but use of coal and water would reduce that and the absence of hammer blow on the tender wheels meant that the list of restricted routes was limited. Locomotive wheels were individually balanced for rotating forces but only 40 per cent of the reciprocating masses were balanced. As this was divided between all ten coupled wheels the mass applied to each individual

Scheme for 2-10-0 standard Heavy Freight locomotive, as finally constructed.

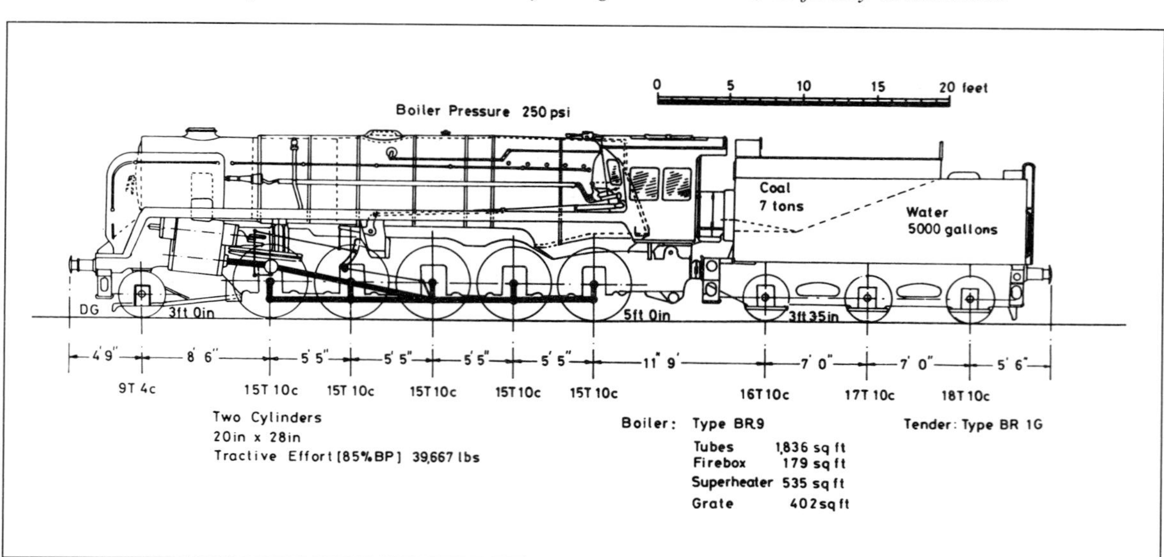

The third 9F class 2-10-0, No 92002 at Banbury in April 1966. Fitted with double chimney and BR 1G tender. (D.K. Jones Collection)

wheel was very small. This reduced hammer blow at each coupled wheel to a very low value and hence the total loading, static plus dynamic, on any axle was well within the limits designated by the Civil Engineer. At a rotating speed of five revolutions per second the 9F had a hammer blow effect of 0.78 tons (0.79 tonnes) per wheel, the lowest of the standard classes, contrasting very favourably with the 2.12 tons (2.16 tonnes) of the 'Britannia' class.[3] (At five revs per second the 9F would be running at 53½mph (85.6km per hour) whilst the 'Britannia' would have a speed of 66mph (105km per hour).

In service the efficacy of the arrangement was proven by the reputation the 9Fs had for smooth running even at high speeds. In order to allow for the negotiation of relatively tight curves without the risk of derailment the centre driving wheels were flangeless whilst wheels on the second and fourth coupled axles had tyres with thin flanges. Wheel centres were made from cast steel, tyres being secured by means of Gibson rings.

Frames were substantial, 1¼in (3.2cm) thick, in order to support the rather long locomotive structure but being of the plate type the design was flexible enough to compensate for the relatively long wheelbase of 21ft 8in (6.6m). Plain type axlebox

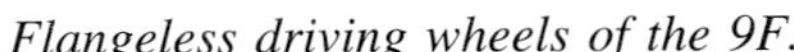
Flangeless driving wheels of the 9F.

bearings used for the coupled wheels were similar to the LMS pattern consisting of steel castings with pressed-in horse shoe brasses lined with white metal. The decision whether to fit roller or plain type bearings to standard classes was not an easy one and in true British tradition turned out to be something of a compromise, Classes 5, 6 and 7 being provided with roller bearings and all others, including the 9Fs, plain bearings. Roller bearings strong enough for the purpose were available but they cost much more than the plain type, however, roller bearings had a much longer operating life than the plain type and maintenance requirements were lower. The decision became one of first cost against later life costs and the lower initial costs tended to find favour. In retrospect the decision proved to be correct as subsequent substitution of plain bearings for roller bearings on some locomotives produced very little difference. The 9Fs appeared to fare quite well with their plain bearings and in view of the relatively short operating lives some of the class were to have anything else would have been a waste of money. That the class was withdrawn so soon was political and had nothing to do with engineering, thus it will not be discussed.

A major departure from the standardization scheme was in the boiler which had to be specifically designed for the 9F. In order to clear the loading gauge and the rear driving wheels it became necessary to compromise on several features including barrel diameter and depth of firebox. For the entire fleet of Standard designs two loading gauges were introduced, L1 and L2, the latter covering larger types from Class 5 upwards and the former, smaller locomotives from Class 4 downwards. The L2 gauge covered all routes where 9ft (2.7m) wide corridor stock would be used whilst the L1 was a universal gauge covering all regions. As the 9F would be for heavy freight use which did not require access to all routes the L2 gauge could be adopted but even that imposed restrictions particularly with respect to firebox width. The two ring barrel tapered slightly from 5ft 9in (1.75m) diameter at the smokebox end to 6ft 1in (1.85m) diameter at the firebox, the length between tubeplates being 15ft 3in (4.65m).

As the firebox needed to sit above the coupled wheels its depth was of necessity limited, further restriction applied because the grate also sloped for part of its length. Grate width had to be limited because the loading gauge restrained the firebox width and length was restricted by the fact that a long grate was extremely difficult to fire manually. A grate length of 7ft 5½in (2.27m) and maximum width of 7ft (2.13m) produced an area of some 40.2 sq ft (3.7 sq m). Overall the tube heating surface of the boiler appeared small for such a large locomotive but it was larger than the 'Austerity' 2-10-0. Free surface through the tubes represented 13.6 per cent of the grate area, the lowest for any of the Standard designs but it was considered adequate for a freight locomotive. In fact the boiler steamed very well and that low free surface value appears to have had little effect on performance. In original form, but with the blast pipe diameter reduced from 5.375in (13.65cm) to 5.25in (13.35cm), the boiler could evaporate 29,000lbs (13,182kg) of water per hour whilst burning Blidworth coal at the rate of

Single chimney 9F No 92013 at Rugby Central with an easy load in May 1964. A BR 1F tender with 5,625 gallon capacity is fitted. (D.K. Jones Collection)

Double chimney 9F No 92247, fitted with BR 1G tender. (D.K. Jones Collection)

4,655lbs (2,116kg) per hour. These figures represented the front end limit of the 9F in its original single chimney form. The shallow grate did, however, limit maximum performance somewhat but not such that normal freight operations were restricted.[4]

The outer firebox was constructed from steel but copper was used for the inner firebox, that same material also being employed for the smokebox end tubeplate. A practice adopted from the LMS was use of Monel metal for stays in the water space, the advantage of this material being its resistance to corrosion from electrolytic action. In common with other types a standard rocking grate was incorporated, there being six sections on each side of the centre line allowing one half of the grate to be rocked independently of the other. Each of the sections contained twelve grid firebars. Due to space limitations the triple hopper pan as fitted to the Standard 4-6-2s could not be fitted and the 9Fs had a conventional ashpan arrangement with twin hopper doors at the base. Front and rear dampers regulated air flow to the fire.

The wide firebox design presented a problem with respect to the frames which had to be stepped down in order to accommodate it. This reduced the frame depth in the vicinity and it became necessary to rivet stiffening plates to the main frame in order to provide sufficient strength.

Following construction of the first 20 members of the class a decision was made to build ten with Crosti type heat exchangers in order to assess the claimed advantage of this device. The Crosti system, invented by the Italian engineer Piero Crosti, was used successfully in Europe, particularly Italy and Germany, where improvements in coal consumption up to 20 per cent had been achieved, thus the idea offered considerable potential. Due to the fact that

Crosti boiler-fitted 9F class 2-10-0 No 92024, showing position of the chimney. (BR LM Region)

Non-chimney side of Crosti boilered 9F No 92024. (BR LM Region)

the 9F was already at the limit of gauge restriction it was not possible to utilize the standard Crosti arrangement and a new system had to be designed for the British locomotive. The basic principle of Crosti's idea was to make use of heat remaining in the exhaust gas to heat incoming boiler feed water and that required additional heat exchangers. For the 9F only one could be used and that had to be positioned between the frames underneath the boiler, even then there were problems and the standard 9F boiler, designated BR9, could not be used. A smaller diameter unit needed to be designed and that gave a reduced heating surface area for tubes, firebox, and superheater. Comparative figures are:

Boiler	Tubes		Firebox		Superheater	
	sq ft	(sq m)	sq ft	(sq m)	sq ft	(sq m)
Standard	1,836	170.6	179	16.6	535	49.7
Crosti	1,274	118.4	158	14.6	411	38.2

The heat exchanger provided 1,021 sq ft (95 sq m) of tube surface whilst the exhaust steam jacket gave an additional 57 sq ft (5.3 sq m) of heating surface. That exhaust steam jacket around part of the heat exchanger allowed additional waste heat to be

Diagram of Crosti boiler.

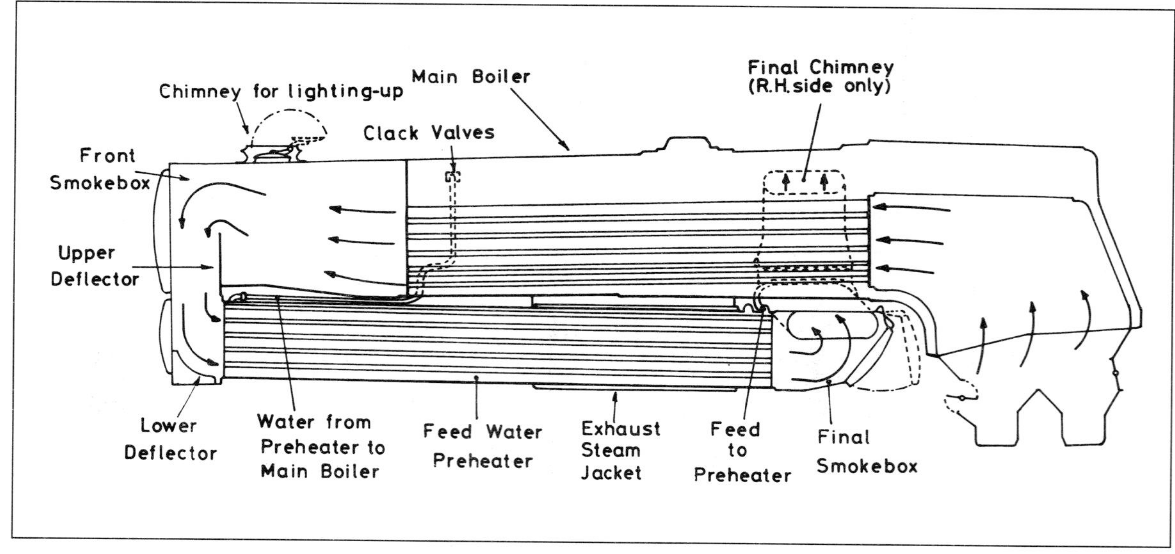

utilized for feed heating at the cold water inlet end of the unit. Condensate drained from the steam jacket via a Spirax steam trap.

Modification had to be made to the smokebox in order to redirect hot gases from the normal chimney through the heat exchanger to a chimney positioned on the right hand side of the locomotive just in front of the firebox; a set of blast nozzles and blower unit applied to this chimney just as they did to a normal chimney. The normal chimney was retained for use when lighting up but was blanked off whilst running. Smokebox doors were fitted at both ends of the heat exchanger to allow for cleaning.

Two injectors, one BR standard live steam unit and a Davies & Metcalf type K exhaust steam injector, were available for supplying water to the boiler. That water would normally be directed to the heat exchanger or preheater but a two-way cock was provided to allow water from the live steam injector direct access to boiler clack valves. Under normal circumstances cold water from the injectors passed through the preheater and hot water entered the boiler thus reducing the heat required to turn it into steam. Theoretically the steam generating plant became more efficient and less coal had to be consumed for a specific power.[5]

That at least was the theory and BR agreed to test the system with royalties being paid on a sliding scale in proportion to the savings made. Full royalty would be paid if a reduction in coal consumption of

Chimney and blast arrangement of Crosti boiler.

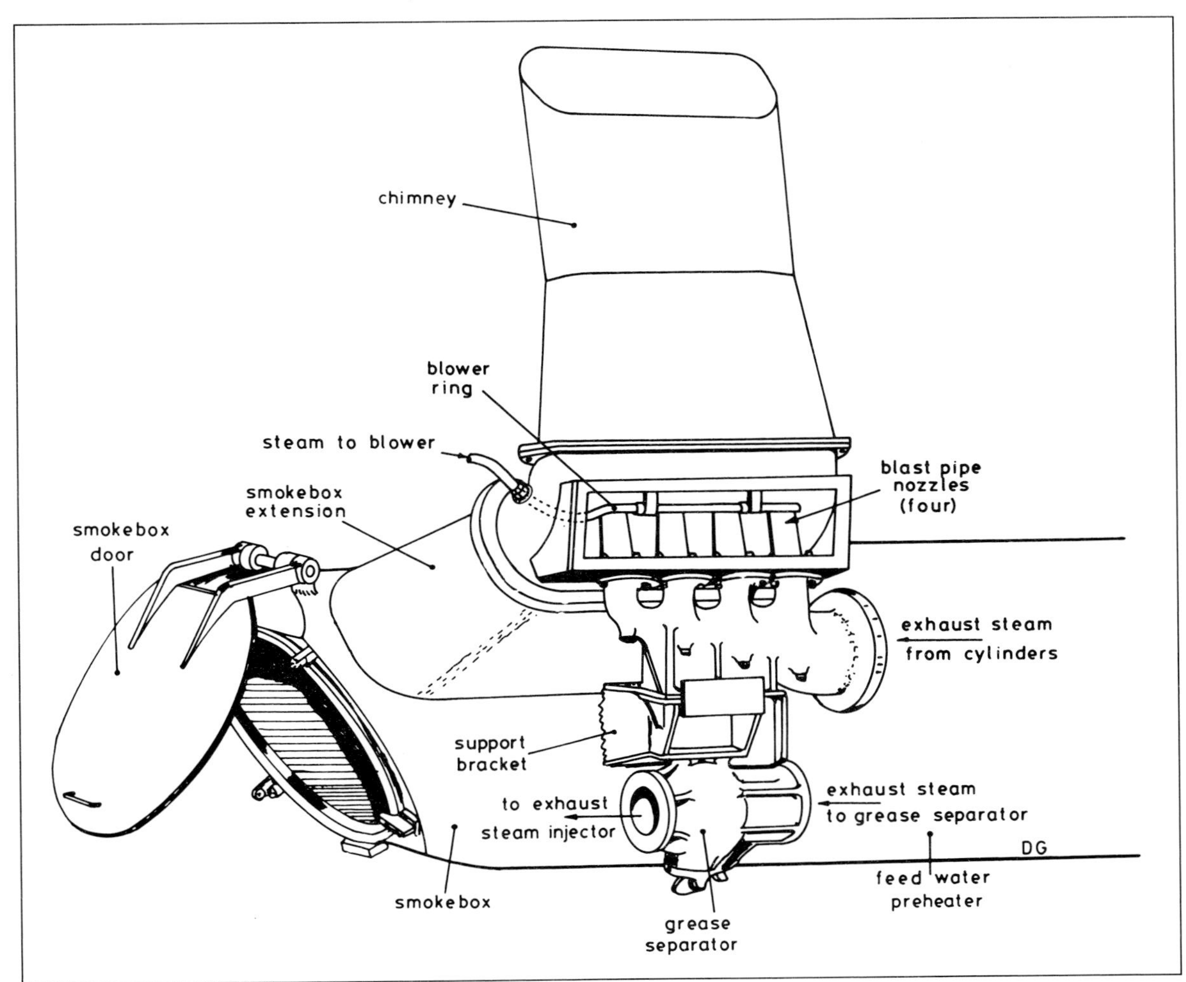

18 per cent could be achieved but if the savings fell below 12 per cent no royalty would be paid. The agreement was drawn up in March 1953 and the ten Crosti boilered 9Fs turned out in 1955. They were immediately put to work on normal freight duties and consumptions monitored. In addition specific trials were organized to compare performance of standard and Crosti versions.

No 92050 was the representative standard 9F whilst Crosti versions were represented by No 92023, trials being conducted at the Rugby Stationary Test Plant and on the road. Use was made of live and exhaust steam injectors in order to assess performance with each type, the exhaust steam injector acting as a feed heater in its own right as well as a means of forcing water into the boiler. Results of the trials were published in 1956 and they showed that overall there was little to be gained from using the Crosti principle; detailed results are given by E.S. Cox in his book *BR Standard Steam Locomotives* and in the official test report,[6] thus there is no need to repeat them in detail here.

As might be expected coal and water consumption was lower in both cases when using the exhaust steam injector compared with the live steam unit. Consumption figures obtained on the stationary test plant when generating 16,000lbs (7,273kg) of steam per hour were:

	Standard (No 92050)		Crosti (No 92023)	
Type of injector	live	exhaust	live	exhaust
Water (lbs/hr)	16,000	14,880	16,000	15,320
(kg/hr)	7,273	6,764	7,273	6,964
Coal (lbs/hr)	2,018	1,852	2,162	2,050
(kg/hr)	917	843	982	932

On the road results depended upon power being developed and tests were conducted at different speeds, the average results being:

	Standard (No 92050)		Crosti (No 92023)	
Indicated power	1,122HP (837kW)		1,088HP (812kW)	
Drawbar power	930HP (694kW)		866HP (646kW)	
	live	exhaust	live	exhaust
Coal consumption				
lb/DBHP/hr	2.318	2.138	2.322	2.202
kg/kW/hr	0.786	0.725	0.787	0.746

Although there were variations during the trials the figures indicated that the Crosti fitted 9F was 3.03 per cent less powerful than the standard locomotive. Allowing for differing weights and internal restrictions between the two locomotives the conclusions drawn with respect to savings were:

Saving	Operating condition
3.93 per cent	both locomotives using live steam injectors
7.33 per cent	both locomotives using exhaust steam injectors
11.74 per cent	Crosti with exhaust injector, standard with live

No matter which way the figures were manipulated the conclusion had to be drawn that the Crosti fitted 9F could not achieve the 12 per cent saving which would trigger the payment of royalties.

There was some disagreement between the parties after the event and André Chapelon was called in to adjudiate. A lengthy report from the eminent French engineer detailed factors concerning heat transfer and drew the conclusion that the preheater of No 92023 had been seriously fouled. As the report was presented two years after the initial trials any inspection at that stage would have been meaningless; there had been no reason to inspect the preheater after the initial trials and so the matter remained unresolved. A small payment to the Franco-Crosti company concluded the issue with no real decision being made for so obvious a failure of the system.

Even small improvements in efficiency could have been beneficial but a number of other factors also had to be considered not least the additional cost of the system and the royalty payment. Crosti fitted locomotives were also marginally less powerful thus reducing maximum load which could be hauled. Footplate crews did not like them because the exhaust blew into the cab in cross winds, even the fitting of deflector plates near the chimney failing to cure the problem. Corrosion of the preheater smokebox and chimney was severe due to the relatively cold exhaust gas precipitating sulphuric acid (due to sulphur in the coal). Replacement of parts would have been a frequent event and there was a need for additional maintenance due to cleaning of the preheater. Overall the system failed because the 9F design was already highly efficient anyway, at least as far as steam locomotives are concerned. The Crosti system had proven itself to be

Class 9F 2-10-0 with Crosti heat exchanger removed, No 92024, as running during 1964.
(D.K. Jones Collection)

a success when fitted to older less efficient Continental designs but the new 9Fs offered little scope for improvement. The ten locomotives subsequently had their preheaters removed and operated as normal locomotives, retaining their smaller boilers.

One other European device tried on the 9Fs was the Giesl ejector but in this case only one locomotive was so fitted, No 92250 being given the unit during 1959. Following the Crosti incident a carefully worded prior agreement was reached with the inventor, Dr Adolf Giesl-Gieslingen of Vienna, regarding conduct of the tests and what would be regarded as success. The Giesl ejector had a sound reputation having produced marked improvements in performance for a number of locomotive designs, a particular claim being that it allowed for the economic burning of low quality coal. A Giesl ejector would produce an adequate smokebox vacuum without imposing excessive back pressure on the cylinder exhaust system thus enabling output power to increase. It was, however, the claimed ability for a locomotive so fitted to burn lower quality coal which attracted BR as the National Coal Board was actively marketing its lower grades of coal at that time.

The primary objective of the tests was to determine how well a Giesl ejector fitted 9F would work when burning lower grades of coal and to assess the cost savings involved. It was agreed that success in this area would be achieved if the £500 cost of the ejector could be liquidated in two years from the burning of lower quality coal alone. The Rugby Stationary Test Plant was used to simulate road operations, the control condition being a standard locomotive operating at 40mph (64km per hour) with an evaporation rate of 18,000lbs (8,182kg) per hour on Blidworth coal. When burning low grade coal for the same operating conditions savings of 7.5 per cent on fuel costs were to be made. A further condition was that when burning any coal the boiler had to be capable of producing 21,000lbs (9,545kg) of steam per hour.

Agreement was reached on the three grades of coal to be tried, these all being of lower quality and less expensive than the Blidworth coal. The test report[7] gives full details of the trials together with information regarding calorific values and costs of these fuels. Firemen in Britain had little experience in the firing of boilers with low quality coal and a firing instructor was brought over from Austria to advise. It would appear that BR went to great lengths to ensure fairness and avoid any recriminations of the sort which followed tests of the Crosti system.

Whitwick large coal was found to be too large for normal firing and even after considerable effort had been expended on breaking it into smaller pieces large void spaces in the grate were still present thus reducing efficiency. With both types of slack coal clinkering of the grate took place resulting in a fall off in performance. Under the agreed speed and steam generation conditions coal consumption figures were:

Coal Type	Fuel consumption lbs/IHP/hour	kg/kW/hr	% increase over Blidworth Hards
Blidworth Hards	1,993	676	
Whitwick large	2,462	827	20.1%
Whitwick 1in slack	3,390	1,149	63.8%
Cossall slack	5,180	1,756	150%

A standard 9F with double blast pipe had an equivalent consumption on Blidworth coal of 2,070lbs/IHP/hr (702kg/kW/hr).

There was nothing in the results which encouraged adoption of the Giesl ejector or even further trials, particularly as the price difference between Blidworth coal and the low quality coals was not significant enough; at the time Blidworth cost £4 8s 3d (£4.41) per ton whilst the cheapest of the low quality coals cost £2 17s 6d (£2.87) per ton. In consumption terms with a good locomotive under test plant operation there just might have been some advantage in the Giesl ejector but other factors had to be taken into account, not least being the necessity to recover initial costs by savings in coal consumption over two years. A further important point mitigating against the burning of poor quality coals was the readiness with which clinker formed, thereby reducing performance and increasing the fireman's work.

No 92250 retained the ejector during its remaining life but did not distinguish itself amongst other 9Fs even when burning the same high quality coal.

The 9F was used for a further trial of a device aimed at improving the output of its boiler, namely a mechanical stoker. The ability of any steam locomotive to develop high levels of power over prolonged periods depends ultimately on the fireman as he is the person who must maintain steam in the boiler. Being of power class 9 this Standard heavy freight locomotive was expected to haul large loads and the expectation was that such loads would increase in size and that required operational speeds would be increased. Investigations had been carried out into the abilities of an average fireman, if there was any such creature, and it had been concluded that with a good boiler sufficient coal could be moved to maintain a steam output over one hour of 30,000lbs (13,636kg); the limit over a prolonged period was 24,000lbs (10,909kg). These figures depended upon the burning of good quality coal and during the late 1950s there were views that poorer quality of coal could present advantages; but as indicated above the Giesl experiments proved that view incorrect.

In order to test the maximum sustainable output which could be achieved by a 9F it was decided to equip three members of the class, Nos 92165, 92166 and 92167, with American designed Berkley stokers. This device essentially consisted of a screw feed conveyor system which supplied coal to a distributor

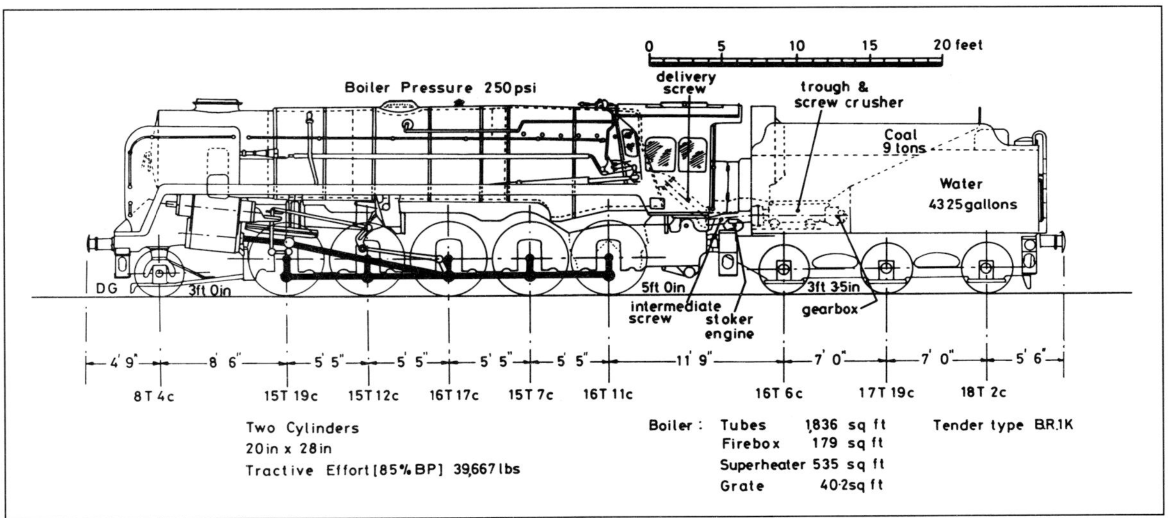

Diagram of 9F fitted with mechanical stoker, illustrating the changed weight distribution.

plate just inside the firehole, four separately controllable steam jets then being used to blast the coal to the front, back, left or right side of the grate. The conveyor screw system was operated by a small steam engine, the speed of which could be regulated by the fireman; hand firing was also possible should the system fail. For best results graded sizes of coal were required but the system did include a crushing grid and it was made reversible should blockage occur.[8]

The system was put through its paces on the Rugby Stationary Test Plant and out on the road with the mobile test unit. Results were no more encouraging than obtained for the other two devices mentioned above thus indicating that the 9F was as close to the ideal steam locomotive as was possible under British operating conditions. The report issued in October 1959 mentioned the possibility of operating heavier and faster freight trains in the future but concluded that the device was no real advantage under the then present conditions and with the locomotive as designed. With a redesigned grate and other modifications the report stated that the locomotive might be made to steam at a higher rate, but for the situation then existing, adoption could not be economically defended.

With the usual quality of coal a maximum steaming rate of 29,000lbs (13,182kg) per hour was obtained, no higher than for manual firing. However, the mechanically fired locomotive consumed 6,000lbs (2,727kg) of coal compared with 4,750lbs (2,159kg) for the manually fired locomotive at the same steaming rate. Clearly mechanical stokers were wasteful but the claim that they could fire at high rates could be employed advantageously if lower quality coal was used, greater quantities of this being required compared with good quality coal. Again there appeared to be no advantage in the mechanical stoker and with certain types of low quality coal the screw caused problems as it tended to break down the lumps into dusty slack.[9]

One clinching argument against the mechanical stoker lay in the fact that no real work could be found where sustained heavy steaming could be employed. Even on the longest and heaviest freight runs there were slacks, speed restrictions and other delays which put any run within the bounds of hand firing.

One modification which did suit the 9Fs was the fitting of double blast pipe and chimney. As with other standard locomotives this device produced an improvement in performance but even then it was not so great as to convince those in power that existing locomotives should be so converted.

From trial and operational results it would appear that, right at the end of steam, the railways of Britain had a heavy freight locomotive which was as nearly perfect a machine for existing conditions as could have been designed. Nothing is absolutely perfect, certainly not a machine, but as a steam locomotive for British operations in the 1950s and 1960s the 9F was as close to perfection as economy would allow.

The impact of the 9Fs on freight services was immediate and impressive. They were put to work throughout the railway system and proved their worth in hauling heavier trains at speeds greater than had previously been the case. Limiting factors were, however, still at work as train sizes were restricted by the length of refuge sidings and certain items of rolling stock had speed restrictions imposed. On the Southern Region oil trains from Fawley were taken via the Didcot, Newbury and Southampton line to the Esso depot near Birmingham. The 9Fs managed 1,200-ton (1,222-tonne) loads along the severely graded line without difficulty and to time.

Traditional coal traffic formed much of the work but imports of iron ore steadily increased and dedicated fleets of 9Fs could be found servicing these trains. Traffic from Bidston to the Summer's Steel Works at Shotton became a preserve of the class whilst others were put at full stretch on Tyne Dock to Consett iron ore trains. For the latter duties the ten allocated locomotives were fitted with air pumps for operating doors on the hopper wagons. These Consett trains were probably the hardest duties to which the 9Fs were put as the nine loaded hopper wagons gave a total weight of about 800 tons (815 tonnes) and gradients were as severe as 1 in 35 at times. Not surprisingly banking had to be provided.

On the Settle to Carlisle line anhydrite trains would be hauled from Long Meg to their destination at Widnes whilst limestone trains would be taken from Shap quarry. In fact the class served all parts of the system, even Scotland which did not have its own allocation, on freights of any kind. The group sent to operate on the Somerset & Dorset line certainly revolutionized traffic operations, even if they did fail to save that route. It was there that they found regular employment on passenger trains including the 'Pines Express'. Accounts of their adventures on such traffic have been recounted a number of times particularly in books devoted to that line.

S&D trains were not the first passenger duties given to the 9Fs as soon after they entered service summer relief and excursion work was performed, and performed well. One of the earliest high speed runs with passenger stock is recalled by E.S. Cox. This refers to a Crosti fitted locomotive, No 92023, hauling 14 coaches at speeds in excess of 80mph (128km per hour) when heading for the test area north of Carlisle in connection with the controlled road tests of the Crosti system. High speed express running on the Western Region became almost common place until some 'high-up' put a stop to it, again speeds were regularly in excess of 80mph.[10]

Free running at speed on passenger trains with a capacity for being flogged hard on heavy freights, the 9Fs were without doubt excellent locomotives but their end came too soon. It is difficult not to be political when common economic sense dictated retention of these machines, albeit in set areas, but dogma required that steam traction should cease on a set day. In the end the class was better than the railway management deserved.

8

Diesel Freight Locomotives

The 1953 Transport Act heralded a new era for British Railways with the Modernization Plan forming an essential part of the reorganization. Although steam traction would be retained in the short term the future firmly lay in diesel and electric traction and immediate plans were laid for the acquisition of a pilot group of diesel powered locomotives. Nowhere in that pilot scheme nor in the subsequent widespread ordering of locomotives under the Modernization Plan was there any place for a dedicated heavy freight locomotive. It seems strange that there should be such an omission as extensive mineral traffic still used the railways of Britain and the experience of overseas railways illustrated the potential of such machines; October 1962 actually saw production of the 25,000th General Motors (EMD) diesel locomotive for the world market.

Relatively new Class 9F and former LMS Class 8F steam locomotives were capable of handling all freight traffic as visualized in the late 1950s, and it is doubtful if even the most ardent anti-steam faction could have contemplated the rapidity with which relatively modern steam locomotives would be despatched to the scrap heap. Even when the end of steam was imminent it appears to have been considered that heavy or fast freight traffic could be handled by the diesel locomotives then in service or on order. An advantage frequently claimed for diesel traction was that multiple heading allowed for increased hauling power without the need for an additional crew. Certainly there was, and still is, truth in that fact but what appears to have been forgotten by some was the continuous tractive effort limit of the electric motor at low operating speed. High output power of the diesel engine was not the sole criteria for performance, if that power was not available at the rail during periods of starting or sustained low speed operations then the high powered diesel locomotive was a reduced power diesel locomotive.

In order to produce a particular rotating wheel speed and hence locomotive speed the electric driving motor of a diesel electric locomotive is actually geared down, but the characteristics of the electric motor only allow full power to be available continuously in a certain speed range. That severely limits the capability and so, like the steam locomotive which may be constructed with a particular wheel diameter, gearing is arranged to suit fast running or slow running, depending upon requirements. Express steam locomotives have large diameter wheels whilst express diesel electric locomotives have high gear ratios; for the shunter which needs high power at low speed small diameter wheels or low gear ratios are employed. Diesel-electrics of the pilot plan all had a relatively high continuous rating speed; for the Class 47s this was 27 mph which meant that full tractive effort was only available above that speed. When starting a heavy freight train or hauling such a train up a prolonged gradient that speed might not be reached for a considerable period and so haulage capability was limited. To exceed the tractive effort rating at low speeds would result in overheating of traction motors and care had to be exercised under such circumstances.

Action following implementation of proposals detailed in the Beeching report changed the railway scene and the 'good doctor' has since then been castigated as the destroyer of Britain's railways. It was, however, not all gloom as Beeching did actually propose expansion in the area of heavy freight operation, a proposal which is conveniently overlooked by most railway enthusiasts. This proposal gave birth to the concept of the merry-go-round train for the transport of coal from pit to power station and that has proven itself to be a money-spinner for British Rail and an environmental blessing as it has kept convoys of heavy lorries from the roads. Loading and discharge of hopper wagons would take place whilst they moved at slow speed through terminals at colliery and power station. That slow speed was to be 0.5mph (0.8km per hour) and it had to be maintained as load gradually changed during loading or discharge. Certainly no steam locomotive could be controlled with such precision but it was no easy matter for a diesel-electric either, particularly on rails covered in coal slurry. Problems were overcome and Class 47 diesels performed merry-go-round services satisfactorily during the 1960s. Development of the merry-go-round system required the co-operation of BR, the CEGB and the NCB, and it improved operating performance as well as reducing operating costs. An account of its introduction has been provided by one of the original instigators, R.T. Munns in his book, *Milk Churns to Merry-Go-Round*.[1]

Despite the advantages there were limitations, not least in terms of the locomotive stock which had not been designed for prolonged slow running. Train capacity was restricted by the continuous tractive effort which could be made available during those slow speed runs through loading and discharge terminals.

Abandonment of the 1955 Pilot Plan resulted in the introduction of many new locomotives and a proliferation of classes. This ill-considered scheme was not only financially unsound but it essentially failed to meet the needs of the new railway system. Many classes were unsuitable for the work expected of them and availability was low. In retrospect the absence of a heavy freight diesel from the range is difficult to understand but at the time there did not appear to be a need to respond to a market merely to provide a set service, whether required or not. The fact that the diesel locomotives were essentially for mixed traffic, with the exception of specific express passenger types such as the 'Deltic', is indicative of the then current British Railways Board (BRB) thinking.

Class 56 Locomotive

By 1970 some ideas had changed and there was a proposal for a high powered fast freight locomotive.[2] This was to have been of Co-Co wheel arrangement with power supplied by two Ruston-Paxman diesel engines giving a combined output of 3,360kW. Nothing came of the idea and a dedicated heavy freight locomotive of class 5 designation had to wait until the middle of that decade. Even then its design and introduction was a rather hurried affair in response to a very brief procurement specification. This called for a locomotive of 2,424kW output power with a maximum speed of 130km/hr and a capability of hauling heavy, slow speed merry-go-round trains or fast Freightliner and Speedlink services.

Rapidly increasing oil prices of the early 1970s caused concern amongst many parties in government and outside that Britain might be at an economic disadvantage if too great a reliance was placed on imported fuel. Plans were drawn up for construction of large coal fired power stations and an expansion in coal mining was forecast as a means of producing the necessary fuel for these stations. That events did not actually turn out as predicted or expected is of no consequence here but the result was that the BRB called for tenders for construction of diesel locomotives to the specification outlined above. Brush Electrical Machines of Loughborough received the order for 60 locomotives, that organization probably being the most experienced British locomotive builder as far as heavy freight diesel locomotives were concerned. That experience was based upon a single prototype type 5 express passenger/freight engine, No HS4000 *Kestrel*, and that illustrates the parlous state of the remaining British locomotive construction industry. So well stocked had British Rail become with diesels during the modernization programme that no further orders were forthcoming once that scheme had been completed and British builders cut back their capacity or even turned from locomotive construction. The folly of that rush to modernize not only haunted British Rail for years to come but it dealt a body blow to the locomotive industry from which it never really recovered.

The subsequent sale of *Kestrel* to Russia in 1971 aroused interest in the Eastern bloc and Brush reached an agreement with a Romanian state counterpart for a co-operative venture in production of a high powered freight locomotive. When the British need arose a substantial amount of design work had already been done and Brush was able to tender on the basis of that existing design and offer a very early delivery date.

Delivery was not the deciding factor but it was an important one as far as the railway was concerned. Brush did not have facilities for construction of the locomotives and so the initial batch of 30 were built at the Electroputere Works in Craiova, Romania whilst the balance was allocated to the BREL workshops in Doncaster. Government approval for construction abroad was granted on condition that a large proportion of the components were to be of British manufacture. All 60 bogies for that initial order were, however, of Romanian construction and that subsequently caused problems as they were all found to be defective. A further 75 locomotives of the class were subsequently ordered, construction of these being at Doncaster and Crewe.

The first Class 56 locomotive entered service early in 1977 although delivery from Romania had commenced in August 1976. In many respects these overseas built engines failed to meet BR's minimum requirements and a considerable amount of time, and money, was spent rectifying faulty workmanship as well as design defects. The catalogue of serious problems was alarming and included leaking traction motor gearboxes, corrosion of bearings due to inadequate protection in transit, inadequate tightening of bolts, defective dressing of welds resulting in stress concentrations, loose tyres etc. The average time taken to commission each Romanian built locomotive was $4\frac{1}{2}$ months but eventually they were all accepted.

Design defects were rectified as they became apparent and redesigned features built into the locomotives under construction at Doncaster. Staffing difficulties at that establishment slowed construction but in the light of the need to modify several features that was no bad thing. Apart from details with respect to the cab and bogies British and Romanian machines were identical and so was their relatively poor availability. The design was something of a compromise to suit the loose specification for general heavy freight traffic. Over the years repair levels and costs have remained high causing considerable difficulties in relation to their repair and allocation to duties. During 1987 it was stated that availability was 71 per cent,[3] a figure which is hardly likely to inspire confidence.

The BR definition of availability used in this case may be defined as;

$$\frac{\text{TOPS hours the locomotive is available to work}}{5 \times 24} \times 100\%$$

The normal working week comprises five days. The definition is somewhat crude in terms of current market demands as a locomotive which is undergoing repair during that five day period could be considered as unavailable, even though there is no work for it to perform. Such a definition takes no account of availability to haul the desired trains and the more logical measure of availability is that adopted by Foster Yeoman for its Class 59 fleet;[4]

$$\frac{\text{Number of trains actually worked}}{\text{Number of trains scheduled to be worked}} \times 100\%.$$

This definition covers business requirements and that is what British Rail is, a business. A business which requires trains to operate, not a business requiring machines to operate.

It must be conceded, however, that the Class 56 locomotives are not very good no matter which definition of availability is chosen. Poor performance and reliability soon became evident but at the time of ordering hopes were high that they would fulfil the freight needs for years to come. Compromise designs seldom produce the desired effect and in retrospect it was folly to rush into ordering a large fleet of such locomotives but then, as is often stated, hindsight is always 20-20 vision.

The heart of the Class 56 locomotive is its 16-cylinder Ruston four-stroke diesel engine. This engine, classified 16RK3CT, is of 'V' form which means that two pistons are attached to each crank, this arrangement allowing for increased power potential from a shorter engine. Pairs of cylinders set at an angle of 45° to each other, the cylinder bore being 0.254m and piston stroke 0.305m. Although originally designed for an output of 2,626kW with a mean cylinder pressure of 14.0bar, the engine operates in a slightly derated condition producing 2,424kW at 900rpm with a mean cylinder pressure of 13.0bar. Pressure charging by means of two exhaust gas driven turbo-chargers allows more combustion air to be supplied to the engine than is the case with a normally aspirated engine, thus more fuel can be injected and so specific cylinder output power is increased. In order to keep cylinder

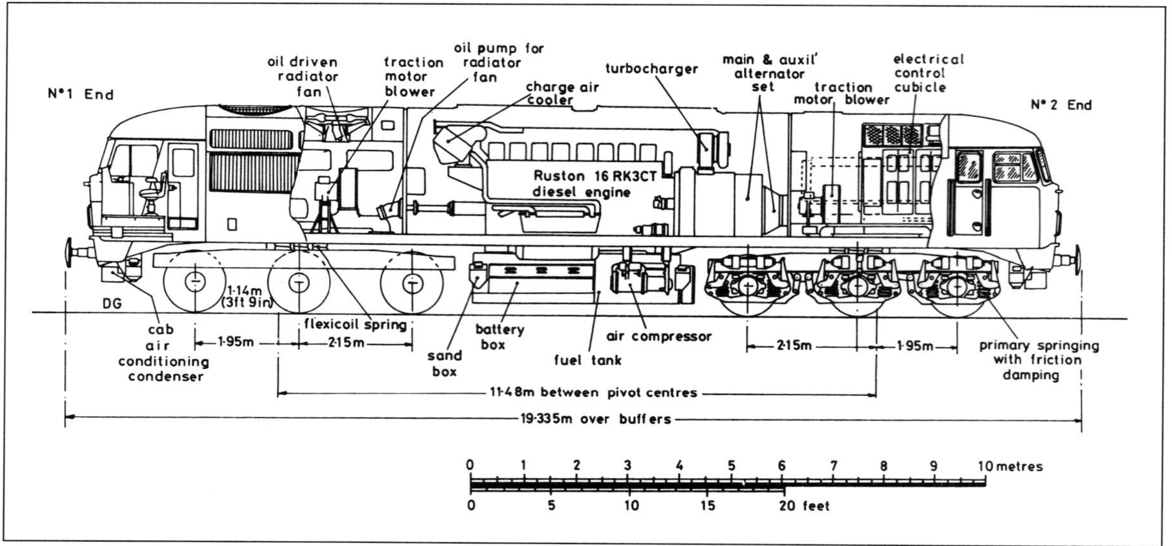

Arrangement of Class 56 locomotive.

temperatures reasonable the air leaving the turbochargers is cooled before it enters the cylinder.

The engine itself is water-cooled and the lubricating oil is also cooled by water in order to ensure that its temperature remains at a reasonable level to give optimum lubrication. There is, therefore, a high cooling requirement for the engine alone and this is met by two radiators positioned at the sides of the cooler compartment at the No 1 end of the locomotive. One of these coolers deals with engine cooling water whilst the other deals with coolant from the lubricating oil cooler and charge air cooler. Two roof-mounted radiator fans draw air over the radiators, these fans being hydraulically driven with oil supplied by a main engine driven pump unit. This form of fan drive allows for thermostatic control of the fan speed to suit the cooling load.

For the first time in the production fleet of BR diesel-electric locomotives, apart from the concurrently constructed HST power cars, alternating current (ac) power generation was employed with the Class 56 locomotives. Main and auxiliary alternators were connected directly to the engine output shaft, each alternator being a three-phase, star-connected machine with its own brushless self exciter. Brush constructed both alternators the main being a 12-pole BA1101A type whilst the auxiliary was an 8-pole BAA602A type. The main alternator provides power for the traction motors whilst the auxiliary alternator supplies power for such devices as traction motor blowers, brake system, control units and lighting. All auxiliary circuits are supplied with ac but the traction motors require direct current (dc) in order to allow for speed control.

Six type TM 73–62 traction motors are provided, one for each axle, the dc power for these coming from a diode rectifier located in the electrical compartment at the No 2 end of the locomotive. Rectification of the full power output is provided by 36 diodes allowing a continuous rating of 840V/2,730A or 1,520V/1,520A, or a one hour rating of 760V/3,000A. Traction motors have a maximum continuous rating of 420V/910A and are connected in a series-parallel form with three parallel lines of two motors in series. Each motor has four main poles and four compoles, or interpoles, designed to minimize sparking. Force ventilation is provided via ducting from electrically driven fans in the body unit, one fan to each bogie. Motors connect with drive axles using single reduction gearing with a ratio of 16:63; gearboxes are totally enclosed and contain an oil bath.

The generation of alternating current is less problematic than the generation of direct current but speed control of ac motors does pose difficulties. For this reason the three-phase traction power generated by the main alternator is rectified to give a supply voltage which is relatively steady and may thus be regulated in a similar way to dc. The 36 silicon diodes used for rectification in the Class 56 are

No 56054 viewed from No 1 end.

connected in six banks of six and produce an output which exhibits very little ripple. A considerable amount of heat is developed by the diodes and this must be dissipated if these devices are to function effectively. Each parallel grouping of six diodes is connected to an aluminium heat sink which in turn is cooled by means of air circulation.

The bogies fitted to the Class 56 locomotives are of the CP2 type which is based upon an earlier Swiss design. Compared with later bogies it looks rather cluttered but that is primarily due to the brake gear arrangements. The main bogie frame comprises two longitudinal welded box structures joined by similarly constructed cross members, this form providing strength and rigidity with relative lightness. The axleboxes are attached to the bogie frame by means of helical springs, two for each axlebox, the loads on the outer axles of each bogie, Nos 1 and 2 and Nos 5 and 6, being equalized by means of levers. In addition to this the centre axleboxes of each bogie, Nos 2 and 5, are provided with parallel roller bearings which permit lateral movement within the axlebox and so allow displacement of the wheelset whilst negotiating curves. This arrangement serves a similar purpose to the use of flangeless driving wheels on many freight steam locomotives. All other axleboxes are provided with rigid spherical roller bearings. In order to accommodate the traction motors wheelsets have unequal spacings as may be seen from the drawing.

Individual air brake cylinders are provided for each wheel, these actuating clasp type brake linkages forcing cast iron brake shoes onto the tyre. These cylinders are controlled as a group during brake application; the cylinders at one end of each centre axle are also actuated as handbrakes. Automatic slack adjusters are provided at each brake cylinder thus avoiding the need for a mechanic to make manual checks and adjustments. The first 60 locomotives, except for No 56042, were fitted with separately tyred disc wheel centres whilst the remainder of the class had monobloc wheels. The disc wheels had a maximum diameter of 1.143m whilst the monobloc type were 1.150m when new. Sand ejectors are fitted to the bogie frames at the leading wheel position in each direction of travel, these being fed with sand from boxes attached to the main frame structure. Four sand boxes are connected to the outer corners of the main underframe with four more being fitted to the underframe between the bogies.

Flexicoil springs provide secondary springing between the main body structure and bogie frames, this being in the form of triple sets on each side of the bogie. Hydraulic dampers constrain vertical and lateral movement whilst traction and braking forces are transmitted to the body by means of a bogie pivot pin, pre-loaded rubber traction pads being positioned in front and behind the pin. The initial 60 locomotives of the class were provided with four

Maintenance in progress on No 56068; engine compartment covers have been moved back and the silencer may be observed away from the engine.

bogie restraint brackets around each pin, these essentially holding the bogie to the body. However, derailments caused bogies to become parted from the body resulting in a decision being made to modify the design and incorporate brackets and bogie restraining slings.

The actual body structure is a monocoque affair which means that it consists of a single strength shell just like most modern automobiles. This arrangement was not new being based upon the design successfully used for the Class 47. The merits of a monocoque form include a saving in weight compared with a chassis type arrangement having a body placed on top and this was the primary reason for its use with the Class 56 design. Just as with an automobile the body acts as a strength member, in the case of the Class 56 allowing the whole unit to take machinery and buffing loads in excess of 200 tonnes.

Welding was used extensively for Class 56 body construction and new techniques originally developed for North Sea oil rig construction, were utilized for mass locomotive building for the first time. Jig assembly allowed for easier and more accurate construction. The underframe was erected from five jig-built sub-assemblies of box form and onto this the jig-assembled body-side framework was welded. With body skin plates in position the body sides were tensioned and the two internal bulkheads welded into place. Driving cabs were originally of aluminium construction but fabricated steel structures subsequently came into use. During construction of the later locomotives several other modifications were made to suit problems discovered during testing or to ease construction difficulties. These included the cab changes such as use of glass reinforced plastic for the cab desk and for the double skinned cab canopy. Other design improvements included a simplified air trunking system and incorporation of cable trunking in kit form. Although many of the modifications were forced upon the design and construction teams they did provide valuable experience for use in future locomotive design.

An important aspect with any locomotive is that of control and for a diesel-electric freight locomotive rapid response to any control signal is essential in order to maintain traction. Wheel slip detection plays an important part in any control system and the ability to start and haul heavy loads depends upon the response and accuracy of that detection and control system. Class 56 locomotives have been unfavourably compared with more recent freight locomotives but it is only fair to state, however, that at the time of their introduction wheel slip detection and control techniques were not as sophisticated as they were later to become.

Traction motors are connected in a series-parallel arrangement with three parallel groups of two motors in series, each group being provided with a single permanent divert resistance. In order to protect the main rectifier and traction motors from current surges due to earth faults or diode failures a high speed short circuit breaker is connected across the main alternator output. Wheel slip detection is by comparison of individual traction motor voltages in each series group. If wheels on an axle slip the voltage across that drive motor will change and that change will be noticed when the voltage across that motor is compared with the voltage across the other motor in the group. Power to that pair of motors would be reduced by the control system until the voltages across both motors was the same. Power would then be reapplied gradually up to the level previously selected by the driver. If any slipping was detected during this reapplication power would be reduced and then reapplied however many times was necessary. Manual sanding facilities could be used by the driver in order to assist in restoring traction at the wheels. With this arrangement simultaneous slips on two or all three motor legs could be detected provided that only one axle in each leg was slipping.

The system is both simple and reliable within the limitations mentioned, although it was discovered that problems did exist when hauling merry-go-round trains at slow speed on track covered with coal slurry. Under such circumstances it was possible for an axle in each pair to slip thus allowing the control system to remove power from all drive motors. The train would consequently come to a standstill. Only careful control by the driver and judicious use of sand would minimize such incidents. Driver skill and knowledge of conditions was still as important as it was during steam days even though technology had eased conditions somewhat.

Those eased conditions included cab comforts which were not to the liking of everybody as complaints soon came concerning cab floor vibration, noise from the bogies, cab temperature, draughts, seating arrangements, etc. The level of complaints during the winter of 1977–78 put continued operation of the class in doubt but an urgent program of action cured most of the problems, or at least pacified the drivers. Details of these problems and their solution has been given by D.F. Russell and P.J. Lowe in a paper to the Institution of Mechanical Engineers during 1980 and there is no need for repetition here.[5] These points have been raised, however, to indicate the difficulty in producing a new design which satisfies all parties, especially those who do the driving.

It was accepted at the time that the Class 56 was only an interim design, its purpose being to deal with the immediate freight haulage problems as they existed in the mid to late 1970s.[6] Success, or otherwise, of the class must be judged on that basis and comparisons with subsequent classes designed or purchased for operation on BR are not really justified in a business sense although they are in engineering terms. Hopes were high for the class when it was ordered but with hindsight it is apparent that the order was somewhat rushed. More work could have been done in assessing actual requirements and the locomotive design actually tailored to those requirements. One of the more obvious areas which required attention was that of operation. Whilst a mixed traffic steam locomotive was a reasonable proposition a diesel-electric mixed traffic locomotive presented difficulties. Electric traction requirements for haulage at high speed and slow speed are different and heavy merry-go-round trains on slurry covered tracks present a different proposition to fast Freightliner trains on frequently used main line track.

Diesel engine problems plagued the Class 56 during its early service years. Leakages of engine coolant and of oil from the hydraulic system presented major problems. Engine failures resulted from low coolant levels whilst leakage from hydraulic systems used to drive the radiator fans caused overheating. Many of these problems emanated from incorrect choice of pipe, poor quality pipe or defective seals. Bad design and inadequate quality control certainly caused most of the difficulties. Exhaust manifold failures were regular occurrences requiring urgent redesign of the exhaust pipework. At one stage welding was employed as a means of sealing leakages from exhaust pipe joints but that

No 56122 Wilton-Coalpower *supported to allow its bogies to be removed.*

presented problems for subsequent maintenance. This, however, indicates the desperation involved in attempting to keep the fleet operational. During 1985 a 'stop leaks' campaign was instigated and that improved matters but it took a number of years for the entire fleet to be checked and corrected.

The diesel engine itself was not perfect and required attention to major components, particularly the turbo-chargers. With the later locomotives camshaft failure caused difficulties whilst individual cams also tended to break up. The latter appears to have been a problem of fatigue resulting from the high loading and stress raisers caused during hardness tests carried out at the factory. Such failures should not have occurred and they were the responsibility of the engine builder, Ruston's not BR or the locomotive design team. Type testing of all items of equipment used in locomotives is now standard and such incidents provide the reason why. It has become the lot of BR's fitters and mechanics to keep the fleet in a reasonable state of repair and fitness for service. With ageing machinery the procurement of spares can also present difficulties and many components, such as exhaust pipework and silencers are specific to the Class 56. If these spares are not available locomotives stand idle.

Class 56 as viewed from No 2 end.

Ingenuity is required to deal with the problem otherwise the availability, 71 per cent in 1987, would be even lower. Judicious use of parts from locomotives already stopped awaiting other spares allows the number of traction units out of service to be kept to a minimum. Such common sense engineering has a price for valuable time is taken removing parts from one locomotive and then replacing them when spares are available. That price shows up on the balance sheet as labour costs but the price of not taking the common sense action does not.

Class 56 locomotives were initially allocated to merry-go-round services based on Shirebrook and Toton depots but with completion of the order the Western Region received an allocation for hauling iron ore and stone trains. This was the heavy freight work for which they had been designed and, within the limits imposed by failures or traction problems, they were able to handle with a degree of success. The other string to the intended bow, fast Freightliner work, did not in the end form a major part of their duties. Had more consideration been given to the expected type of work a better design might have resulted, at least in terms of hauling capacity on heavy slow freight trains, especially coal trains. However, machinery limitations and failures would still have existed.

To a certain extent sectorization and the allocation of locomotives to sub-sectors has focused attention on the need to provide specific hauling power for particular types of train. Such an idea was not around when the Class 56 design was being developed and these locomotives were essentially a general engineering solution to a vaguely defined problem. It is obvious now to most people that fast freight trains and slow heavy mineral trains require different traction. As an interim solution they were an advance on existing lower powered traction and did eliminate double-heading. They still perform a valuable service in the early 1990s but it is really a pity that so many were constructed straight from the drawing board. The money could have been more wisely spent.

Class 58 Locomotive

Barely had the first Class 56 locomotives entered service than proposals were afoot for a new heavy freight design. From early service experience it was obvious that many features of the Class 56 offered scope for improvement and that locomotive was only seen as an interim measure anyway, thus a new design was only to be expected. British Rail Engineering Limited (BREL) initiated a feasibility study in 1977 aimed at investigating the potential of a Type 5 heavy freight locomotive which would not only suit the changing requirements of the railways in Britain but also open up export markets. Such an intimation towards overseas sales now appears to be somewhat naive, or overly optimistic, as the American companies General Motors and General Electric had, more or less, sown up the world wide diesel locomotive market. Then again aspirations towards overseas sales might simply have been a ploy to obtain funding for the project. Whatever the reason authority was given for the design scheme to proceed.

Certain conditions had to be satisfied and these

No 58049 Littleton Colliery *showing the underframe form of construction.*

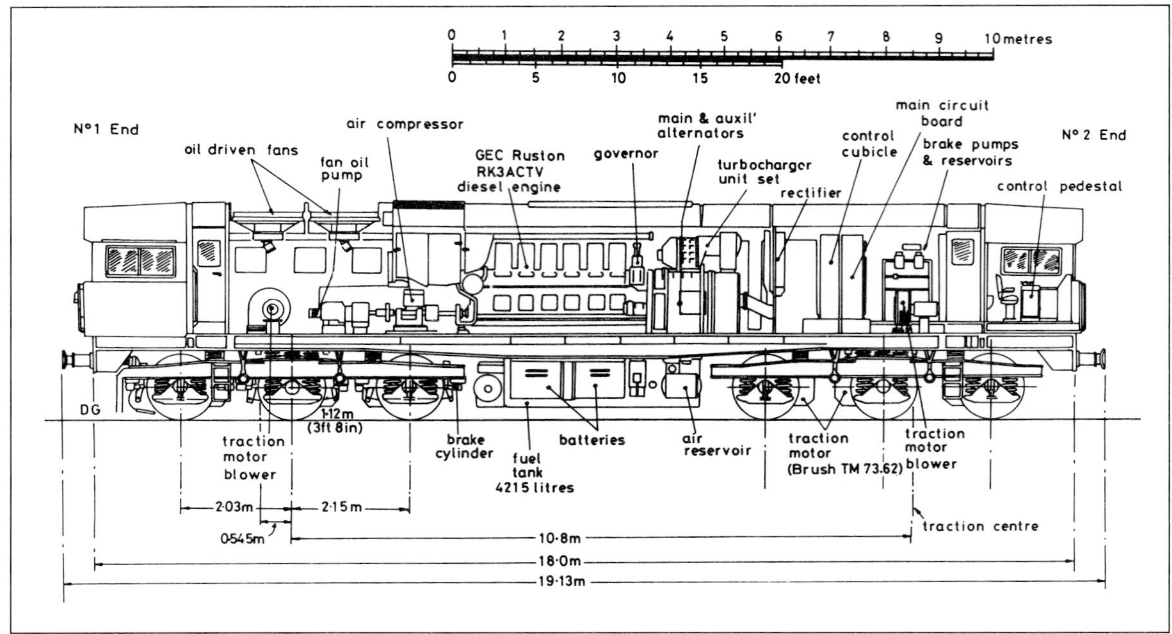

Layout diagram of the Class 58 locomotive.

included reduced weight, simpler construction and better accessibility compared with the Class 56. Several other conditions also had to be satisfied and these involved compliance with Union Internationale des Chemins de Fer (UIC) requirements for frame end loading and noise control. Although several tried and tested items of equipment from the earlier freight locomotive were to be utilized the basic concept of the Class 58, as the new design was to be known, differed radically from its predecessor. Adaptability to overseas markets in terms of different gauges could be satisfied through the bogies and so the actual body structure could be designed with different criteria in mind. Reduced construction cost was important but so was accessibility and the monocoque form of body structure did not suit either.

The design approved made use of a simple load bearing underframe constructed from girders, this frame carrying all static loads and being capable of withstanding the 200 tonne UIC end loading. Use of standard sized rolled steel joists (RSJs) would have made construction easier than it was but no joists of the size required were actually produced and the limited number of locomotives to be built did not make the organizing of a special roll economically acceptable. The main frame girders were actually fabricated from plate and although the concept was as envisaged the cost of the process was somewhat greater than anticipated. That frame supported all operating equipment and the two cabs, a modular form of construction being adopted for all items of equipment. This allowed for the fitting of complete modules away from the erection shop and also permitted equipment modules to be replaced as complete units should that be considered necessary. A bonnet or hood style of superstructure surrounded the modules on the frame with bulkheads keeping the modules isolated from each other. That arrangement provided for optimum air management enabling air flow through various compartments to be regulated. As has already been stated a diesel locomotive makes conshderable use of air for cooling purpose and the Class 58 design aimed at producing the best cooling and combustion effect for the locomotive whilst minimizing filter contamination.

The body between the two cabs is divided into four separate compartments, that closest to the No 1 end cab containing the cooler group and traction motor blower. Radiator panels are fitted at the compartment sides and unfiltered air is directed through these panels and expelled through the roof by means of hydraulically powered fans. The

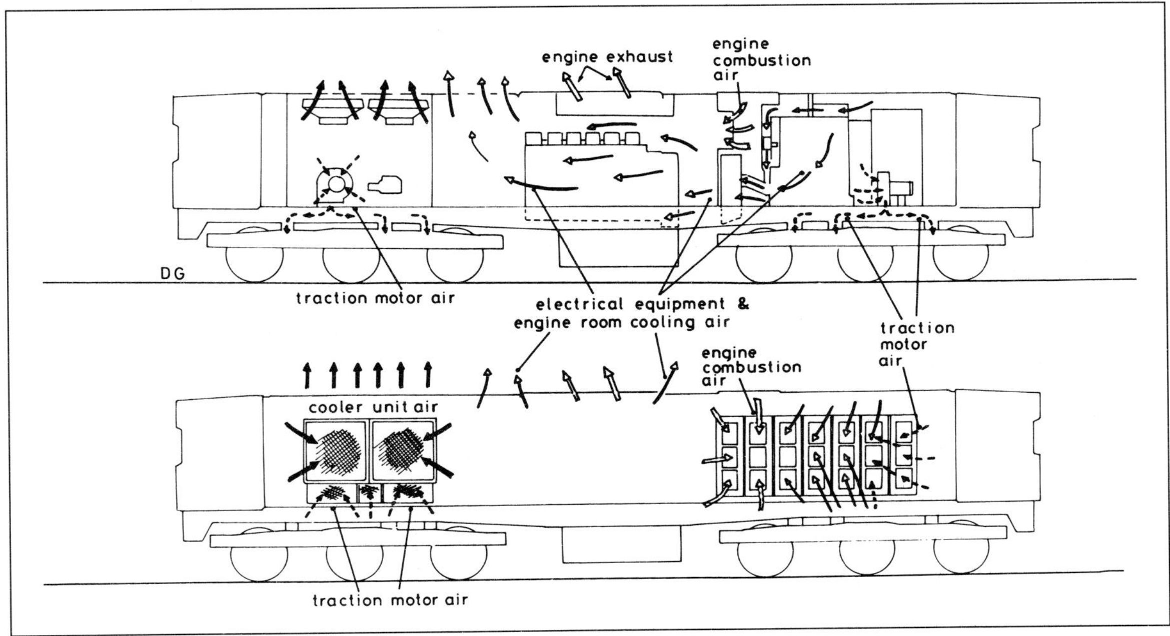

Class 58 air management system.

radiators cool the water from two separate circuits:

a. The primary circuit which cools the engine jacket water.
b. The secondary circuit which cools the engine lubricating oil and the combustion air inter-cooler.

The common fan system did allow some degree of interaction between the cooling circuits in the original design but this was subsequently altered to keep primary and secondary circuits separate. Independent operation of the fans could then provide the optimum cooling effect for each circuit. Within the cooler group compartment is the traction motor blower and this takes air through a separate bank of filters positioned below the radiators. This air is drawn over the air compressor intercooler and aftercooler thus providing a cooling effect for those units. Two further small inlets provide air for the brake system air compressors. Apart from these openings the cooler module is sealed from other air flows.

Next to the cooler module is the engine compartment which only draws filtered cooling and combustion air from the alternator compartment situated further along the structure. Filters in side panels behind the engine room bulkhead direct combusion air towards the engine turbocharger. This small compartment, to the rear of the engine module, contains the engine turbocharger filter, alternators and some electrical equipment. Filtered air is also drawn into the clean air compartment which houses the main rectifiers, brake gear and electrical control gear. This air provides a cooling effect for the compartment and also exhausts through the alternator housing to the engine compartment. The clean air compartment situated next to the cab at the No 2 end also contains a traction motor blower.

Such a system of air management reduces the risk of dirty air passing through the various compartments causing contamination whilst at the same time it ensures optimum cooling and adequate engine air supply. Access to engine, alternator and clean air compartments is by means of side doors which are sealed against a hardwood frame to prevent ingress of water or air. These doors allow for engine inspection and adjustment but roof sections may also be removed in order to allow for better access to compartments. One innovation which allows this is the mounting of the engine silencer on the exhaust manifold instead of the roof panel. The top of the silencer forms part of the roof and the exhaust piping system is greatly simplified, requiring only ten components compared with the 28 needed for the

Class 58 cab.

Class 56 turbocharger exhaust system. Admittedly the Class 58 engine only has a single turbocharger whilst the earlier locomotive was fitted with two.

Silencers had to meet the UIC noise limit of 100dBa at 1 metre distance and the 95dBa limit proposed in draft EEC environmental regulations. Two manufacturers were approached to produce a design which would comply with these limits within designated size restrictions but neither achieved complete success and a larger silencer had to be used. The type produced by Gloster Saro was eventually approved and became the standard for the 58s, however, Southampton University was contracted to conduct research into silencer arrangements and the reactive design developed has considerable potential for future use.[7]

Cabs at each end of the locomotive were an improvement on earlier designs as some attempt had been made to consider the driver. Waste heat from engine cooling water provides the main form of cab heating with the air flow across the heat exchanger being by means of an electrically driven fan. A 2kW electric heater is available when the engine is not running. The ventilation fan provides an air flow of 330m^3/h of which 70m^3/h is fresh filtered air from outside the locomotive, the remainder being recirculation. Air may be heated or not as required by the driver. Commissioning trials indicated that at higher speeds a large air flow into the cab through the air entry duct could be expected thus reducing the comfort level. As a consequence of this discovery the air intake was repositioned. Entry to the cab is by means of a single door in the rear bulkhead and so there is no direct access to the outside, thus reducing the risk of draughts. Services to the cab enter via a central duct and that also minimized the risk of draughts and noise.

Careful consideration was given to the layout of controls and the result was a more ergonomically arranged control and monitoring unit. Gauges were placed together on the dashboard in front of the driver, brake controls to the left hand side of the seat and power controls on a plinth to the right of the driver. This eliminated the traditional knee-hole found on most other BR locomotives. The seat itself is also a departure from tradition and is similar to that found in modern heavy duty, long distance lorries. In order to arrive at the optimum cab design a full scale mock-up had been constructed, an idea borrowed from certain designers during the steam age.[8] This cab design became the basis for future locomotive cabs and subsequent freight locomotives purchased from overseas have had cabs arranged to suit the 'standard'.

As a structure the cab is a bolt-on unit and can be replaced as a complete entity should that be necessary. This idea allows for easier damage repairs but also permitted different cab arrangements to be utilized should overseas orders have been forthcoming. UIC strength and collision requirements insist that the structure be able to withstand a 300kN force uniformly distributed across the cab immediately below the window. This was achieved with the Class 58 cab by means of a hollow, rolled beam positioned in that region and braced to the cab floor. Such regulations are essential in order to protect drivers in the event of minor collisions; no practical structure could ever be devised to afford complete protection against higher speed impacts.

Whilst the aspects of the design outlined above were novel as far as BR was concerned the power unit and electrical equipment were very much the same as that employed for the Class 56. There were, and still are, very good reasons for that. Tried and tested equipment was type approved and had a reasonable track record (the pun is intentional). When the Class 58 was being designed many of the leakage problems with the Ruston 16RK3CT diesel engine had not become serious and it was reasonable to choose an engine with which maintenance staff were familiar. Use of similar spares also had advantages. The diesel engine was not identical to that fitted in the Class 56 but was its shorter and more powerful younger brother. The 12RK3ACT was of similar Vee form but only had twelve cylinders, however, the bore of 254mm and piston stroke of 305mm were the same, allowing for interchange of mechanical parts. Being shorter it required a shorter engine compartment and that was one of the reasons for the reduced length of the 58 compared with the 56. A single turbocharger also simplified the engine system and, as mentioned above, the exhaust manifold system. Despite the fact that the engine has fewer cylinders its rated output is greater than that fitted to the Class 56, this being achieved by a more effective turbocharger allowing for higher mean cylinder pressure. Service rating of 2,460kW is achieved at 1,000rpm with a mean cylinder pressure of 15.9 bar (mean cylinder pressure on the Class 56 engine is 13.0 bar). Compared with the 16RK3CT engine the newer version also produces fuel savings of some 5.6 per cent.[9]

There were, however, penalties to be paid for such improvements and one was a difficulty in starting from cold. It became accepted practice to keep engines idling for long periods in order to avoid the need for starting but this was wasteful of fuel and caused fuel dilution of the crankcase lubricating oil. There are other reasons for fuel oil finding its way into the crankcase past piston rings, including faulty injectors and fuel dilution has tended to be a problem throughout the BR fleet. However, idling for prolonged periods is a major cause. A test version of the diesel engine was fitted in locomotive No 47901 for evaluation purposes and that provided much valuable data but there were anomalies. The Class 47 engine did not suffer from fuel dilution and cold starting was not so much of a problem. No

Engine as viewed through door in engine compartment.

Flywheel end of the engine showing position of the governor.

47901 had the Class 56 form of charge air cooling which provided a higher combustion air temperature, that higher temperature improving ignition and combustion of the fuel in the cylinder. With complete combustion there is no fuel impingement on the cylinder liner walls and so no fuel is scraped into the crankcase. A better injection system which allows for more complete combustion was tried and appears to have overcome the problem, although dilution is something of a long term effect and only time can tell how effective any measures are. The new injectors also seemed to cure the difficulties of cold starting especially when linked with modifications to fuel injection timing.[10]

Electrical equipment fitted to the 56s had proven itself to be reliable and there was no need for a change, items fitted being more modern, rather than more powerful developments of their earlier sisters. Naturally, updated plant was provided but alternators and traction motors were completely interchangeable with those on the 56s. The way in which those traction motors were connected electrically did differ slightly but it was still a series-parallel arrangement. Motor pair connections are 1+6, 2+5, and 3+4 whereas the 56 arrangement is 1+2, 3+4 and 5+6; numbering being 1 to 6 from No 1 end of the locomotive. A single divert line was provided across one motor in each pair in order to weaken the field, which motor had the divert depended upon the direction of travel. The idea behind this arrangement being to counteract the possibility of wheelslip during weight transfer when starting. The same divert, which reduced the motor field strength to 70 per cent of its full value, was connected across all traction motors at speeds in excess of 76km/h.

Alternator with air ducting from clean air compartment.

In conjunction with this motor field weakening arrangement a current balance system of wheelslip detection and correction was devised. This system compared values of current flowing to each motor in a pair, adjustment in power to the motors would then be made if there was any discrepancy. Theoretically it was an ideal arrangement but practice proved otherwise as out-of-balance currents of 40 per cent remained undetected in certain circumstances, resulting in high axle speeds and rail burn. Multi-axle slips were also common. Increasing the sensitivity of the current comparator unit did not improve matters due to the fact that when slip occurred it was equally likely to take place at each axle in a pair. This was basically due to the way in which the axle pairs had been coupled, 1+6, 2+5, and 3+4, and because of the permanent field diverts. When starting a 'sitting down' effect takes place as the load is taken and that increases the load on one of the axles in a pair. However, the divert tends to balance out the effect allowing each motor in a pair to draw approximately the same current. In order to encourage one of the motors to slip first the field divert was removed but this did not cure the problem. Fundamentally the system was at fault due to the inability of the current comparator to detect changes in current quickly enough. The time interval between motors in a pair commencing to slip could be in the order of milliseconds and a domino effect would be produced as motors in the pair slipped successively at higher and higher speeds. The fault was not actually in the sensitivity of the system but in its inability to react quickly enough. A voltage balance system as applied to the Class 56 locomotives became the only option and that was fitted retrospectively to the class.

For merry-go-round working slow speed control is provided at one of three pre-selected speeds, 0.8, 1.6 and 4.3km/h, with a fourth position on the controller being available for starting heavy trains in low adhesion conditions. The latter provides a fixed value of tractive effort at a speed determined by load and gradient. Under such control all traction motors are connected in series and the main alternator output voltage is maintained at a level slightly above that which normal slow speed working would require. The purpose of this is to actually encourage slight wheelslip which cuts through the coal slurry and conditions the rails for trailing wheels. Consistent higher levels of adhesion should then be maintained. Output power from the alternator to meet varying power demand from the motors is adjusted by altering the field excitation through the control unit and load regulator; engine speed remains constant during slow-speed control.

The slow-speed control system was designed to maintain tractive effort when a slip was detected, by limiting the alternator output voltage in order to obtain a particular current required for the designated track speed. By this means the voltage across a slipping motor would be limited and so would its speed. Again the theory proved to be more effective than the practice. The idea had been developed in order to prevent merry-go-round trains from coming to a standstill as had been the case with Class 56 haulage when tractive effort was removed from all axles simultaneously during wheelslip correction. Because all motors on the 58 are in series during slow speed control voltage reduction is across all motors and not just the slipping motor. That does not allow for a sufficient reduction in voltage across the slipping motor which, because it is slipping, can reach high rotational speeds. (Trials indicated a motor speed of 32km/h could be reached when train speed was only 0.8km/h.) Additional problems resulted because reduced current to a slipping motor means a reduced current to all motors causing loss of tractive effort. Although this series system was fitted throughout the class from new certain locomotives have been modified to the Class 56 series-parallel form of slow speed control. Neither system it would appear is ideally suited to merry-go-round operations where indifferent track conditions exist.

The bogie fitted to the Class 56 had performed reasonably well but it was never considered to be the ultimate as far as freight or other traction was concerned, and even before the delivery of the class was complete, plans were afoot for a more effective design. This new design, designated CP1, was applied to locomotive No 56042 and underwent extensive testing. It was intended to provide a good quality ride with fewer wearing surfaces than the CP2 bogie and thus have lower lifetime costs, that lifetime expectancy being 35 years.

The CP1 bogie frame is a mild steel fabricated unit employing box sections although steel castings were used for transoms which incorporated the traction motor mountings. Secondary springing, between bogie and locomotive underframe, was by means of flexicoil springs located directly on the sole bars. Instead of conventional horn guide arrangements the primary suspension, between axles and bogie frame, consisted of a rolling rubber ring which provided lateral stiffness and allowed wheelset yaw. Coil springs provided vertical suspension stiffness and in order to permit negotiation of small radius curves centre axles had floating bearings. The CP1 design showed many advantages over the CP2 version, though not enough to make it economic to convert all Class 56s. It could not be directly used for the Class 58 due to the underframe and body structure of that locomotive.

A novel traction connection had been incorporated in the CP1 bogie and that involved the use of inclined traction links from the headstocks at each end of the bogie. The idea behind this arrangement was that it would avoid the need for equalization of load between individual bogie axles. To some extent this did work as weight transfer tests carried out by BR illustrated but, as mentioned above, the bogie could not be used for the Class 58. The CP3 bogie actually used for the 58 incorporates a conventional pivot with rubber traction pads positioned fore and aft of it as in the standard Class 56 bogie. The CP3 frame also comprises a combination of fabricated sections and castings. Side frame centre sections, which provide the flexicoil spring seatings, are castings as is the circular transverse section which joins the two side frame sections. This circular casting provides supports for the outboard traction motor and the housing for the traction pad. A fourth major casting of the CP3 bogie is the rectangular section transverse girder, connecting with the two outer parts of the bogie frame, which provides support for the inboard traction motors. The remainder of the bogie frame is fabricated box section, a headstock being fitted at the inboard end only.

The positioning of the axles in relation to the traction centre is a critical part of the design and extensive mathematical analysis was required before

CP3 bogie fitted to the Class 58.

an ideal arrangement could be devised. Design is not simply a case of placing pieces of equipment where they will fit; it is necessary to consider aspects such as vibration, stress and flexure before any components are actually put together. The bogie must be considered in relation to the locomotive superstructure and the track conditions over which it will operate at speed. Analysis indicated that the traction centre required to be lowered compared with earlier bogie designs, the position being some 595mm above rail height. This placed the traction centre almost on the same level as the axle centres and that position is close to the optimum for minimizing weight transfer between axles when driving. Weight transfer between axles is critical for there is a limit to axle loading and if there is likely to be a large degree of transfer the static loading must be reduced.

With a driving centre some way above the axle centres of a two-axle bogie there is considerable weight transfer to the trailing axle as the locomotive 'sits down' as load is taken; wheels on the leading axle would tend to leave the rail. If the traction centre is on the same line as the axle centres there should, at least in theory, be no 'sit down' effect and so no weight transfer between axles. Adding a third axle complicates matters because weight tends to be transferred to this axle as the traction centre approaches the axle centre. A further complicating factor is that locomotives are provided with two bogies and the locomotive tends to 'sit down' on the bogie nearest to the train as traction force is applied. A trailing bogie, therefore, tends to take most of the weight transferred and the larger proportion of that is taken on its rearmost axle. Considerable testing is required to obtain the optimum but even the optimum degree of weight transfer does not mean that all axles are equally loaded; they never are when a load is being hauled.

Initially Westinghouse brake gear was fitted to the CP3 bogie, as it had to the CP1, sanding arrangements being provided for the outer axles, ie the two axles at the extreme ends of the locomotive. This sanding operated only in the direction of travel and was activated by means of electro-pneumatic valves, being under automatic and driver control depending upon circumstances. Early service indicated problems of slipping in colliery sidings due to track condition and it was decided to modify the sanding arrangement. It was found that the rear bogie, which was subject to higher traction loading due to the 'sitting down' effect, was being inadequately sanded. The solution was to provide additional sandboxes at the inner ends of each bogie but that resulted in the need to modify the brake equipment in order to provide the necessary space. SAB brake gear replaced the Westinghouse arrangement, this system being more or less self contained in that a single compact unit incorporates the operating system, brake lever and block carrier mechanisms. Modifications were undertaken on the bogies of No 58020 in order to test the new design and these proved satisfactory. The new bogie, classified CP3a, was designated for the second batch of 58s, Nos 58036 to 58050.

A second modification to the bogie was the fitting of softer primary springing to the middle axle in order to equalize loading. During 1983 a value analysis study of the CP3 bogie was undertaken with a view to reducing total costs, maintenance as well as construction, over the anticipated 35-year life. Other aims of the study were to reduce weight and improve maintenance. The need for a new bogie frame and other modifications were identified, including those mentioned above, but because only 15 locomotives instead of the anticipated 39 were ordered in the second batch a completely new bogie design was not considered to be cost effective. The CP3a modified bogie proved to be the next best solution. This work illustrates the ongoing design process which BR's engineers followed but the absence of orders limited practical application of solutions to identified problems. That sort of development took place during steam days and the steam locomotive, passenger and freight, progressed but it was only possible because there happened to be a steady demand for locomotives. Design is not a single step affair is a continuing process which cannot exist without orders. Unfortunately British locomotive manufacturers had lost their way in terms of world markets and British Rail Engineering Limited (BREL) became the major locomotive supplier to its parent BR. Although BREL was able to compete for overseas contracts American locomotive manufacturers had cornered the market and so it was the limited BR orders which kept locomotive design and construction work alive. Rather than being steady development with improvements being incorporated in long production runs the British locomotive industry has had to exist on a stop-go diet of orders. Little wonder then that innovations tend to be initially problematic — there is little scope for development. A similar situation existed with the British civil aircraft and shipbuilding industries, and their demise is obvious to all.

During 1985 tests were carried out to investigate the relationship between axle load equalization and wheelslip. Locomotive No 58004 was provided with soft springing on the central axles whilst No 58005 retained its normal primary springing. Static tests at Derby indicated that the standard Class 58 exhibited a greater variation in centre axle loading than did the Class 56 for track deviations of plus and minus 25.4mm. Softer springing improved matters but the Class 56 was still better at load equalization during static and running tests. These results did, however, confirm the results of the bogie analysis and allowed for incorporation of softer centre axle springing on the CP3a bogie. Adhesion trials carried out at the same time also indicated that sanding increased adhesion by between 5 and 6 per cent and that also confirmed the plan to increase sanding arrangements. Trials were also conducted into the most suitable form of motor connection during slow speed operation and, as mentioned above, modification was made to certain locomotives in order to allow this. Slurry on tracks at collieries and power stations does not help either of the systems and it would appear that no real solution exists for these locomotives working in such conditions.

Although certain aspects of the design may have presented problems and a number of defects have become evident over the years the 58s can be considered as successful. Construction time and cost were both less than for the Class 56 whilst running costs are also lower. Better access to the machinery compartment and a simpler bogie design provide for easier, and less costly, maintenance. Availability, measured on the BR system of TOPS hours available for work, also shows an improvement on the Class 56, being 78 per cent in 1987.[11] By no stretch of the imagination can this be considered as ideal but it must be judged alongside the maintenance facilities available, stock of spares kept per locomotive, size of total fleet, the nature of work for which the locomotives are utilized, but more especially the definition of availability employed.

Class 58 locomotives do their work well but problems have been experienced under extreme conditions on merry-go-round trains, to which they are almost exclusively diagrammed and for which they were designed. Facilities were provided in the design to allow up to three locomotives to operate in multiple but rarely has it been necessary to employ two on service trains due to the high tractive effort available relative to the size of normal train load. As in steam days there are still limits to the length of train which may be formed, not least because of facilities available at collieries and power stations.

Despite the problems the 58s do have a number of

No 58024 leaves Rugeley after delivering coal to the power station.

positive attributes not least of which is the cab design which has been particularly successful and is the basis for the 'standard' BR cab. The modular arrangement certainly eased manufacture and has made maintenance simpler than for earlier designs. Modifications to several components and systems have been made over the years as already mentioned and these have served to improve both performance and availability. Due to the size of the 58 fleet, only 50 locomotives, 35 from the first batch and 15 from the second, it has not been an economic proposition to design absolutely new systems to overcome certain of the difficulties encountered, but within that restriction the machines have performed well. Availability has steadily improved as problems have been rectified and this has also had the effect of increasing the number of miles per casualty. Expectation must be that the 58s will play an important role in heavy freight operations on BR for many years to come. Even in their present compromise condition they are very good locomotives.

Class 59 Locomotive

The story behind the purchase of Class 59 locomotives for use on BR metals is generally well known but some repetition is required in order to set the scene for a technical description of the locomotives. The Somerset quarrying company, Foster Yeoman Limited, has for many years shipped stone from its Torr Works near Shepton Mallet to depots in the South East of England. Rail shipment found extensive application for the longer routes although road haulage was still practicable. Stone is a relatively low value commodity and so its production is only profitable if it can be transported to the consumer at the least possible cost. It might be considered that quarrying and delivery to the consumer can be carried out at a steady rate but that is not the case, for the aggregate industry can be a rather volatile affair with periods of bad weather influencing road and other forms of construction. This reduces the need for stone which cannot be stored at depots due to space limitations hence delivery requirements are variable. When weather improves the demand for stone increases and the supplier must be able to respond quickly otherwise the order is lost. Flexibility is required of any transport system but the cost of that system must also be minimized, a few pence per ton difference in delivery cost can make all the difference between winning an order and losing one.

During 1983 Foster Yeoman delivered 3.7 million tonnes of stone to its own and other depots using British Rail. A fleet of wagons, many purpose built, was employed and full utilization became a necessity in order to ensure a return on the capital or hire charges involved. Over the years a number of different classes of locomotives had been employed but in 1983 trains were diagrammed for exclusive Class 56 haulage. The length, and hence weight, of train varied and double heading could be required at times. However, the 56s were not particularly reliable with the result that up to 40 per cent of Foster Yeoman's trains were not arriving on time. That caused the company concern as it disturbed relations with its customers, the knock-on effect of delivery delay could have been costly in terms of building and construction work, thus incurring the risk of lost orders in the highly competitive aggregates market.

Foster Yeoman is a well run business — it has to be in order to survive in such a competitive field, and its management lost no time in seeking a solution to the locomotive problem. Foster Yeoman reasoned that if a small stud of dedicated Class 56 locomotives were allocated exclusively to its traffic they could be maintained close to Torr Works at convenient times thus increasing potential availaibility. BR's Railfreight management could find no argument with the proposal, in fact it broadly adopted the idea for sections of its own operations at a subsequent time. It was estimated that six locomotives, with an availability of 95 per cent, could meet all anticipated traffic needs but the Somerset businessmen were not prepared to let matters lie there. If BR would agree to a dedicated fleet of its own locomotives would it also agree if the quarry company purchased a small stud of diesels? Naturally, costings had been carefully considered but a renegotiated haulage contract would make it a worthwhile proposition and allow Foster Yeoman to have control over the traction for its trains. The British Railways Board agreed in principle and a search began for suitable locomotives.

From subsequent events it would appear that the 'simple quarry men' were not that simple at all, they knew exactly what they wanted and also where to get it. A specification was drawn up which, on the surface appeared to be quite basic, but covered the exact business requirements as perceived by Foster Yeoman. There were only four requirements but they were as rigorous in intention as any more detailed specification.

a. The locomotive manufacturer had to prove that similar products of its making were achieving elsewhere consistently the levels of performance and reliability required in other parts of the specification.
b. A minimum level of availability of 95 per cent had to be consistently maintained. The definition of availability was:

$$\frac{\text{No of trains actually worked}}{\text{No of trains scheduled to be worked}} \times 100\%$$

c. Reliability had to be such that six of the chosen locomotives had to be capable of conveying four million tonnes of stone per year at the same times and speed achieved by Class 56 haulage.
d. Maintenance must be carried out at a depot with limited facilities during normal periods when the quarry was not operating. Other downtime must be minimal.[12]

BR's Class 56 and 58 locomotives were quickly ruled out; they certainly were not achieving consistent levels of performance and reliability anywhere, nor could six locomotives expect to convey the necessary stone as some double heading with Class 56 was required. Whether conditions (b) and (d) could be met was purely academic. If British products were not suitable the net had to be cast wider but Foster Yeoman already had experience of one overseas product, its General Motors Type SW1001 Bo-Bo switcher (shunter). This locomotive had performed reliably on the quarry sidings, on call 24 hours per day, Monday to Friday, since 1981. Foster Yeoman had actually set out to purchase two such machines but General Motors (GM) Electro-Motive Division (EMD), more concerned with reputation and the future, indicated that only one would be needed; they were right and the managers of Foster Yeoman obviously knew who to call on in order to meet its mainline locomotive requirements.

GM-EMD had no problem in meeting requirements regarding proven reliability nor, on the evidence of the switcher, would there be problems in complying with availability targets. Worldwide operation of GM locomotives indicated that they were capable of being maintained in the most rudimentary workshops. Although a number of locomotive manufacturers were consulted, there was probably only one horse in the race. However, as they stood no GM-EMD product could comply with restrictions imposed by BR and considerable redesign would be needed. However, a number of people in BR, Railfreight in particular, were keen to see how well a high powered, high availability locomotive would perform on British tracks. At the end of 1984 an agreement was reached between BR, Foster Yeoman and General Motors-EMD whilst the quarry company also signed a 15-year agreement for rail transport of up to 4.2 million tonnes of stone per annum.[13]

From the power and traction requirements General Motors knew which locomotive in its range would fit the bill but the locomotives in its range were way outside of BR's loading gauge and weight limit. That, as far as EMD was concerned just happened to be another design restraint and the company would not let such a prestigious order slip on a mere size and weight restriction. Redesign of the basic structure would be needed and some equipment had to be left out whilst others had to be included to satisfy local BR requirements. It has been admitted that some 40,000 man hours were expended on the redesign work but the real figure was probably double that.[14] There was no way in which that sort of investment could be recovered from the Foster Yeoman contract but EMD obviously considered it to be worthwhile in order to obtain that vital foothold in the UK market.

One of its proven locomotives, the SD40–2, formed the basis for the design, its power and tractive effort being close to Foster Yeoman's needs. It was also a proven design with large numbers in regular service worldwide. Restrictions on weight and height posed major problems, the SD40–2 having an axle load of nearly 28 tonnes whilst the limit for BR operations was 21.5 tonnes; its height above the rails was 4.75m but BR's height restriction amounted to 3.9m. A very large quart had to be squeezed into a rather small pint bottle. In effect the locomotive had to be redesigned as it was impossible to simply produce a scaled down version. Engine, alternators, auxiliary systems, traction motors and the highly successful HT-C bogie would be taken from the SD40–2, although in the case of the bogie certain modifications had to be made in order to remain within gauge restrictions. In a relatively short technical description it is impossible to convey the amount of work which went into producing a design which satisfied all requirements and simply outlining aspects of the design does not do justice to the efforts of EMD's engineering staff. Regrettably space does not permit a thorough description of the procedures involved which, as far as this author is concerned, are the real triumph of the Class 59 project. For some strange reason the average railway enthusiast does not consider engineering to be of real interest, and the same can be said for the specialist press which has devoted almost as much space to paint schemes as to the technical aspects of the Class 59s. Therein probably lies the reason for Britain's decline as a manufacturing nation.

Use of the HT-C bogies imposed certain constraints as they are rather tall units. In order to

Layout arrangement of the Class 59 locomotive.

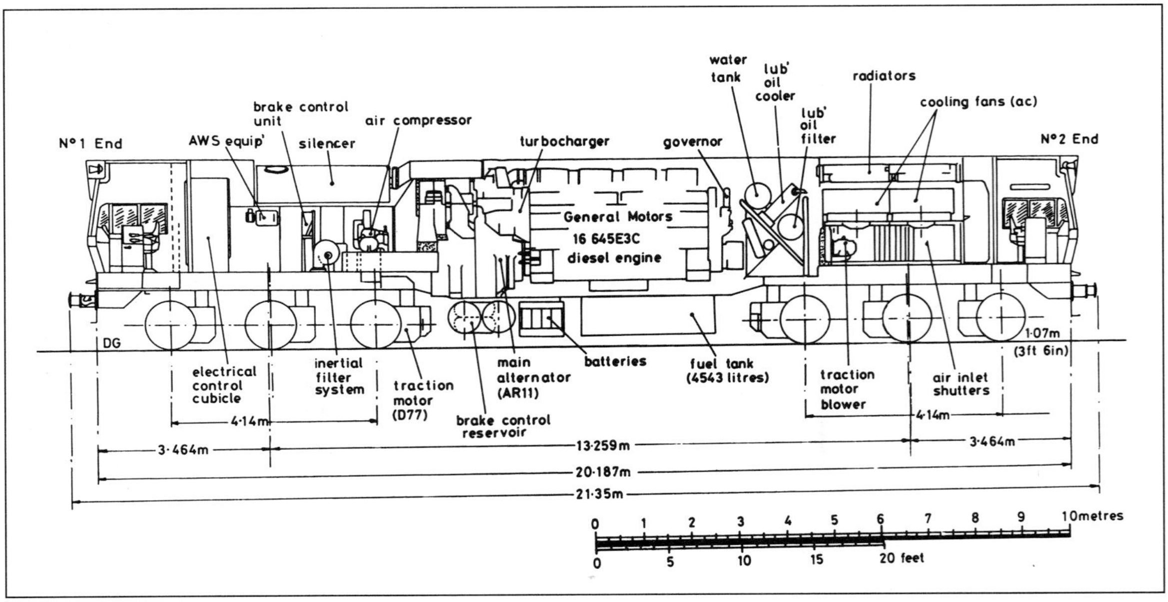

comply with height restrictions the underframe and body structure needed to be specially designed, even then space would be at a premium. Bogies are of cast steel construction with relatively soft primary suspension using coiled steel springs and comparatively stiff secondary suspension employing rubber springing. Primary damping results from hydraulic dampers mounted on the leading and trailing axleboxes and that is assisted by friction between the horn guides and axleboxes. Liners at the horn guides are of a nylon based material rather than the more usual manganese steel. Secondary damping is achieved through the rubber springs and friction at the bolster longitudinal stops. The standard HT-C bogie employs large brake cylinders which would infringe the British loading gauge but replacement by SAB units, as fitted to the Class 58, overcame the problem and produced a degree of standardization with other locomotives on BR. The SAB cylinders also eliminated the brake rigging and so avoided problems regarding later pin and bush wear with that rigging.

Whilst British main line diesel locomotives, apart from the 'Deltics', have made use of four-stroke cycle engines GM has found success with a two-stroke cycle engine. A number of restrictions apply to the use of a two-stroke cycle, the most important of which is the fact that air above atmospheric pressure must be supplied to the cylinders in order to remove exhaust gas and provide a fresh charge for the next cycle. Such air can be supplied by means of fans driven by chains from the crankshaft but the more usual modern means is to employ exhaust gas powered turbochargers. At low speed a turbocharger may not supply enough air causing poor combustion and high fuel consumption. As locomotives idle for prolonged periods this could be a problem but GM provides its turbocharger with an automatic clutched drive from the engine enabling sufficient combustion air to be supplied at slow speeds. Two-stroke engines tend to have a better power to weight ratio than four-strokes and usually contain fewer moving parts as air enters cylinders through ports in the cylinder liner, thus eliminating the need for air inlet valves and valve operating gear. Because the two-stroke cycle engine has one power stroke for every crankshaft revolution a faster response to control is available compared with a four-stroke, an advantage when attempting to control wheel creep. The GM 16-cylinder Vee form 645E3C engine is rated at 2,460kW with a maximum speed of 904rpm. Cylinders are of 230.19mm bore and 254mm stroke whilst the compression ratio is 16:1. GM has done much to improve efficiency but a two-stroke engine tends to be less fuel efficient than a four-stroke, although specific fuel consumption depends upon

Class 59 under construction with the alternator at No 1 end and the engine in view. (Courtesy GM-EMD)

Interior arrangement of an ARC Class 59/1; the cooler units may be seen at the end of the engine.
(Courtesy GM-EMD)

The size and positioning of the silencer may be seen from this view of a Class 59 under construction.
(Courtesy GM-EMD)

engine condition. A slightly higher fuel consumption can be more than offset by improved reliability and availability; the cost of fuel is but one consideration when operating any form of traction.

American operating practice does not call for strict control of noise levels and so the standard SD40–2 engine silencer is relatively compact but British operation required a much quieter exhaust. The maximum level in the cab was to be 82dBa whilst at the UIC defined 'Q' point, a set position some 1m away from the exhaust outlet, it needed to be kept below 105dBa. That necessitated a large silencer which, because of height restrictions, could only be positioned in the control compartment at No 1 end. Like their SD40–2 progenitors the Class 59s, as the Foster Yeoman locomotives were to be designated, were originally specified with dynamic braking. This is similar to regenerative braking as used on electric locomotives where traction motors act as generators during braking and convert kinetic energy of the locomotive into electrical energy, that power being fed into the electrical supply system. With a diesel locomotive the energy so produced cannot be fed back into the electrical supply system as there is not one and so it must be dissipated in some way. The method adopted by EMD was to use a bank of electrical resistors but these need to be cooled in order to prevent overheating. Large roof-mounted fans are employed to cool the dynamic brake resistors on the SD40–2s, but space prohibits their fitting on the 59s, the large volume silencer taking up a considerable space. Dynamic braking, therefore, could not be supplied with the Foster Yeoman locomotives. The use of such a braking system has considerable merit as it avoids the friction which causes wear to brake blocks and tyres.

Electrical generation produces alternating current which is then rectified to produce a supply for the dc traction motors. As with other heavy freight diesel locomotives discussed here the 59s are provided with main and auxiliary alternators. The main alternator (type AR11) has a rectifier housed within its casing thereby avoiding the need for a separate

Beneath a Class 59; traction motors and sanding arrangements can be seen. (Courtesy GM-EMD)

A Class 59 is lowered onto its bogies at the General Motors La Grange Works. (Courtesy GM-EMD)

rectifier compartment. The D14A companion auxiliary alternator provides current for the main alternator field. The traction motors, model D77B, are rated continuously at 900A 537kW which is well above the Class 59 traction requirements and indicates a standard unit in the EMD range. Use of larger motors than power requirement dictates might seem a waste but economy is served by the fitting of a standard unit which, having a higher continuous rating is not liable to overheat when subject to high starting currents. All motors are connected permanently in parallel across the main alternator rectified output. Alternating current is used to power cooling fans, traction motor blowers and inertial filter fans.

The use of inertial air filtration avoids fitting maze type filter elements which must periodically be cleaned or replaced. The main problem with a maze type filter is that, of necessity, it gets dirty and that impairs air flow. The inertial filter does not, however, become blocked in the same way as particles of dirt are thrown to the side of the filter tubes and clean air flows through. This arrangement is used for primary air filtration with bodyside elements of filter tubes producing the inertial effect as air swirls through. Within the locomotive structure secondary filter elements are provided in the usual way for the likes of the compressor and turbocharger. This principle has been used in Britain but it is no longer common practice, but experience with the Class 59s, which operate in a rather dusty environment, indicates that the system employed is very effective.

Although basically happy with EMD's Class 59 arrangement BR did insist that several items common to British practice were incorporated. Some of these were necessary in order to comply with stricter UK and European regulations whilst others were needed in order to maintain a degree of standardization with other locomotives in the fleet, this being particularly important as far as the drivers were concerned. Exhaust noise control has already been mentioned but adequate insulation had to be provided around the cabs in order to ensure that the driver's working environment was comfortable; this also applied to heating and ventilation systems for the cabs. An early requirement of BR was that the 59 cab had to be similar to that fitted to the 58, both in terms of comforts and layout. EMD worked closely with BR in order to ensure that this was the case and even produced a mock-up so that arrangements could be checked. The steps to which EMD went in order to guarantee satisfaction illustrates a strong

Comparison of a Class 59 with the standard American parent Class SD50. (Courtesy GM-EMD)

desire to please a customer and to break into the British market.

The cab structure was designed in order to meet stringent UIC collision requirements whilst the large windscreens, which contained electrical elements for demisting and defrosting, were manufactured from high-impact resistance glass. Air-operated windscreen wipers were provided for both wind-

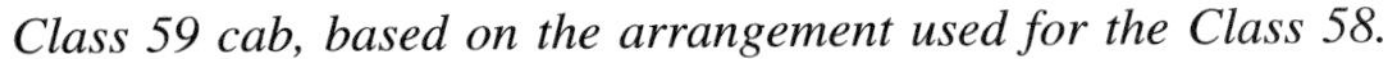

Class 59 cab, based on the arrangement used for the Class 58.

screens and these had in-built wash water nozzles to ensure that cleaning fluid would be sprayed at the correct position. Pinch roller blinds allowed drivers to adjust shading to suit individual requirements. The instrument control panel arrangement mimics that of the 58 apart from some minor variations. At the driver's right is the pedestal-mounted master controller which is moved forwards to increase power, whereas that of the 58 is pulled backwards. This is a standard EMD arrangement and was retained as it fitted closely enough to BR standards not to cause undue confusion. The controller has nine notch positions, idle and 1 to 8, plus a stop position. With traditional BR locomotives the controller is generally manipulated with caution, care being taken to ensure that the ammeter reading does not go above the red line indicating maximum current. Engineers from EMD do not regard that red line as such a restriction and high traction motor currents, compared with those for Classes 56 and 58, may be employed should circumstances dictate. This flexibility is possible because of the high continuous rating, 900amps, of the traction motors.

All light switches are positioned conveniently for the driver and are capable of being reached from his seat which is to current BR standards. A second similar seat is provided in the 'second man' position whilst a cab to cab telephone is also fitted should such communication be required. Sound insulation is fitted at the cab nose-end, sides and rear bulkhead and the floor is provided with heavy rubber matting. In order to maintain driver comfort levels there is no direct access to either cab. At the No 1 end doors on each side of the locomotive open into small vestibules which allow entry to the cab and at No 2 end locomotive side doors access a corridor which has a single door into the cab. For fire protection portable extinguishers are fitted in each cab with a fixed system operational in the body of the locomotive. The fixed system can be activated electrically by means of buttons from either cab or mechanically by handles on the sides of the locomotive.

A number of British built components have been incorporated in the Class 59 in order to comply with BR requirements for standardization of certain equipment, and to provide for security of supply from a local manufacturer should replacements be needed. Standard items included the PBL brake system, advanced warning system and DSD equipment. Although the power plant and traction equipment are strictly American, layout of cab and the use of items of equipment with which British drivers are familiar ensures that the locomotives could be operated effectively with a minimum requirement for training. Operations indicated that drivers quickly became accustomed to the 59s and were able to deal effectively with the minor idiosyncrasies of the class. One of these was the hydraulic parking brake which tended to leak 'on'; this was overcome by ensuring that drivers pressed the 'off' button long enough to ensure complete ventilation of the parking brake system.

An item included in the 59 specification with which no British driver had experience was the 'Super Series' creep control system. This had been developed by Bruce R. Meyer of General Motors as a means of maximizing the tractive output of a locomotive under heavy load and/or difficult track conditions. An important aspect to consider with respect to any diesel-electric locomotive, or any locomotive for that matter, is that high power does not mean high hauling potential. If power is not transmitted to the rail then the locomotive is effectively overpowered and the purchaser has spent more money on capital equipment which can never be fully utilized. On level track or even modest gradients full output power is never required – it is only when starting a load or hauling one up steep gradients that maximum power might be required. However, during these periods there is increased tendency for slippage between wheels and track, thus reducing the effective traction power and it was this area that Meyer and the General Motors team set out to tackle. The reasoning was that if adhesion could be improved then an increased portion of engine power output would be available for haulage and so a smaller prime mover could be utilized.

Tests had shown that friction/creep curves could be obtained for different track surface conditions and each of these curves gave different positions for maximum friction. Friction levels were not always a maximum at low levels of creep and in certain cases, with water or oil on the track, the percentage friction level was greatest at higher levels of creep. These studies, therefore, indicated that attempting to eliminate creep was not the best policy because at very low creep values friction between wheels and rail could also be low thus reducing tractive effort. Use of sand indicated an increased level of friction, as might be expected, and moved the peak level towards the lower values of creep, again as might be expected. However, the tests also showed that indiscriminate use of sand could be wasteful and even harmful as sand produced increased rail and tyre wear. At higher creep levels it was found that the leading wheels on a bogie tended to condition the track for the following wheels thus improving their adhesion, this effect being better than the use of sand with bogies where wheels were not allowed to creep.

Normal wheelslip control systems attempt to regulate slip first by detecting it and then eliminating it by removing power from the slipping wheels until that slipping ceases. With tractive power removed from one or more axle motors the locomotive can slow down and even stop thus negating any control effort. Whether a voltage balance or current balance system is used the purpose is the same, to stop wheels slipping. These systems tend to operate in the region up to 1.5 per cent slip which is considered to be the maximum allowable. However, tests mentioned above indicate that friction between rail and wheel can be a maximum at much higher values of slip. Meyer decided to make use of this situation and decided that slip between wheel and rail could be allowed to go to higher values, the limit depending upon the nature of rail surface, thus maintaining traction and even accelerating the train. The situation is similar to that of attempting to drive a car on an icy surface. If the foot is removed from the accelerator when driving wheels begin to slip forward motion is lost and the car will tend to slip sideways. On the other hand if the foot remains on the accelerator and wheels are allowed to slip at a controlled amount forward motion can be maintained and control of the car remains with the driver.

'Super Series' is a total control system not just a wheel creep control system as it attempts to maximize adhesion under all conditions whether that be on heavy grades, curves or under adverse track conditions. The basic principle of the system is to provide a motor voltage which will allow that motor, and hence its axle, to rotate at a particular speed which will give the required amount of slip. The value of terminal voltage required to give the desired value of creep may be determined for a known ground speed if the applied current, motor resistance and motor characteristics are known, which they are. The system hinges on the ability to monitor actual operating conditions and one of these is the true ground speed. In order to obtain an accurate value of true ground speed a doppler radar unit is provided on the locomotive. The control system monitors operating conditions so that actual wheel speed may be determined and a value of creep may be ascertained.

Depending upon adhesion conditions a limiting value of creep is set and if the actual value of creep remains below this then 'Super Series' is inoperative. Should, however, creep exceed this limiting value 'Super Series' takes over and regulates supply voltage such that a particular level of creep may be obtained to give the desired adhesion. Sand is not applied immediately 'Super Series' takes over but it is applied automatically when power supplied to the motor falls to 90 per cent of normal power. (With 'Super Series' in operation, for reduction in adhesion the speed remains constant and applied current falls thus reducing supplied power.) As adhesion improves and hence motor speed reduces the sand will be turned off at 95 per cent normal power. Sand is not, therefore, applied at all times with 'Super Series' but is only used when the control system indicates that adhesion is being lost due to adverse conditions. Tests have shown that 'Super Series' operation reduces sand usage by 70 to 90 per cent when compared with normal wheelslip correction systems. In many cases allowing an axle to slip by a certain amount produces improved adhesion and so traction is maintained. Under such circumstances 'Super Series' is not operative but if a normal wheelslip control system was used it would have reduced power to the motors as soon as slip commenced and so would have reduced traction. In simple terms 'Super Series' waits to see what happens and then allows slip within limits.

The above outlines the general situation but it is essential to know which of the friction/creep curves the locomotive is encountering; there are different curves for different wheel-rail conditions, eg oil, water, dry, dry/sand, water/sand, oil/sand, etc. Each of these curves gives a different maximum value of friction and a different value of creep at which it occurs. Within the electronics of the control system is a circuit which determines the friction/creep curve being encountered at a particular time. By sampling the current eight times per second the circuitry determines a current trend and any change is used to signal an alteration in the desired value of creep. The actual control system is extremely sophisticated requiring complex electronic circuitry and considerable time and thought went into its development. Anybody interested in more detail on the matter should consult Meyer's paper which gives details of the 'Super Series' development and provides references to earlier work.[15]

An important aspect of any control system is the response time of the prime mover which provides for power generation. As already mentioned it is considered that the two-stroke cycle engine responds faster to load changes than does a four-stroke cycle engine but there are other factors to be taken into account and EMD have addressed these in devising 'Super Series'. The entire locomotive system is integrated and not just a collection of parts: engine, control system, monitoring systems, electric motors, etc. have been chosen and designed carefully to react with each other in order to ensure the rapid and smooth response so essential to heavy freight train handling.

When starting both 'Super Series' and a specially tuned current difference rate of change system are employed. For operating speeds below 2.4km per hour the 'Super Series' ground reference speed is set to this value and the rate of change system is tuned to provide high adhesion operation. In this mode the rate of change system deals with the main control function whilst 'Super Series' operates to limit wheelslip. When ground speed reaches 2.4km per hour the rate of change system is turned off and 'Super Series' takes over control. This combined starting arrangement is considered to have an adhesion rating of 1.4 to 1.5 times the rating at continuous speed. Overall the ability of the 59s to start a heavy load and keep it running under adverse conditions lies in the way in which these systems have been integrated.

As mentioned above Foster Yeoman originally indicated a need for six locomotives as the heaviest trains, 4,300 tonnes, required double heading of Class 56 locomotives. EMD pointed out that its product, although not necessarily more powerful than the 56, had a much higher tractive effort and was able to start and haul heavy loads under adverse conditions. The company stated that double heading would not be needed and suggested that Foster Yeoman would only require four Class 59s and not six. When the contract was signed it was for four locomotives, a fifth being ordered later to meet increasing demand, and neither the quarry company nor BR have had any cause to doubt the confidence EMD had in its product.

During trials carried out in February 1986 No 59002 developed a sustained tractive effort of 111,000lbs with a peak of 114,000lbs, these representing adhesion coefficients of 40 per cent and 41 per cent respectively.[16] Initially a maximum load of 43 102-tonne PTA wagons was set for the 59s representing a load of 4,386 tonnes but this has been raised gradually as the EMD locomotives showed that they were capable of loads well in excess of Class 56 and 58 locomotives. The critical factor is always the ability to start a load and BR also organized tests to determine the limit of these American machines. On the 1 in 136 Savernake bank No 59001 started a load designed to simulate 46 102-tonne PTAs, that load actually consisting of 43 PTAs plus dead Class 56 and 59 locomotives. Conditions were not good but the 59 proved its worth and the worth of 'Super Series'. That ability to start a train has avoided the need for double heading which would have been needed with Class 56 haulage, however, the maximum power of a single 59 is less than that of two 56s, thus a lower maximum speed with a full load is to be expected. Journey times between the quarry at Merehead and distribution terminals is, therefore, greater but effective scheduling still ensures that each 59 can perform two round trips each day.

Prior to allowing the 59s to run on BR metals a series of acceptance trials had to be carried out and this was undertaken at Derby. Following delivery to Southampton Docks in January 1986 the four 59s were taken to Merehead where EMD personnel checked them over prior to commissioning. Later that month they were towed to Derby for acceptance testing. This series of tests is carried out on all new locomotive designs and it was not just a case of testing overseas products. Certain of the tests are carried out whilst the locomotive is static but others require the use of a mobile test car, the aim being to ensure that the locomotives will operate safely on the BR system within the route restrictions applied and also to ensure a degree of driver and environmental comfort.

Weight Distribution Test – on the weighbridge at Derby the loading on each wheel is determined to ensure that distribution falls within specified limits.

Torsional Stiffness Test – also carried out on the weighbridge this test simulates twisting of the bogies to detect if there is a risk of derailment when operating over severely distorted track.

Rotational Resistance Test – using a special rig the ability of bogies to steer into a curve without losing stability is checked.

Parking Brake Test – the parking brake must be capable of holding the locomotive on a gradient of 1 in 30.

Painted but as yet without a number, original style Foster Yeoman Class 59 ready for delivery at GM's La Grange Works. (Courtesy GM-EMD)

Power Brake Test – stopping distances are measured at various speeds with the locomotive running light. These tests ensure that the locomotive can stop within signalling distances.

Ride Test – condition of the ride, for comfort purposes and to avoid excessive shock loading on the locomotive components, must fall within certain values. Locomotive suspension has a considerable influence in this area.

Noise Test – the ability to meet stringent noise levels is assessed (mention has already been made of the need to provide a larger silencer than is normally the case with EMD products).

Driving Compartment Heating and Noise Test – carried out whilst running this test ensures that the driver will have a reasonable environment in which to work.[17]

In service the 59s quickly proved themselves and allowed loads were steadily increased. By 1989 Foster Yeoman had received approval to run trains consisting of 51 102-tonne wagons giving a total train load of 5,202 tonnes, the largest daily scheduled train in the UK. The limit of 51 wagons is not set by the locomotive's haulage ability but by the size of main line siding links which are 640m long.[18]

Again it has to be emphasized that the story of the 59s is essentially a joint effort between GM-EMD, Foster Yeoman, and British Rail. Without the enthusiasm shown by all concerned, including 'shopfloor' workers such as BR drivers and maintenance staff, the entire venture would have been something of an impossible dream. However, the dream did come true and it bodes well for future freight traffic on BR.

The story does not, however, end with entry of the locomotives into service as they do have to be maintained in service. High levels of availability are only possible if the machines are reliable in the first instance and if routine maintenance can be carried out at times when they are not required to haul a train. The business definition of availability men-

The clean engine compartment of No 59001 after three years of service; the absence of oil leaks is most impressive.

tioned above indicates what is required. There are free periods between service trains and the quarry does not operate at weekends thus, logically, these are the times to schedule routine maintenance. Although BR tested and accepted the locomotives for operation on its metals it is still bound to ensure that they can continue operating safely so regular inspections are required. Again logic prevailed and an agreement was reached with BR for its personnel to assist with maintenance, working alongside the Foster Yeoman workshop supervisor, Steve Hannam, so that inspection would be undertaken at the same time as maintenance. All routine work is carried out at the reorganized facilities at Merehead with BR mechanics from Bristol Bath Road travelling there for shift work on a rota basis. The system works and a dedicated group of maintenance men have become very familiar with a small stable of locomotives. There are advantages for all concerned as Foster Yeoman keeps its trains running, BR knows that the locomotives will be reliable out on the road and the service personnel have a high degree of job satisfaction as they see 'their' locomotives regularly. Teamwork is important and seeing a job through promotes enthusiasm, as was the experience of Volvo when it changed from a production line form of automobile manufacture to team manufacture.

Faults have occurred but over the years reliability has improved as the teething troubles have been rectified. By 1989 availability stood at a level in excess of 98 per cent, despite a new locomotive, No 59005 entering service that year. During that year only three technical casualties were reported giving a staggering 165,620km per casualty average for the fleet.[19]

High locomotive utilization is helped by arranging daily reliability checks at Merehead and weekly 'A' examinations, these being fitted in between turns. The total examination requirements are met by twelve balanced 'B' examinations organized on a 5-week cycle thus giving a 60-week programme for completion of the work involved in the total examination. This rolling programme of work means that every aspect is covered during the 60-week period but it avoids the locomotive being out of service for the long period needed to complete the total examination in a single stage. There are other advantages to 'rolling' inspections (the same system having been employed for many years in the survey of ships), not least amongst these is the fact that an experienced mechanic is involved in a detailed inspection of some part of the machine at frequent intervals. Defects can be detected more readily as it is difficult to inspect one part of the vehicle without actually noticing other items of plant in the vicinity.

Without a doubt the Foster Yeoman 59s have been a great success since they entered service, more than meeting initial expectations as far as reliability and availability are concerned. Expanding trade required that fifth locomotive to be ordered during

On shed at Foster Yeoman's Torr Works, No 59003 Yeoman Highlander *undergoes routine inspection between trips.*

1988 for delivery in July 1989. Such is the performance of these American locomotives that a number of people from BR have cast eyes enviously but so far they remain in privately owned fleets working on BR. The plural is used because another quarrying concern, ARC, has now followed the lead of Foster Yeoman and purchased four 59s, classed as 59/1 in order to account for slight changes in equipment.

Purchase of these machines by two companies indicates faith in rail haulage and for that we must all be grateful. These companies must be satisfied

ARC Class 59/1 ready for delivery; changes in arrangements at the cab front may be seen, compared with the original style. (Courtesy GM-EMD)

that possession of their own small fleets allows them to keep customers for their products happy by delivering the goods on time. British Rail must be happy because it now has a long term commitment to rail haulage by two major concerns in the construction materials supply industry. Railway employees will be pleased that these long term contracts exist, although neither company ever stated that it would transfer haulage away from the railway if the purchase of private locomotive fleets was not allowed. The British public also has an interest, not only because it has a stake in the railways but because of the horrendous problems which would have existed had any of the stone traffic been moved from rail to road. Although tonnages vary from day to day, during 1991 these nine locomotives will have moved per day between 8,000 and 10,000 tonnes each from the Somerset quarries to depots in the South East of England. The number of lorries required to haul that tonnage can be calculated but the pollution and road damage which would ensue is difficult to imagine.

Whilst the quarry owners are to be praised for their foresight and business acumen considerable merit must go to British Rail and its employees. Management grasped the nettle and, after initial scepticism on the part of some, employees welcomed the move. Like good employers everywhere BR kept its staff aware of the situation by means of a series of publications entitled *Changing Horses*. Three of these, published at intervals, gave details of the locomotive design, management attitude, testing procedure, maintenance arrangements and the views of Foster Yeoman. Only future years will tell how well the initial promise has fulfilled expectation but if operation of EMD products overseas is anything to go by then the future looks secure for these quarry companies as far as their locomotives is concerned.

Class 60 Locomotive

Under pressure from the government BR was forced to come to terms with the financial reality of the market place during the 1980s and that included the Railfreight Sector. Although it is hard to imagine road transport being in a position to cope with the heavy traffic currently carried by Railfreight, the effect on the environment being even more unimaginable, there are some who appear to see nothing wrong with the idea of shifting all freight to road haulage. It is not surprising, therefore, that the government indicated that Railfreight should be yielding a return on capital of some 5 per cent by 1990. The Railfreight Sector was profitable during the 1980s, a 1987/88 turnover of £550 million producing an operating surplus of £44 million, but the current rolling stock was generally old and important decisions had to be taken. Whether such constraints and demands should be placed on BR is political and does not fall within the remit of this work.

Unfortunately old rolling stock does not produce high yield and even the newer Class 56 and 58 designs could not achieve the levels of availability or reliability to come anywhere near the goal. The only effective solution was to construct new locomotives capable of achieving high levels of availability and reliability as had been achieved by the Class 59s. Other factors also had to be addressed including the provision of dedicated fleets for certain duties and suitable maintenance facilities. The Foster Yeoman experience had shown the way and Railfreight had to do the same but on a massive scale by comparison.

During August 1987 BR invited tenders for the construction of 100 high power Type 5 heavy freight locomotives, issuing a performance specification which was very much to the point. Installed power had to be in the range 2,200kW–2,400kW whilst the locomotive had to be capable of hauling trains of 4,000 tonnes at 100km per hour and start one of 2,800 tonnes on a 1 in 100 gradient. A minimum starting tractive effort of 410kN (92,168lbs) was required whilst continuous tractive effort was to be not less than 290kN (65,192lbs); all of this had to be accomplished for a maximum weight of 126 tonnes. Additional restrictions applied including an expected technical life of 40 years and compliance with standard restrictions relating to noise level, loading gauge and body strength at buffer and cab ends.

A number of concerns tendered but the Brush offer was accepted, although it would be fair to say that some people would have preferred a design based on the Class 59. Brush had had considerable experience in the manufacture of electrical equipment, such plant being successfully operated in BR service, but the company had no engine building base and the body structure would also need to come from outside as Brush no longer had facilities for such construction. Apart from those restrictions it was all down to Brush and a myriad of small suppliers. Brush undertook all design work and made a full size wooden mock-up of the locomotive

No 2 end of a Class 60, No 60061 Alexander Graham Bell, *showing the positioning of the silencer.*

in order to optimize layout of equipment. The mock-up allowed underfloor piping and cable runs to be properly arranged, these then being used as templates for the production locomotives. Cab design, equipment layout, access, maintenance and safety were all proved on the mock-up before being adopted for production. The cab layout was based upon that of the Class 58, this having been stipulated by BR in order to ensure a degree of standardization and familiarity for the crew.

Choice of the Mirrlees Blackstone MB275 four-stroke cycle engine was based upon its proven record in marine and industrial application, together with the traction experience gained during trials of a six-cylinder version in four different Class 37 locomotives. Intensive diagramming of these locomotives on South Wales steel trains provided valuable experience and upheld many of the claims

Mirrlees engine prior to fitting in a locomotive, with cooler fan units to be seen to the right.

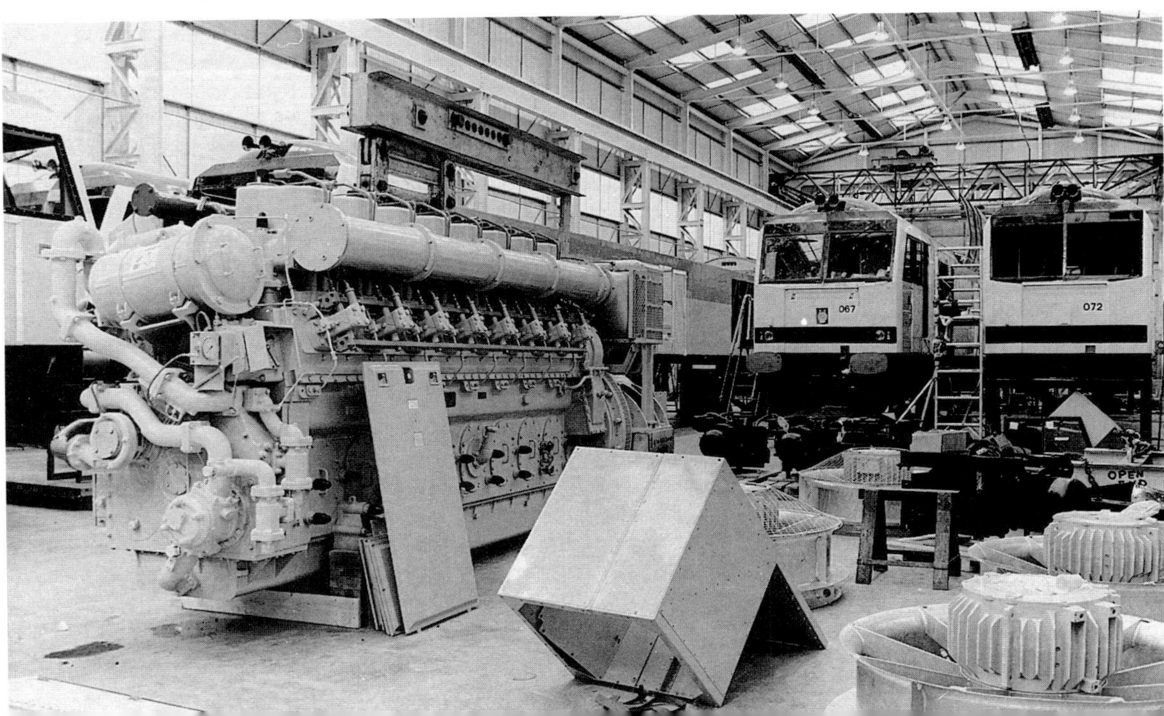

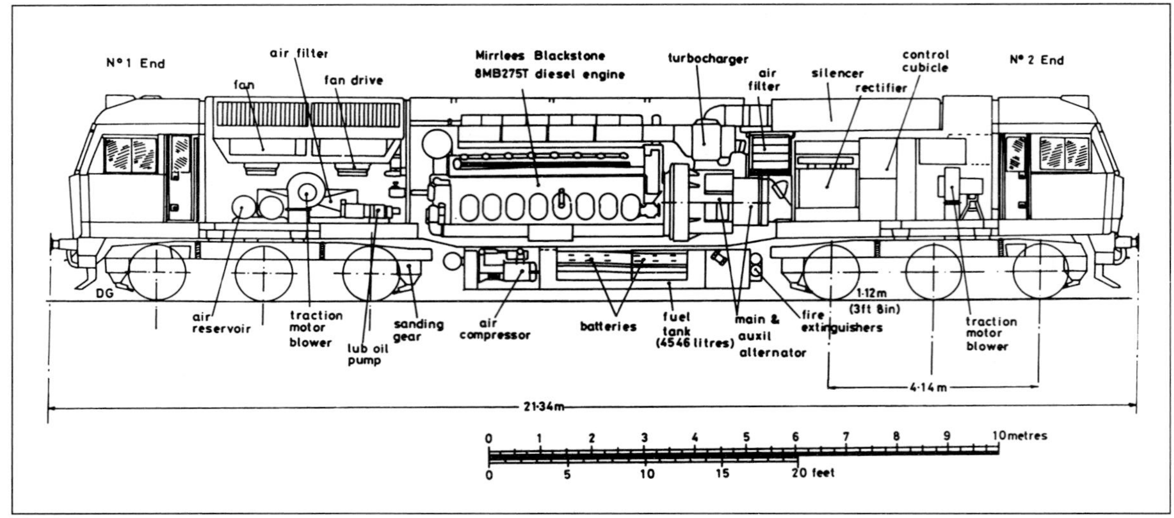

Layout arrangement of Class 60 locomotive.

made for the engines. Amongst such claims was one of low specific fuel consumption, in fact the MB275 has the lowest specific fuel consumption of any of its type on the market. Over the anticipated life that could represent considerable savings as a total life costing exercise carried out by BR indicated that 47 per cent of a diesel locomotive's operating costs were for fuel and lubricating oil. Maintenance accounts for nearly 40 per cent of operating costs and the expectations are that the MB275 with only eight cylinders will require less maintenance than the Class 56 or 58 engines which have 16 and 12 cylinders respectively.

It is not just the number of parts which influence maintenance costs but engine design itself and the use of better materials. For the MB275 major items such as pistons, cylinder heads and bottom end bearings only require inspection after 20,000 hours, a major improvement on earlier engines where about 12,000 hours between overhauls was the norm. The in-line configuration of the engine allows more room for walkways either side within the locomotive structure and at the same time enables items such as cylinder heads and pistons to be lifted directly upwards. Hydraulic tensioning of all large nuts ensures correct loading and ease of assembly.

In order to comply with BR's requirements for type testing an engine of the design to be fitted in the Class 60 was submitted for approval at a rating of 2,315kW. An important part of the test consisted of cycling the engine between idle and overload in order to determine capabilities with respect to thermal fatigue resistance. Initial operations proved to be successful but running after completion of the test programme produced cracking in the cylinder head. The design was of conventional form with cooling water passageways cast into the structure and Mirrlees considered that a major departure from that form of construction was necessary to achieve suitable resistance to thermal fatigue. The form adopted was of the thick section bore-cooled arrangement where water is circulated through a large number of small diameter holes drilled in the cylinder cover close to the combustion face. These holes, suitably plugged and interconnecting with other holes provide a cooling effect just where it is required. Subsequent testing revealed that the new head was suitable.

Turbochargers were type tested separately and after initial problems of blade cracking due to vibration and thermal stress had been overcome the turbochargers also received approval.

The Class 60 body is divided into three main sections plus two cabs, the structure being of the stressed skin monocoque form, two bodysides forming the main load bearing members. An arrangement of cantrails, waistrails and solebars form the basic structure and onto these are welded steel cladding panels. Vertical and diagonal pillars connect the main structural units and provide additional rigidity. Fabricated cabs are designed to meet all strength requirements with respect to crash and buffing loads, end trusses being incorporated to transmit these loads to the cantrails and solebars. The floor area consists of dragbox assemblies and stretchers for bogies and power unit, these being welded to the cab and bodyside section with the aid of jig alignment. At the assembly stage floor plating and internal bulkheads are fitted. The roof consists of four sections manufactured separately, bolted connection to the main structure being used in order to allow for removal when necessary. Brush subcontracted body construction to Procor of Horbury, West Yorkshire although it did undertake the design itself. Finite element computer analysis was employed in order to identify those highly loaded body areas which would require particularly close attention. However, in order to meet tight delivery schedules it was necessary to commence construction of some body structures before full results of the analysis were available. These indicated certain areas which required modification in design, bodies already built were provided with additional strengthening.

The main body consists of three separate sections, the engine room being placed in the centre of the locomotive. At No 1 end is placed the cooler group, air reservoirs and engine auxiliaries whilst a clean air compartment at No 2 end houses the electrical equipment. Two walkways are provided through the locomotive, one each side, with access being via a single door to a vestibule at each end. These vestibules may be entered at either side of the locomotive and they also allow entry to the adjacent cab, again via a single door. This arrangement avoids direct access from outside to the cabs and main compartments of the locomotive, thereby reducing the risks of draughts or dirty air entering these spaces.

The cooler group compartment is open at the sides in order to allow free access for air flow and in addition to the fans and cooler radiators, contains other equipment which is able to withstand the rigours of moisture and atmospheric pollution. Two roof-mounted radiators were originally designed to operate in series, water first flowing through one cooler then the other, but early problems were experienced due to element failure. After extensive testing vibration as a cause was eliminated and the problem traced to pressure pulsations in the water flow. Reconfiguration of the pipework and modifications to the system reduced pressure pulsations to

Cooler air inlet at No 1 end showing the spin tube filter element.

No 1 end of a Class 60, No 60008 Moel Fammau, *showing cooler air inlet from the other side.*

the extent that they were no longer a problem, the main modification being conversion of the system to one of parallel flow. Cooler performance has been reduced slightly but it is still possible to effectively cool an engine at full load with ambient temperature of 30°C whilst still allowing a margin of 20 per cent for fouling of the radiator panels. Radiator panels are protected from damage by stones and other foreign bodies by sloping stone guards. Fans are driven by three-phase induction motors, thermostatic switches being used to start up the fan when the water inlet temperature to the cooler reaches a preset value.

Side inlets to the cooler group compartment, and

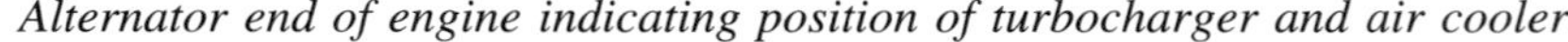

Alternator end of engine indicating position of turbocharger and air cooler.

the stone guards, had to be designed very carefully in order to avoid excessive pressure drops which would reduce air flow efficiency. Mesh grills protect the fan units from large objects and also prevent access whilst they are running. Within this compartment are two air reservoirs and an air dryer, the two compressors and a third air reservoir being positioned outside, beneath the locomotive structure.

Engine auxiliary units comprising fuel supply pump, lubricating oil priming pump and crankcase extractor fan are also located in the cooler group compartment. These units are driven by dc motors, the first two from the battery as they are required to operate at times when the diesel engine is not running, whilst the third is driven from the dc power supply. A spin tube, or swirl type inertia filter directs air to the No 1 end traction motor blower which is driven by a three-phase motor. The spin tube filter also provides primary filtration for the compressor air supply.

The clean air compartment at No 2 end is essentially closed with the air supply being through a spin tube filter positioned at the bodyside. This air is directed to several paths for particular purposes. The traction motor blower supplies cooling air to the traction motors at the No 2 end but some air from this blower is bled off to pressurize the control cubicle and so prevent ingress of dirt. The main alternator is arranged so that it draws air from the clean air compartment and over the rectifier thus exerting a cooling effect on that unit, suitable ducting being provided for that purpose. This air also cools the alternator before being expelled from the locomotive. Originally it had been intended that air from the alternator would be expelled into the engine compartment and then be discharged through louvres in the roof by natural circulation. Testing on a locomotive at full power revealed that very high temperatures were reached in the engine compartment. The fitting of two ac driven centrifugal fans in the roof of the engine compartment was found to be necessary in order to remove hot air from the alternator and draw in air from outside to cool the engine compartment. A baffle arrangement directs hot air from the alternator to the outlet fan and so prevents it from circulating in the engine compartment.

Combustion air requires two stages of filtration, the first of these being by the spin tube filter in the clean air compartment. Air for combustion is drawn from this chamber to the turbocharger inlet via a filter box containing a replaceable fibre filter element. The very effective silencer is positioned above the clean air compartment.

In keeping with the policy of building upon proven items the bogies are derived from the designs successfully used on the Class 56 and the electric Class 89, locomotives. The layout arrangement has

Class 60 wheeled axles with drive gears fitted.

been modified slightly in order to minimize weight transfer during traction, this being accomplished by a number of measures including the positioning of all traction motors on the side of their respective drive axles nearest to the locomotive centre. Other measures included a reduction in distance between axle centres and drive connection to the structure, together with optimization of primary and secondary springing. With these arrangements there is zero weight transfer between axles within a bogie, and minimum transfer of weight between leading and trailing bogies.

Bogie frames are constructed from fabricated steel plate with top and bottom plates being cut from a single plate. This is rather wasteful in terms of plate but it avoids welds in these critical sections. All welds in the structure are radiographically tested in order to detect flaws which could give rise to subsequent fatigue cracking. This technique is costly but it indicates the thoroughness employed to ensure a long working life. Wheelsets comprise 1,120mm diameter monobloc wheels connected to hollow axles, these axles showing a reduction in weight compared with solid axles but larger diameter also limits torsional stress when the locomotive operates under creep conditions. The axle-hung traction motors connect with the axles by means of single stage reduction gearing which has a ratio of 19 to 97. Coil springs provide for primary suspension at the axles, the axleboxes being allowed to move vertically in sliding guide posts, four hydraulic dampers at each axle being used to control vertical motion. Outer axleboxes on each bogie have taper roller bearings but the centre axle is provided with parallel roller bearings which allow a 22mm movement either way, in order to enable the locomotive to negotiate small radius curves.

Secondary suspension between bogie and structure consists of four laminated rubber/steel stacks which support the body and a further two stacks

Axle fitted in a bogie showing casing around the gear wheel and the double brake shoe arrangement; the rubber and steel laminated secondary suspension pack may be seen on the bogie frame top and the lateral stop can be seen to the left of that.

The plumbing beneath a Class 60; the battery unit is to the right and the fire extinguishing bottles are in the centre of the picture; to the left is a flexible pipe for conveying cooling air to a traction motor.

mounted fore and aft of the traction centre. Two hydraulic lateral dampers control sideways movement of the bogies whilst rubber bumpstops limit lateral travel. Cast iron brake shoes act on each wheel of the bogie, a hydraulically operated parking brake acting on one of the axles. The Westinghouse system employed consists of two arrangements, one an electrically controlled air brake and the other a straight air brake. The automatic arrangement allows for actuation of both locomotive and rolling stock brakes whilst the straight brake allows the driver to apply the locomotive's brake independently of the train. Westinghouse DSD/vigilance equipment and BR standard AWS equipment are provided in order to afford safe operation as required by the BRB specification. To allow for satisfactory starting and haulage under indifferent track conditions sandboxes are fitted at the four corners of each bogie.

Electrical equipment for traction differs from Class 58 arrangements in several ways but it has all been type tested and has the enviable Brush pedigree. The main alternator is a Brush BA1006A type, the stator windings of which are arranged to provide two balanced three-phase outputs. These outputs are connected to separate diode bridges which are subsequently paralleled on the dc side of the electrical system, the idea being to limit fault currents in the event of any diode short circuiting. The auxiliary alternator is a Brush BA702A type, it is indirectly excited and has two output windings, one of which provides three phase for the induction motor-driven auxiliaries, whilst the other provides a six-phase output used to supply traction motor fields, alternator rotors and the 110 volt system. Sliprings are used to feed current to the excitation windings of the alternators, the reason for this being to provide faster response to wheelslip. In order to allow for easier maintenance sliprings are fitted outboard of the main bearing (see appendix).

The main alternator has continuous ratings of 2,015kW (1,055V and 1,910A), or 2,009kW (478V, 4,200A) at 1,000rpm. The one-hour rating is 1,996kW (423V, 4620A) at 1,000rpm. The auxiliary alternator has a 168kVA rating for the three-phase windings and 354kVA for the six-phase windings.

Direct current traction motors are used, these

being fully compensated and separately excited, marking a departure from normal practice for diesel-electric locomotives, the choice of such an arrangement being dictated by requirements of the control system. Although the form of excitation is new, construction of the armature, commutator and roller bearing systems are based upon motors designed for Class 56 and 58 locomotives. Other aspects of motor construction have been proven on the Class 59s and Brush built locomotives for service in New Zealand. Separate excitation of traction motors, described as SEPEX, has a number of advantages compared with the more usual series excitation and these characteristics can be exploited by a carefully designed control system (see appendix). The separately excited dc motor allows for stepless field variation which can be used to effect in providing for accurate speed control and reversal without the use of contact switches. Each axle is provided with a Brush TM216A motor which has a continuous rating of 300kW (462V, 700A) at 472rpm.

Control plays an important part in the operational effectiveness of any locomotive but there is no single arrangement which has all the advantages, and the Brush design engineers recognized that fact. In order to allow for rapid response to driver demand and at the same time enable the control system to exercise control over all events, the driver power demand is fed to the controller which then sets engine speed to deal with the requirement. This differs fundamentally from conventional control systems where the driver requests an engine speed and the control system reacts to that. The other part of the control system philosophy lies in the use of separately excited traction motors which are utilized in order to enable full use to be made of available adhesion.

Separately excited traction motors have two distinct operating regions which, for the level of gearing employed, change at a road speed of about 46km per hour. In the first region the field excitation current is at a set full value and speed variation is met by changing voltage applied to the armature. In the higher speed region, above a base speed, armature voltage is kept constant at the maximum value and the field current is decreased with increasing speed. Compensation and the use of separately excited fields mean that the voltage applied can be considered as directly proportional to the motor speed alone, and this fact may be employed in developing a creep control system.

Because motor voltage varies with speed alone the creep control system may be treated as one for voltage control and organized accordingly. A doppler radar unit enables true ground speed to be measured and this may be used to compute the voltage of a non-slipping motor, say V1. For particular conditions it is known that the maximum value of adhesion may be obtained when the wheels slip a certain amount (see the section on the Class 59s) and the control system can determine what that value of slip is for conditions encountered. For this value of slip a value of voltage, V2, may be calculated and the sum V1 + V2 gives the expected motor voltage for the true ground speed at which the locomotive is operating. This is compared with the actual applied voltage, and any difference used to control the main alternator excitation, in order to bring the applied voltage to the value expected for the road speed and level of slip required.

This voltage control system deals with variation in set conditions whilst the parallel current control system produces change in current in response to driver demand. Both control systems work together and each produces a desired value of main alternator excitation current, the lower of the two being used for control. In many situations only one might produce a change, for instance if the driver speed control was not changed but the train encountered wet track which caused slipping, only the voltage control system would react. The voltage system only operates up to a certain speed, the base speed, and at speeds greater than this it is isolated and the traction motor field current is changed in order to bring about motor control. Above the base speed a conventional slip control system operates and this also provides back-up for the voltage balance creep control system working below base speed.[20] It should be noted that the creep control system of the Class 60 operates down to a speed of 2km per hour.

Accurate control is essential to the effectiveness of the arrangement and a microprocessor based system provides that control. Signals from the radar unit and each of the traction motors are monitored every fraction of a second in order to ensure accuracy and rapid response to any change in condition. Only time will tell how effective the control system is at enabling heavy loads to be hauled on indifferent track. Early results are encouraging thus illustrating that there are alternatives to the GM-EMD 'Super Series' system but the real test is in the hauling of maximum loads on colliery tracks covered in coal slurry. Expectation is that a single Class 60 will be capable of pulling 63 loaded

No 6008 Moel Fammau *ready for duty at Toton depot.*

coal wagons giving a gross trailing weight of 3,000 tonnes.[21]

Details of the Class 60 electrical system and control arrangements have been included for completeness but the average reader should not become too involved in either arrangement if interest does not lie there. The important thing to realize is that the systems work and allow the locomotive to haul heavy trains under adverse conditions as found in colliery and power station sidings.

A number of modifications were necessary with early members of the class in order to meet the BRB specification, such modifications being made retrospectively to locomotives in service and incorporated in others during construction. British Rail also required changes to be made and the redesign of certain systems had to be undertaken. Close co-operation between engineers from BRB and Brush enabled that work to be carried out whilst delivery of the class was taking place, changes to existing Class 60s being made when convenient.

It would be easy to attempt direct comparisons between Class 59 and 60 locomotives but care is necessary as operating conditions differ. The Class 59s operate as small groups from distinct sites on definite routes. Maintenance is also carried out by dedicated teams of artizans at those home depots. The much larger Class 60 fleet ranges far and wide over the BR system and only reaches home depots infrequently. Under current maintenance systems small dedicated bands of artizans cannot be allocated to the class, maintenance staff having to be familiar with several classes of locomotive all having different mechanical, electrical and control systems. Ideally the arrangement as used for the Class 59s should be applied but on the large BR system it would be uneconomic. Like can only be compared with like but both classes are fine examples of locomotive engineering and worthy successors to classic heavy freight steam designs such as the Stanier 8F and BR Standard 9F.

Appendix Electrical Machines

An electric motor functions due to the interaction of magnetic fields whilst the generator, for direct current, or the alternator, for alternating current, produces electrical power when an electrical conductor cuts through a magnetic field. There is much more to electrical machines than that simple statement and the real situation can be extremely complex and mathematical but as this is not an electrical text book only sufficient detail will be given here to enable the electrical aspects of Chapter 8 to be appreciated.

Electric Motors

The electric motor functions because like poles of magnets repel and unlike poles attract; this fact may be proven by the individual who has access to two magnets. If one of those magnets is fixed, the stator, and the other allowed to move, the rotor, there is the basis of an electric motor. By supplying current to the coils wound on the rotor an electro-magnet is produced and that will function in the same way as a solid iron magnet, but by changing the direction of current in the electro-magnet coil it is possible to alter polarity of the coil, ie change a particular end of the coil from north to south pole or vice-versa. If the polarity can be changed at the correct time such that, say, the polarity of one end of a coil can be altered to a north pole just as it passes a north pole on the stator then there will be repulsion and the rotor will turn. With similar reasoning the polarity of

Arrangements of excitation for dc electric motors.

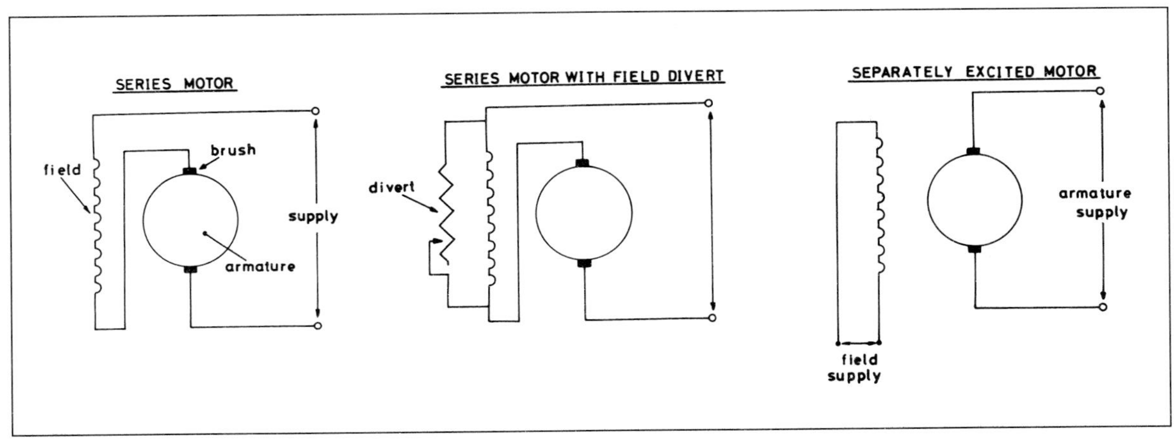

a coil on the rotor should be south just as it approaches a north pole on the stator in order to achieve attraction. This is the basic of an electric motor.

Motors in general use for traction purposes are direct current (dc) for reasons which need not be considered here and so only the dc motor will be described. For small motors, such as those used in electric train sets, stators are provided with permanent magnets but larger motors use electro-magnets. The principle of operation is still the same but an essential difference is the fact that the strength of the stator magnetic field may be changed with an electro-magnet but it cannot wth a permanent magnet. The ability to alter stator magnetic field strength is important in traction motors as it influences the power developed. The term 'excitation' is used to describe the application of an electric current to the stator magnetic coils (the field coils) in order to produce a magnetic effect. With a model railway the rotor (armature) current is changed by means of the control unit and that alters the strength of the rotating magnetic field whilst the stationary magnetic field strength remains constant due to the permanent magnet. Speed variation is, therefore, achieved by changing the armature current whilst direction change can be made by changing the polarity of the voltage supply, positive becomes negative and vice-versa. The larger the number of poles employed in a motor the smoother will be its drive and the greater will be its power, for the same pole strength. There are limits to the number of poles which can be fitted to a motor of given size.

Electrical power is passed to the rotating electro-magnets via static brushes which contact the rotor at a commutator. Brushes are made from carbon because of its ability to transmit electrical current and because carbon is soft and will not wear away the commutator too easily. The commutator segments connect with windings of the rotor coils and insulated slots in the commutator keep the segments apart thus avoiding a short circuit. Sparking takes place between brushes and the commutator for a number of reasons and this increases the wear of these parts.

Traditionally the series wound electric motor has been used for traction purposes. The arrangement is such that the electric circuit for the stator (field) coils is in series with the supply to the rotor (armature) coils. Changing supply voltage or current alters supply to the stator and rotor magnets together and that gives particular motor characteristics. In some cases a divert resistance is connected across the stator coil windings in order to modify the motor characteristics. The series wound motor gives a high starting torque making it ideal for traction purposes. At very low loads, however, such as exist when slipping occurs, there is a great tendency for speed to increase and that can result in considerable problems. Slip control is a complex matter and some additional correction to the electrical supply must take place to prevent high speed.

A recent idea has been to employ separately excited dc motors for traction purposes. The rotating coils, or armature coils, are supplied from the main electrical supply as for the series motor but the stator (field) coils are excited, or energized, from a separate supply. In basic terms the strengths of the rotating and stationary magnetic fields are independent of each other and may be adjusted independently. It is possible to keep one supply constant and vary the other but in practice that achieves no useful

Series/parallel and parallel arrangements for motor connections.

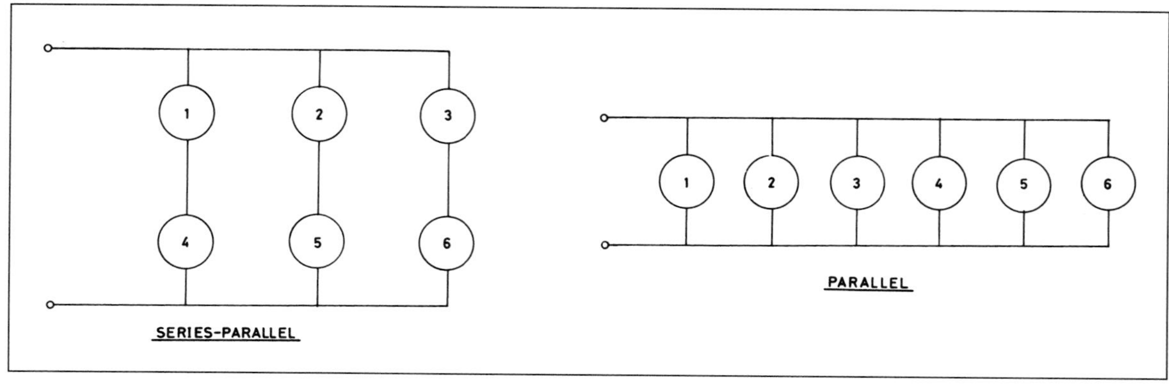

purpose and both are varied to suit load and speed requirements. Careful control is required in order to achieve the necessary effect and produce the required torque at the desired speed whilst avoiding the tendency to slip. Because armature and field supplies are independent the range of operating conditions is wider than for the series wound motor where armature and field are in the same electrical circuit. Reversal of direction is also simpler, supply to the field coils only having to be altered to give the new coil polarity. The separately excited motor may be considered as similar to the permanent magnet motor used for model railways except in that case the stator (field) has a constant strength and is not variable. Reversal of direction is achieved in the same way except that with the separately excited traction motor field supply polarity is changed whilst for the model locomotive the armature supply polarity is reversed.

Traction motors may be connected in a series-parallel arrangement across pairs of motors in both bogies or as a parallel arrangement across all motors (as used for the Class 60). The method chosen suits the form of excitation and the control system used. The actual motors grouped in the series pairs for a series-parallel system depends upon a number of factors including the form of slip control adopted. In general there will be a traction motor from each of the bogies in each series pair.

Alternators

The diesel electric locomotives considered in this book generate alternating current which is then rectified to direct current for supply to the traction motors. The reasons for this are many and need not be discussed but they include efficiency and reliability of plant. Rectification of alternating to direct current supply is achieved by means of diodes, description again being beyond the scope of this book. Alternators operate in a similar way to motors except that a prime mover, the diesel engine, is used to bring about relative movement between a magnetic field and an electrical conductor in which an electric current is induced. In practice there are three separate electrical conductors giving three separate electrical supplies which are slightly out of phase with each other, a three-phase supply. After rectification the supplies are merged to give a very steady direct current supply.

Either the stator or the rotor can be the magnet with the current being induced in the coils of the other unit. In order to simplify the system the rotor is usually provided with the magnet and current is collected from coils in the stator; that avoids the problem of brushes for current collection from the rotating unit. However, there is still the problem of how to produce an electro-magnet in the rotor. The most direct way would be to supply a direct current to the rotating field coils via brushes but brushes cause problems and so the brushless alternator was developed.

The brushless alternator has a separate excitation alternator fitted at the end of the main alternator shaft and alternating current is induced in its rotating coils, the stator being fitted with the field coils. A rectifier unit, also fitted on the shaft, converts alternating current from the excitation alternator into direct current for supply to the main alternator field coils. Thus to change the main alternator output the excitation alternator field coil supply must be changed and that in turn alters the strength of the rotating magnetic field of the main alternator. The system is effective and avoids problems involved in electrical transmission via brushes but it does take time for the main alternator output to respond to an instruction for change in power. That time is only short but it could be critical in the event of wheelslip.

In order to minimize the risk of wheelslip due to time delay between control signal and alternator response the use of brushes and slip rings has been resorted to by one manufacturer. Excitation current for the alternator rotor coils is thus supplied from an external source, in the case of the Class 60 the auxiliary power supply, and the strength of the field produced by the current will determine the alternator output. Unlike commutators which are slotted, slip rings are complete rings and so the brushes do not have to pass over gaps. Slip rings can be used because direct current is supplied to the rotating field coils in order to produce an electro-magnet which always has its north and south poles in the same physical position relative to the coil. As the coil rotates the magnetic field will interact with the stator coils and induce in these an alternating current. There are problems resulting from the use of slip rings and brushes, not least that of brush wear, but the alternator may be made to react much more quickly to control signals than can the brushless alternator.

Footnote References

IME – Proceedings, Institution of Mechanical Engineers
ICE – Minutes of Proceedings, Institution of Civil Engineers
ILE – Journal, Institution of Locomotive Engineers
IT – Journal, Institution of Transport

Chapter 2

1. 'Some Modern Goods and Mineral Locomotives' by E.C. Poultney. *Railway Magazine* Vol 10, 1902, p544–5 also *Locomotives of the GWR, part 10.* RCTS 1966, pK34–K37
2. *The British Steam Railway Locomotive 1825–1925* by E.L. Ahrons. Locomotive Publishing Co. 1927, p304. also *Locomotives of the GWR, part 10.* RCTS 1966, pK43–K44
3. 'The Late G.J. Churchward's Locomotive Developments on the GWR' by K.J. Cook. ILE paper 492 March 1950, p131–4
4. *Heavy Freight 28xx & 38xx Consolidations of the GWR* by C. Veal & J. Goodman. GWR Society. Didcot 1980, also *Locomotives of the GWR, part 9.* RCTS 1962
5. 'Organisation & Control of Locomotive Repairs' by R.C. Bond. ILE, paper 520, March 1953, p183
6. *New Light on the Locomotive Exchanges* by C.J. Allen. pub Ian Allan, 1950, p10–13
7. Allen, *New Light on Locomotive Exchanges*, p16–27, also *Railway Magazine* vol 95, p331–334. *Railway Gazette* 29 July 1949, p116–7
8. *Chronicles of Steam* by E.S. Cox. pub Ian Allan, 1967, p51
9. *Railway Gazette*, 4 March 1921, p325–6
10. *Railway Gazette*, 18 Jan 1946, p64–9
11. 'The Standardization of GWR Locomotives' by A.J.L. White. *GWR Magazine*, vol 25, 1913, p68–9
12. *An Outline of GWR Locomotive Practice 1837–1947* by H. Holcroft. pub Locomotive Publishing Co., 1957, p133
13. *GWR Magazine*, vol 46, 1934, p498–9
14. *Locomotives of the GWR, part 9*, RCTS, 1962, pJ53

Chapter 3

1. 'Coal & Mineral Traffic on the Railways of the UK' by H. Kelway-Bamber; ILE paper 60, March 1918, p137–9
2. *Railway Magazine vol 10*, 1902, p547
3. *Locomotive Magazine vol 11*, No 70, October 1901
4. *The McIntosh Locomotive of the Caledonian Railway* by A.B. MacLeod. pub Ian Allan, 1948, p31
5. 'Horwich Locomotives' by G. Hughes. IME, June 1909, p605
6. ICE 1901–2, vol 150, part 4, p115
7. *The Engineer, vol 68*, 18 Oct 1884, p326
8. *The Engineer, vol 94*, 15 Aug 1902, p112
9. Hughes, 'Horwich Locomotives', p570–1
10. *The L&Y Railway in the 20th Century* by E. Mason. pub Ian Allan, 1954, p144
11. 'Compounding & Superheating of Horwich Locomotives' by G. Hughes. IME, 1910, p400–5
12. Hughes, 'Compounding & Superheating' p405–25
13. Mason, *L&Y Railway in 20th Century*, p146–9
14. Hughes, 'Compounding & Superheating', p450
15. Mason, *L&Y Railway in 20th Century*, p146
16. 'A Modern Locomotive History' by E.S. Cox. ILE paper 457, 1946, p108–11
17. *The Engineer, vol 83*, 28 May 1897, p707
18. 'Modern British Goods & Mineral Locomotives' by E.C. Poultney. *Railway Magazine, vol 10*, 1902, p545 also 'Eight Coupled Locomotives on British Railways' by E.C. Poultney. *The Engineer*, 4 May 1945, p348

19. *Some Recent Developments on Locomotive Practice* by C.J.B. Cooke. pub Whittaker & Co., 1902, p12
20. 'Compound Locomotives' by F.W. Webb. ICE, 1899, vol 138, part 4, p408–9
21. *The Engineer, vol 105*, 11 Dec 1908, p8
also *Railway Magazine, vol 10*, May 1902, p545
22. *The Engineer, vol 83*, 7 May 1897, p458–9
23. *My Life with Locomotives* by 'Rivington'. pub Ian Allan, 1962, p149
24. ILE, paper 457, 1946, 145
25. IME, 1910, p479–81
26. 'Whale Locomotives of the LNWR' by J.N. Jackson. *Railway Magazine, vol 25*, 1909, p137–8
27. *Locomotive Panorama, vol 1* by E.S. Cox. pub Ian Allan, 1965, p24
28. *The Engineer, vol 116*, 2 Nov. 1923, p570
also *Derby Works & Midland Locomotives* by J.B. Radford. pub Ian Allan, 1971, p143–4
29. *Somerset & Dorset Locomotive History* by D. Bradley & D. Milton. pub David & Charles, 1973, p145–6
30. Cox, *Modern Locomotive History*, p125
31. Cox, *Locomotive Panorama, vol 1*, p83

Chapter 4

1. 'Coal & Mineral Traffic on the Railways of the UK' by H. Kelway-Bamber. ILE paper 60, March 1918, p139
2. *Railway Magazine, vol 9*, 1901, p428
3. *Railway Magazine, vol 71*, 1932, p359
4. *Locomotives of the LNER part 6C*, RCTS, 1984, p18–25
5. *Locomotives of the LNER part 9B*, RCTS, 1977, p6–11
6. *Heavy Goods Engines of the War Department vol 1, ROD 2-8-0* by J.W.P. Rowledge. pub Springmead Railway Books 1977, p7
7. *Railway Gazette*, 11 Oct. 1912, p430
8. *Locomotive Profile No 21, ROD 2-8-0s*, by B. Reed. pub Profile Publications, Feb. 1972, p194–6
9. Reed, *Locomotive Profile No 21, ROD 2-8-0s*
also Rowledge, *Heavy Goods Engines of the War Department vol 1*
10. *Locomotives of the LNER part 6B*, RCTS, 1983 p34
11. Rowledge, *Heavy Goods Engines vol 1*, p52
12. *Railway Gazette*, 21 June 1918, p729–30
13. *The Engineer, vol 127*, 25 April 1919, p400–402
14. *Railway Gazette*, 9 July 1920, p60–2
15. Reed, *Locomotive Profile No 21*, p201
16. *Railway Gazette*, 7 Dec. 1906, p64
17. *The Engineer, vol 101*, 20 April 1906, p392
18. *Railway Magazine, vol 42*, June 1918, p353–60
19. 'Locomotives I have known' by O.V.S. Bulleid. IME, vol 152 part 4, 1945, p341–2
20. *The Engineer, vol 93*, 6 Sept. 1901, p252
21. *Railway Gazette*, 4 July 1919, p27
22. *The Engineer, vol 97*, 7 Aug. 1903, p135–6
23. *The Engineer, vol 117*, 23 Nov. 1913, supplement page xv
24. 'Wagons Stock on a British Railway' by H.N. Gresley. IT, 1923, p152–66
also 'Trials with Vacuum Brakes on Heavy Freight Trains' by H.N. Gresley & Sir Henry Fowler. ICE, vol 213, 1922, p223–93
25. *Railway Gazette*, 28 Sept. 1917, p355; 14 Dec. 1917, p649–54
26. *Railway Magazine, vol 43*, 1918, p43–5
27. *The Engineer, vol 126*, 26 July 1918, p71
28. '3-Cylinder High Pressure Locomotives' by H.N. Gresley. IME, July 1925, p927–37
also Bulleid, 'Locomotives I have known', p343
and *Locomotives of the LNER part 6B*, RCTS, p14–31
29. Gresley, '3-Cylinder High Pressure Locomotives', p927–86
30. *The Locomotive, vol 31*, 15 June 1925, p180–1
31. *Railway Gazette*, 26 July 1907, p81–2
also Journal Stephenson Locomotive Society, vol 20, 1944, p201
32. Kelway-Bamber, 'Coal & Mineral Traffic', p139
33. *Railway Magazine, vol 10*, 1902, p546
34. *The Engineer, vol 93*, 29 Nov. 1901, p559–60
35. *Railway Magazine, vol 72*, 1933, p359
36. *Engineering*, 9 Jan 1920, p50
also *Railway Gazette*, 7 Sept. 1919, p595; 9 Sept. 1921, p399–401
37. *Engineering*, 13 Feb. 1920, p208–9
38. *Railway Gazette*, 9 Sept. 1921, p399–401
39. 'Railway Electrification' by Sir Vincent Raven. Trans. North East Coast Inst. of Eng'rs & Shipbuilders, 1921–22, p187–95
40. 'Britain's Most Powerful 0-8-0' by K. Hoole. *Railway Magazine*, Oct. 1978, p472–6

Chapter 5

1. *Locomotive Panorama, vol 1* by E.S. Cox. pub Ian Allan, 1965, p40 & 59
2. *The Railway Engineer*, Dec. 1927, p164
3. *Historical Locomotive Monographs No 1, LMS & LNER Garratts* by R.J. Essery & G. Toms. pub Wild Swan, 1991, p76–82
4. H. Chambers in discussion of Modern Articulated Locomotives by W.C. Williams, ILE, paper 299, Dec. 1932, p139
5. *The Locomotive*, 15 April 1931, p119–21
6. Essery & Toms, *LMS & LNER Garratts*, p19
7. *Living with London Midland Locomotives* by A.J. Powell. pub Ian Allan, 1977, p76
8. 'Compound Locomotive' by R.M. Deeley; *The Engineer*, 17 Dec. 1909, p623–4
9. Cox, *Locomotive Panorama*, p60
10. Essery & Toms, *LMS & LNER Garratts*, p83–91
11. 'A Modern Locomotive History' by E.S. Cox. ILE, paper 457, Jan. 1946, p132–3

12. Essery & Toms, *LMS & LNER Garratts*, p21
13. 'The LMSR 9500 class 0-8-0' by E.A. Langridge. SLS Journal, vol 47, No 546, Jan. 1971, p5–11
14. Powell, *Living with LM Locomotives*, p78
15. Cox, *Locomotive Panorama*, p67
16. Cox, *Locomotive Panorama*, p83
17. Cox, *Locomotive Panorama*, p113
18. *Stanier 8Fs at Work* by A. Wilkinson. pub Ian Allan, 1986
19. *Locomotives of the LNER Part 6B*, pub RCTS, 1983, p108–16
20. Wilkinson, *Stanier 8Fs*, p46
21. Powell, *Living with LM Locomotives*, p81
22. 'Organisation & Control of Repairs on British Railways' by R.C. Bond. ILE, paper 520, March 1953, p183
23. *Locomotives of the LNER part 6B*, pub RCTS, 1983, p152–3
24. 'The Booster' by O.V.S. Bulleid. ILE, paper 228, Jan. 1928, p259–62
25. *The Railway Engineer*, Aug. 1925, p272
26. 'Development of LNER Locomotive Design 1923–1941' by B. Spencer. ILE, paper 465, March 1947, p170
27. *Locomotives of the LNER part 6B*, pub RCTS, 1983, p162
28. *New Light on the Locomotive Exchanges* by C.J. Allen. pub Ian Allan, 1950, p24–7
29. Bond, *Organisation & Control of Repairs*, p183

Chapter 6

1. *Heavy Goods Engines of the War Department vol 3* by J.W.P. Rowledge. pub Springmead Railway Books, 1978, p7–16
also *The Last Steam Locomotive Engineer*, R.A. Riddles by H.C.B. Rogers. pub Allen & Unwin, 1970, p104–14
2. Rogers, *Last Steam Locomotive Engineer*, p115–6
3. *Railway Gazette*, 10 Sept. 1943, p253–8
4. Rogers, *Last Steam Locomotive Engineer*, p119–20
5. Rogers, *Last Steam Locomotive Engineer*, p122
6. *Railway Gazette*, 5 May 1944, p469–70
7. Rogers, *Last Steam Locomotive Engineer*, p123–4
8. *Railway Gazette*, 10 Sept. 1943, p256; 5 May 1944, p469
9. Locomotive Exchange Trial Report; document ERO22258; File Test/BR/10. NRM, York
10. Rowledge, *Heavy Goods Engines of the War Department, vols 1, 2 & 3*. pub Springmead Railway Books, 1977–78
11. Locomotive Exchanges Report; File Test/BR/10. NRM, York
12. *New Light on the Locomotive Exchanges* by C.J. Allen. pub Ian Allan, 1950
13. 'Organization & Control of Locomotive Repairs' by R.C. Bond. ILE, paper 520, March 1953, p183
14. Locomotive Exchange Report; File Test/BR/10. NRM, York
15. *Railway Gazette*, 24 Sept. 1954, p346–8; 1 Oct. 1954, p374–6
16. Report L123; File Test/WD/2. NRM, York
17. General References on USA Class S160
Over Here – The Story of the S160 by R.H. Higgins. pub Big Jim Publishing, 1980
also *Locomotives of the LNER part 6B*, RCTS, 1983, p98–107
and *Locomotive Boiler Explosions* by C.H. Hewison. pub David & Charles, 1983, p123–8

Chapter 7

1. *BR Standard Steam Locomotives* by E.S. Cox. pub Ian Allan, 1966, p51
2. *A Lifetime With Locomotives* by R.C. Bond. pub Goose & Son, 1975, p209–10
3. Cox, *BR Standard Steam Locomotives*, p89
4. Cox, *BR Standard Steam Locomotives*, p136
5. *The Engineer*, 17 June 1955, vol 200, p841–3
6. BR Test reports; File Test/BR/9. NRM, York
7. Test report R18; File Test/BR/9. NRM, York
8. Cox, *BR Standard Steam Locomotives*, p117
9. BR Bulletin 13, Report R17, File Test/BR/9. NRM, York
10. Cox, *BR Standard Steam Locomotives*, p168

Chapter 8

1. *Milk Churns to Merry-go-Round* by R.T. Munns. pub David & Charles, 1986, p148–75
2. *The Diesel Impact on British Rail* by R.M. Tufnell. pub MEP, London, 1979, p76
3. 'Diesel Freight Locomotives of BR' by D.F. Russell & I.A. Brown. IME, paper c94/87, 1987, p31–5
4. 'Foster Yeoman/BR Class 59 Heavy Freight Locomotives' by D.F. Russell. IME (Railway Division) Seminar, 20 Feb. 1990
5. 'The Class 56 Freight Locomotives of British Rail' by D.F. Russell & P.J. Law. IME, vol 194, 1980, p65–76
6. Russell & Law, 'Class 56 Locomotives', p65
7. 'Development of a Successful Locomotive Silencer' by C.D. Saunders; IME Conf., 1987, p77–84
8. 'BR Class 58 Diesel Electric Locomotive' by M.W.J. Etwell. IME, paper D2, vol 200, 1986, p38
9. Etwell, 'Class 58 Locomotive', p140
10. Conversations with D.F. Russell, BR Railfreight Engineer, and Toton Depot maintenance staff
11. Russell & Brown, 'Diesel Freight Locomotives of BR', p34
12. Russell, 'Foster Yeoman/BR Class 59 Locomotives'.
13. 'The Class 59 Locomotives for Foster Yeoman on BR' by R.M. Painter & M.J. Frampton. IME, paper c95/87, 1987, p249–51
14. 'An Overview of Foster Yeoman's Railfreight Dis-

tribution System' by K. Larson. Rock & Rail Seminar, Orlando, USA, 16–18 May 1989

15. 'High Adhesion Locomotives with Controlled Creep' by B.R. Meyer. IME, paper 81/87, 1987

16. Letter D.F. Russell to Foster Yeoman, 5 Feb. 1986

17. BR Railfreight staff newsletter *Changing Horses issue 3*

18. K. Larson, 'Overview of FY Distribution System'

19. D.F. Russell, 'Foster Yeoman/BR Class 59 Locomotives', p7

20. 'Diesel Electric Co-Co Locomotives for BRB' by M.J. Oakland. IME, 14 Jan. 1991

21. *Class 60 – locomotives that move mountains*. pub BR Railfreight, June 1989

Index

Steam Freight Locomotive Classes

Diesel Freight Locomotive Classes

General

Engineers